India and the Third World

Altruism or Hegemony?

Srikant Dutt

Zed Books Ltd., 57 Caledonian Road, London N1 9BU.

India and the Third World was first published by Zed Books Ltd.,
57 Caledonian Road, London N1 9BU in 1984

Copyright © Srikant Dutt, 1984

Typeset by Composer Typesetting
Cover design by Lee Robinson
Printed by The Pitman Press, Bath

British Library Cataloguing in Publication Data
Dutt, Srikant
   India and the Third World.
   1. Developing countries — Foreign economic
   relations — India   2. India — Foreign
   economic relations — Developing countries
   I. Title
   337.9540172'4   HF1590.5.D/

   ISBN 0-86232-090-9
   ISBN 0-86232-095-X   Pbk

US Distributor
Biblio Distribution Center, 81 Adams Drive, Totowa,
New Jersey 07512.

Contents

2258340

Tables

A Tribute to Srikant Dutt

Srikant Dutt's promising future as a committed, radical scholar and journalist ended tragically on 3 December 1981 when he succumbed to injuries sustained in a traffic accident in New Delhi on 20 November, a few hours before his twenty-seventh birthday.

He was born in New York City, America, in 1954, the only child of an Indian father and an American mother. He grew up in New York and graduated from the University of Pennsylvania. In 1981 he was awarded his PhD by the London School of Economics and Politics.

Like Srikant's many friends in London who are now scattered worldwide in Asia, Africa and elsewhere, we were immediately struck by his uncompromising commitment to the oppressed and his encyclopaedic knowledge of history and politics. There were few issues about which he could not provide informed comment. But his convictions were not merely intellectual. Srikant's identification with the oppressed was not disinterested at all, rather, it was personal. He mixed with the less privileged and less articulate easily and without condescension because, like them, he too felt he had no country. And he lived simply and unpretentiously and seemed not to be aware of it.

Srikant had an enviable capacity for work and the prodigious output of his researches and journalistic inquiries was published in a succession of articles in India, Britain and America. Behind the prolific pen of a radical and internationalist with an insatiable desire to know about every battle ground against imperialism and exploitation was an intense, warm and humorous person. Srikant's friends in London were exiles, mostly from the Third World, who fondly remember his remarkable capacity to connect seemingly unrelated information from diverse sources and discover ruling class designs against the oppressed.

The issue central to his concerns was imperialism, in every guise and form. During 1979–81 readers of the Calcutta weekly *Frontier* saw Srikant Dutt's articles on a host of subjects: trouble for US imperialism in the Caribbean; change in Chinese Communist policies towards Tibet; traffic in women in India and Pakistan; insurgencies in Burma; the upheavals in north-east India, India's slums — the 'Bantustans of Hindustan'; Indian multinationals in other underdeveloped countries — these were just a few of the many articles Srikant wrote for *Frontier*.

He rejected contemporary bourgeois Western societies for their self-absorbed materialism, individualism and racism. And he was indifferent to the radical American milieu for its insularity and inadequate concern for the effects of American imperialism abroad. Equally, he denounced the pseudo nationalism of Third World elites and their compromises with imperialism abroad and repression at home. He was particularly irate at the willingness of many Third World intellectuals to ignore oppression within their own borders.

Not surprisingly, one of Srikant's abiding preoccupations was to voice the grievances of the minority peoples of the north-east of the Indian sub-continent. He had finished research on a major study of the area which he unfortunately did not live to write up.

Srikant chose to live in India, despite family ties in America, because he felt he could work effectively towards the things he believed in deeply. But he had little love for Indian middle-class society, which viewed America as a land of milk and honey from where the Indian immigrant comes home as Santa Claus. He was widely travelled himself and understood some Japanese and Chinese, apart from Bengali and Hindi.

He probably would have liked to be remembered for his revolutionary optimism, his sense of urgency about political knowledge and action, his global concerns and his impatience with the enemies of radical change. The pen he had been wielding with growing fluency was to have been the medium of his own personal struggle on behalf of the oppressed and that is what he asked for when he woke up on his hospital bed the day before he died.

Gautam Sen
University of Massachusetts, Amherst

Sanjib Baruah
Bard College
Annandale-On-Hudson, New York
December 1983.

Foreword by James Mayall

Srikant Dutt died in hospital in New Delhi following a road accident while his book was still in the press. It is a privilege, although a sad one, to write this Foreword. My qualification for doing so is simply that, as his Supervisor at the London School of Economics, I was closely associated with him and with the manuscript, originally submitted as a doctoral thesis, on which the book is based. No doubt there will be those who will contest some of his arguments and conclusions. That is as it should be: Srikant enjoyed intellectual controversy and regarded it as his major purpose to challenge conventional attitudes, assumptions and interpretations. But whether the reader accepts or rejects his diagnosis of the underlying causes of India's new foreign policy in the Third World, there will, I think, be no dispute that as a writer he possessed two rare and valuable qualities: one was a natural flair for unearthing information relevant to his theme wherever it was to be found, the other an intuitive sense of justice which gave moral direction to everything he wrote.

Srikant Dutt was at the start of what his friends and all who knew him were confident would be a distinguished career. The only doubt we had was in which of two directions he was most likely to develop, as an academic social theorist or a serious investigative journalist. Most probably he would have continued to combine both roles. Certainly, had he lived, this would have been only the first of several books by him about the emerging geopolitical order in South Asia (indeed he was already well-advanced with a study of India's relations with her small Himalayan neighbours). He wanted to encourage discussion about what he rightly saw as a relatively neglected area of international research. With his death the professional worlds of International Relations and of Indian and Asian Studies have lost one of their most promising young scholars. If this book prompts others, as he hoped it would, to pierce the rhetorical gloom which still surrounds much discussion of intra-Third World relations, it will be a worthy memorial.

James Mayall

Preface and Acknowledgements

There is an increasing need for a reassessment of the basic assumptions concerning the effect of capitalist development in the Third World since 1945. This book is presented as a modest contribution to this reassessment and it is hoped that it will stimulate similar studies to be undertaken to examine the relative impact of development in various parts of the Third World and the effect on international relations.

The author would like to acknowledge the financial assistance given by the Central Research Fund, University of London, which enabled him to carry out fieldwork in India. The staff of the following organizations deserve mention: Punjab National Bank; Punjab and Sind Bank; Indian Bank; Federation of Indian Chambers of Commerce and Industry; Muragappa and Sons; National Research Development Corporation; National Association of Consulting Engineers; Indian Institute of Foreign Trade; Ahmedabad Textile Industry's Research Association; Federation of Indian Export Organizations; National Industrial Development Corporation; Central Bee Research Institute — Pune, Khadi and Village Industries Commission; Hindustan Machine Tools Ltd.; Government of Mysore Sandalwood Oil Factories; Polyofins Industries Ltd; L.G. Balakrishnan and Bros. Ltd.; Kirloskar Electric Co. Ltd.; Engineering Export Promotion Council; Royal Institute of International Affairs libraries; Institute of Commonwealth Studies library; School of Oriental and African Studies library and the India Office Library. The author would also like to thank officials in the Life Insurance Corporation of India, Industrial Development Bank of India, Reserve Bank of India and the Indian Investment Centre for their help, as well as officials in the Ministries of Commerce, Finance and External Affairs of the Government of India. Thanks also to Dr. D.C. Vohra, Mr. Shemoy and several businessmen who asked to remain anonymous.

In addition, the author would like to acknowledge the inspiration, help and support which the following people gave towards bringing this study to fruition: my thesis supervisor at the London School of Economics, James Mayall; Dr. Peter Lyon; Dr. Michael Leifer; Mr. Patrick Davis, Publications Officer at the LSE; Mr. and Mrs. Swapan Choudhuri of Bombay for their hospitality; Mr. A.K. Dutt; Krishna Dutt; Ebrahim Ali; Sanjib Barua; Sugran B. Choudhry; Hassan B. Jallow; Thomas Shopo; Vinoe Thankl;

Gautam Sen and the author's parents. This notwithstanding, any errors that may occur are solely the author's. The author would like to dedicate this work to the people of South Asia.

Srikant Dutt
New Delhi

Introduction:
A New Approach to the
Study of India's Foreign
Relations

The basic tenet of this work is that India's diplomatic and political relations, particularly with countries of the developing world, cannot be fully understood without an examination of the economic relations involved, and that hitherto, conventional studies of India's external ties have afforded only limited insights into these. The term 'relations' is used here to mean the economic and political ties India has fostered with other developing countries since 1947 through overseas Indian populations, and in the fields of aid, investments, banking and insurance. Studies of Indian foreign relations have traditionally focussed on diplomatic and trade policies only, rather than on the forces that have given rise to these ties. The contention of this work is that India's overseas ties are rooted in the nature of the development of the Indian state and the forces it has unleashed.

In order to expound this approach, the book is divided into three sections. The first section of two chapters, sets out to describe the framework of India's foreign relations with developing countries. Accordingly, the concepts of state capitalism and proto- and second-tier imperialism are described as they apply to India. The second section of seven chapters (3—9) describes India's foreign economic policy, aid, technology transfers, investments, contracts, banks, insurance and the role of overseas Indians. The third and concluding section integrates the evidence and concepts presented in the first two.

While the main focus of this study is on an examination of India's economic relationships with developing countries, it is not a study of trade nor, in the conventional sense, of economics. It may be felt that such a study is incomplete without some trade analysis, but a number of studies that have adequately presented such data already exist.[1] Economic relations here are focussed on the more tangible long-term ties which previous studies of India's foreign economic and political relations have neglected to explore.

The argument advanced sets out to describe the nature of the Indian state and how this determines much of its military, economic, political or diplomatic relations. The focus is primarily on those relations formed with other developing countries over the past 30 years. This does not mean that India's relations with the developed world can easily be ignored and isolated from those with the developing world. India's relations with developed countries are essentially those of dependency which has an important bearing upon her relations with the less developed countries. Yet this dependency is not the primary determinant of India's relations with developing countries. Rather, India's relations with other developing countries have been largely based on its own development experience. It is feasible that India's Third World ties may even gradually change her dependency on the industrial countries and possibly provide the Indian state with greater world autonomy.

Conventional approaches to the study of India's external relations have been focussed in terms of theories of international relations, according to which, a state's foreign policy is seen as shaped by such factors as geography, economics, demography, history, strategy and leadership [P1].* It is this last factor which has dominated the field in the study of Indian foreign policy, some venturing so far as to declare that personalities at the top of the hierarchy are crucial to the understanding of Indian foreign policy [C8]. The prevailing thought has been that, in order to understand India's foreign relations, one should concentrate on the concept of non-alignment in a bipolar world — the Bandung spirit and the general impact of Nehru's ideas. This approach is shared by the majority of Western and Soviet scholars. Yet it is no small irony that the prime architect of many of these foreign policy strategies once said: 'Ultimately foreign policy is the outcome of economic policy.' [2] Nevertheless, most studies of India's external relations have been only concerned with non-alignment within the context of superpower rivalries. Countless books and articles have been published which dissect non-alignment and the role it has in understanding India's foreign relations. This approach may provide a fairly coherent picture of India's foreign relations although it is confined to the diplomatic field and a narrow time frame. Therefore it cannot provide a satisfactory framework for understanding these relations without the background of India's own development experience. What has occurred is that the political rhetoric of Indian leaders over the past 30 years has affected the study of India's external relations within India as well as outside. This can be understood because during the early independence period India's low level of domestic development meant that its external relations with other developing countries were largely confined to diplomatic and weak trading relations. Yet, had the veneer of rhetoric worn off, one would have discovered an underlying complex of economic and political relationships formed during the colonial period.

Most studies have agreed that India's external relations are a reflection of a state which, despite internal weaknesses, has played an autonomous and moderately influential role in international affairs. What is overlooked, however, is that India's external links are inextricably connected to its domestic political economy. Therefore, to approach India's external relations through a theory of political economy would be appropriate and provide a better means of understanding these ties. Non-alignment should

* Bibliographical references refer to appropriate bibliography number(s); where figures follow a colon these indicate page numbers, e.g. [D1: 12d].

therefore only be seen as a strategy to shape and safeguard situations for gaining comparative advantage. This is not to deny that other factors, such as the country's strategic location, do sometimes play an important role — as in India's relations with the Himalayan states — but such roles are not the only ones or completely explanatory.

While some writers have characterized India's external relations as being guided by principle and have declared that India does not have the basis of a traditional power — 'overseas possessions, investments, spheres of influence' [R9] — it is the aim of this study to show that India is intent on becoming just such a traditional power. New features, which are growing more apparent in India's external relations, increasingly show the unsatisfactory nature of present analyses of Indian foreign policy. India's expanding economic relations with other developing countries cannot simply be subsumed within diplomatic, trade or political relations. Increasingly, it is the diplomatic and political relations which have to accommodate themselves to the economic forces. Features such as Indian Joint Venture investments, banks abroad, technical, monetary and military aid — all previously a small part of India's external relations — have become increasingly important and cannot be ignored. Indeed these ties illustrate the true nature of India's external relations with other developing states, particularly where India enjoys a position of comparative advantage.[3]

Instead of viewing these phenomena complacently as occurring within an international context of increasing solidarity within the developing world, or 'South-South' relations, it must be shown that these relations embody disturbing parallels to the relation between industrialized and developing states and may thus be adding to the web of unequal international relations.

Notes

1. The many studies and publications of the Indian Institute of Foreign Trade are instructive in this regard. See B7.
2. Quoted in V5: 17–18.
3. This is an important distinction which must be made in any examination of India's relations with developing countries. Where India has no clear advantage, as with states which are economically and politically stronger than it, the nature of the system in India (its weaknesses rather than its strengths) helps to determine these relations differently, manifested in dependent relations. Where India does have advantages, it may seek to form patron relationships with states dependent upon it.

1. India in the Context of Theories of Imperialism

Theories of imperialism are designed explicitly to explain the international system as based upon underlying economic realities. Theories of imperialism can never be only descriptive – they also have inherent prescriptive qualities. As a discipline, international relations assumes that, through understanding, improvements can be made on the present state of international relations [T6c; B25]. This liberal belief pervades most social science research and therefore the prescriptive element in theories of imperialism is at least no worse than any other such approach. What makes imperialism an anathema to some is the claim by one school of theorists that it is the *only* legitimate construct for understanding international relations. To believe that the traditional liberal approach is more value-free and less ideologically tainted than others is to be blind to its own ideological biases; the behavioural approach supposedly the most value-free, is even more ideologically loaded – it shares the traditional assumptions of liberalism while adopting a deeper 'scientific' disguise. Yet all these various approaches have one underlying bias: *they all continue to perpetuate Eurocentrism*, and this includes the current theories of imperialism. Intellectually and historically, imperialism is simply a way of studying international relations from a particular ideological viewpoint. In essence, imperialism merely describes relationships of subordination by a controlling power over another nation, a common enough situation in international relations.

Theories of imperialism have been instrumental in current concern over development and underdevelopment: the existing inequality within the present international system. The call for a New International Economic Order is largely due to the impact such theories have had during the post-war decolonization period. Most theories of imperialism are concerned with exposing the underlying economic structure of the international system, with a view to remedying what is clearly an unequal political, economic, and social order. In this book, the term imperialism is used as defined in the body of literature describing economic theories of imperialism and not the non-economic theories of imperialism advocated by some writers.[1]

The Theory of Sub-Imperialism and Its Pitfalls

The concept of sub-imperialism was first used by Lenin [L7a] when he characterized Portugal as occupying a sub-imperialist position vis-à-vis Britain. He argued that, while nominally an independent state, Portugal was kept in a dependent relationship with Britain, while benefiting from the imperial international division of labour. Other examples were the old mercantile imperial states in Europe, such as Spain, Holland and Denmark which were able to preserve their remnants of empire into the early 20th Century by subordinating themselves to the new and more dynamic imperialisms of Britain, France and later the US and Japan. In this way these old empires were penetrated economically by the new imperial powers although they retained political control in their own hands. This model has also been applied to the West since 1945, when the now old colonial powers — Britain and France — were placed in a sub-imperialist position with a new imperial power, the United States.

Lenin's use of the term sub-imperialism is not completely synonymous with the contemporary usage. His definition suggested the control of new imperialist centres over older established capitalist powers, whilst contemporary usage applies it to states which themselves are in the throes of developing a new capitalism. Another difference is that the older sub-imperialist states generally exercised their dominance over areas far removed geographically from their own region.[2] In contemporary usage, sub-imperialism has been too loosely applied to states which are attempting to exercise only regional dominance, rather than imperial control in its classical economic sense. A distinction must be made between the use of the term to suggest the full panopoly of economic and political control and its use to indicate temporary regional dominance by a power.

Because current definitions of sub-imperialism are imprecise, a variety of disparate states have been thrown together under this label: Israel, Saudi Arabia, South Africa, Iran, Brazil, Indonesia, Venezuela, Mexico, Zaire, Nigeria and India.[3] It should be evident that they are all 'new' states, not only in the sense of sovereign existence but also (except for India) as *'nouveau riche'* powers. They are, in addition, with the qualified exceptions of Israel and South Africa, Third World powers. According to the model, all these states ostensibly act as agents of Western imperialism. Bearing in mind the contemporary simplistic use of the term sub-imperialism as the operation of a dependent power exercising dominance over its own minisphere of influence in conjunction with its patron, a case would have to be made for including other European settler states besides South Africa. Canada, New Zealand and Australia, for example, and perhaps Western Europe too also act in this sub-imperial role. All of these, like the *nouveau riche* Third World states, are dependent upon a centre — the US — for high technology and finance. At the same time they exercise local dominance in their own spheres of influence whether or not they are remnants of empire. Taking this crude stratification model to its logical extent, Japan could also be regarded as having a sub-imperialist role, bearing in mind Japan's defence dependency on the US.[4]

These weaknesses in sub-imperialist theory, creating the possibility of indiscriminate application, are exemplified by Canada and Mexico, both dominated by US capital. Yet until recently, Mexico found its position inferior to Canada's because, for example, she was not allowed to play the agent role that Canada has played in the Caribbean. (This may change now that Mexico has discovered vast oil reserves.) The same theoretical problem arises when one compares the position of Australia with Argentina circa 1900 when both had a similar level of economic development. Economic factors alone cannot explain the subsequent divergence in their development and their role in the world economy; this may be due to the different composition of their respective internal ruling classes. In one, these classes shared direct racial ties with the metropolitan centre as well as political ties, in the other they did not. As a part of the Anglo-American system, Australia was allowed a modicum of autonomous economic growth earlier than Argentina (or for that matter India, Venezuela, Mexico and South Korea).

There is an additional reason for the differences in capitalist growth in dependent social formations: namely, the presence or absence of organized pre-capitalist social formations, which, even after the advent of capitalism, continue to exert influence as an underlying social formation, and, during the transition period, inhibit full-blown capitalist growth. A society need not be fully capitalist in order to participate in the world capitalist economy; imperialism may deliberately seek to stifle capitalist growth by artificially preserving pre-capitalist social formations and thus maintain control over colonial or neo-colonial societies.

The current use of the term 'sub-imperialism' is, therefore, imprecise and generally incorrectly applied to a group of emerging middle-power states which increasingly act in a hegemonic fashion. Most of these powers are located in the Third World. The term 'sub-imperialism' is applied to those states without properly analysing their internal economic and political formations, and external relationships. It is for this reason that current sub-imperialist constructs are somewhat lacking in rigour when applied to a specific case such as India.

Varynen [V3a] has described what contemporary sub-imperialism is not. Sub-imperialism, he maintains, occurs when a state reaches a certain threshold in its economic development and external relations. But he argues that bilateral sub-contracting, such as takes place in Japan's manufacturing outposts in Taiwan and Hongkong, does not automatically transform these countries into sub-imperialist powers. Rationalized production by multinational firms, which leads to sub-contracting in manufacturing, does not automatically create sub-imperialist powers, as patterns of dominance and dependency amongst sub-contracting states can be mutual.[5] The phenomenon of sub-contracting is not without its own set of contradictions. Japan, along with the US, has built up the economies of Taiwan and South

Korea as extensions of its own, only to find these states competing with Japan itself in its home and export markets [P13].

Varynen also defines sub-imperialism as not constituting transit trade, conduit relationships or tax havens. The Bahamas do not control any other state nor does Singapore, but Singapore does act as a sub-imperial agent in some places. Sub-imperialism has a much wider definition than the mere agent role: it not only involves the dominance of one state over other states on behalf of a metropolitan centre, but such dominance must be seen as partly motivated by the sub-imperialists' own economic and political interests. For this operation to be effective, a state must utilize the full array of political, economic and military levers which are applied to weaker states to keep them in a dependent position.

There are other definitions of sub-imperialism: Galtung has described sub-imperialist powers as go-betweens in a three-tiered system defined by the nature of the exchange. In this, the sub-imperialist agent sends semi-processed goods in exchange for highly processed goods from the centre, while at the same time sending semi-processed goods in exchange for raw materials to states under its own domination. Varynen has pointed out the discrepancies and discontinuities in this model [V3a], particularly by analysing the volume and actual direction of such exchanges.

Other definitions of contemporary sub-imperialism suggest an element of superpower sponsorship, in that a state is deliberately built up to play a sub-imperialist role after its national economy has reached a certain level. How it reaches this level is never explained. India's sponsorship, for example, came from two opposing centres, the Soviet Union and the United States. But such a view of India's autonomy is not intended as supporting Warren's thesis [W4] that, as capitalism expands, imperialism declines. The growth of various national capitalisms is not imperialism's death knell, but rather a new form of imperialism's international division of labour.

A better method of explaining rising middle power states in the Third World may be found in examining the development process in these states themselves. Unequal relations between states are the result of differing levels of development. Development occurs at the expense of some other sector from which it draws capital and resources. Capitalist development's insatiable drive constantly seeks to expand, reproduce and exploit new productive forces.[6] As industrial development in Third World post-colonial states takes place, new areas to exploit must be found to avoid premature collapse. In practice, these new areas can only be found elsewhere in the Third World in states relatively less developed than themselves. As a result, middle powers in the Third World may increasingly behave in a sub-imperialist fashion.

Marini [M10] has suggested that market relations are the key to understanding sub-imperialism. The importance of domestic political and economic structures cannot be overstressed. State capitalism, a term used to describe a state such as India, bears in turn some relation to sub-imperialism.[7] Marini sees sub-imperialist states as participating in global imperialism at the expense of their domestic consumption and more equitable development. He describes them as a form of 'rationalized feudalism' under which old social structures are transformed into modern capitalist structures. This analysis may have some validity for sub-imperialist states in the Third World which, in the past, adopted policies of 'export-oriented' growth at the expense of large sectors of the domestic economy, but it cannot fully explain the contemporary sub-imperial phenomenon. 'Rationalized feudalism' may exist among some oil-rich Gulf states such as Oman, which is currently playing a modest sub-imperial role, but cannot explain other states which are seeking to destroy their feudal remnants. The political economy of those states characterized as sub-imperialist do have some points in common. Capital accumulation, much of the time hoarded, is used for speculation or for personal consumption and when investment does occur it takes place abroad, and not domestically. Sub-imperialism then becomes a manifestation of a state's domestic market inadequacies, which forces it to seek outlets abroad. Land reforms in Iran, Brazil and India are all part of an attempt to modernize domestic economies by destroying the feudal remnants and encouraging the capitalist path of development. Marini suggests that maintenance of this transformation, without leading to domestic political crises, may be by means of military expansion.

Marini made a beginning, but contemporary sub-imperialist theory has been marked by lack of rigorous analysis of the class relations within the sub-imperialist state. This can be more clearly seen in some of the examples that illustrate sub-imperial foreign interventions on behalf of an imperial centre. No proper distinction is drawn between foreign interventions undertaken by Third World states in their own interest and Third World states which intervene in a mercenary or agent role on behalf of a capitalist superpower. Many intra-Third World military interventions in recent years can be cited, but each one must be analysed in order to determine whether a charge of sub-imperialism can be sustained. If strict definitions are adhered to, sub-imperialist action is not simply military intervention by Third World states dependent on the West, but must be accompanied by the economic features found in its imperialist parent.

Theories of sub-imperialism identify the control of finance capital as the means whereby the imperial and/or sub-imperial centre maintains its domination over powers subordinate to them. There is no doubt that through control over international financial and economic institutions the West continues to maintain a hold over the fast developing capitalist economies of the Third World. But monopolies over advanced technology also keep these states in a subordinate position. The case of Japan may indicate an interpretation different from the previous definitions of dependence. Japan was, at one time, totally dependent on the US for much of its finance capital and technology [H2]. Nevertheless it has rapidly built itself into an economic and political rival of the US. It was this kind of phenomenon which led Warren to conclude that mutual dependency existed [W4] — a two-way system epitomized by the case of the OPEC states and their relations with the developed capitalist economies after 1973. It is, therefore, far from clear how much one can characterize a sub-imperialist state as being purely an agent, even after allowing for minor contingent contradictions. India is a good case in point in that, while it is tremendously dependent on the outside world for finance and technology, it has also been able to build itself into a state with its own finance capital and technology. Therefore, the Indian state has some autonomy vis-à-vis the superpowers; Indian missiles are being built to enforce an *Indian*, not a Soviet or American, strategic policy.[8]

The Case of India

Very little empirical analysis of India's current status within imperialism exists. The predominant image of India in the West is that of a weak state beset by severe social, political and economic problems and forced to carry an international begging bowl to help alleviate its internal problems. While this image is not completely unrealistic, India remains a country in which the vast majority of its people live under conditions of abysmal poverty and oppression. India's industrial development is ranked tenth in the world. However, India's industrialization has occurred irrespective of, and in fact at the expense of, the majority of the population.

Like other medium-sized, semi-industrialized states, India has created a state capitalist system, in which the public and private sectors of the economy are intertwined. In the next chapter a fuller explanation of this system will be given. And, like any other capitalism, Indian state capitalism needs room to expand, so as not to stagnate. Unfortunately, its impoverished peasantry does not provide a large outlet for India's industrial goods, (which, in any case, are largely produced to meet the consumer tastes and desires of an urban bourgeoisie) and the saturation point was reached long ago. This has led to the chronic problems of the Indian economy, such as under-utilization of capacity, lack of demand and lack of new investment. The capitalist solution to this dilemma is to go abroad. Industries can then expand, open up new markets and exploit productive forces in other developing countries of Africa and Asia. Thus, India is in the process of becoming a donor of services, aid, finance and technology instead of merely being a recipient. In 1980 India had over 107 industrial investments abroad with at least 100 more planned and numerous contracts abroad. The Government of India had given more than 34 monetary loans to over 13 developing countries worth at least Rs. 4,631.57 million; grants worth Rs. 5,234.86 million; and technical aid to 65 countries, and military aid to at least 32. Indian banks are operating in over 26 developing countries.

From the time of Independence the ambition of India's ruling classes has been to make India a great power. As a part of this ambition, many projects have been undertaken, such as the building of heavy industries, a modern arms industry and a well developed technical infrastructure, and in this respect India is different from otherwise comparable states. The aim has been not simply to develop the country economically on behalf of a ruling alliance of capital (although, of course, this has been an important aim) but also to gain for India all the accoutrements of a great power. Nuclear power, missiles, satellites, aircraft, electronics, and an indigenous arms industry are all there to back up the ruling class's image of itself as representing an important world power.[9]

In earlier years the Indian ruling classes were more unrealistic and confidently declared India to be already a world power [G7; W3]. In the debates in the West concerning the reordering of the post-war world, there were early references to India's inclusion in a conscious Anglo-American plan for the world. India, along with Kuomintang China and Brazil, was to play a 'key-nation' role in different regions of the world on behalf of the West.[10] This was an explicit design for global sub-imperialist agents of which India was to be one. It was revived in the early 1970s as the Nixon Doctrine, but now India's place was taken by pre-revolutionary Iran. Dean Acheson notes [A3; B32] that he always favoured this approach to Western post-war planning for the world over the multilateral–unilateral alliance approach which later predominated under Dulles. Chester Bowles saw India having its own sphere of interest protected by a Monroe-type doctrine and receiving American blessing.

This early Western encouragement of an Indian role in international affairs disintegrated in the 1950s as Indian bureaucratic elites steered India into a more equidistant position between the superpowers. After 1953, as hostility from the USSR diminished, this new stance led to increasing Soviet aid. It was precisely this more balanced position which helped India to gain a measure of autonomy in its foreign policies and increased assistance for its ambitious industrial projects. But this autonomy must not be confused with complete independence; India remained particularly dependent in finance and technology. In the early 1960s India's gains in autonomy suffered a setback after the China–India war and the severe economic dislocations caused by this and other factors, such as drought. Western aid poured in, and Indian state capitalism became temporarily even more dependent on the West, although somewhat offset by continuing Soviet aid, particularly in the fields of armaments production and heavy industry. These changes led to a more realistic assessment of India's power by the Indian ruling classes.

But they did not relinquish efforts to achieve what is now called India's 'potential' power. The victory in the 1971 Indo-Pakistan War gave them back some of the old self-confidence. Articles began to appear, heralding India's reassertion as a regional power [R9]; this contrasted with earlier writings in the post-1962 period expressing frustration that India had been pinned down to the sub-regional theatre by a conspiracy of outside powers.[11] It was also during the late 1970s that earlier Indian ruling-class aspirations for world influence were revived. By this time the Indian state had developed far more tangible instruments of power with which to project its influence abroad. In the West, India was perceived as a new emerging power.[12] The US Presidential Security Affairs adviser used the term 'new influential power' to describe India [B29]. This reassessment was the result of a number of converging factors: India's nuclear explosion of 1974 and the growing insecurity of Western interests in the region following events in Iran, Afghanistan and Pakistan. In order to maintain Western interests in regional 'stability', one might have expected this increased US interest in promoting India. Thus, after 1978, India's state capitalist aims and the aims of the West were increasingly converging.

Promotion of India's power has a much longer history with the case of the Soviet Union. After the Sino-Soviet split of the late 1950s and early 1960s and the emergence of the Soviet Union at the 1965 Tashkent Agreement as arbiter between India and Pakistan,[13] the Soviet Union has sought to promote India in order to offset China's influence in Asia and Africa. The signing of the Indo-Soviet Treaty of Friendship in 1971 put a seal on this relationship. In this way both India's aims and those of the Soviet Union have continued to converge. The attitude of China towards Indian pretensions had considerably softened by the late 1970s.[14] While remaining intensely suspicious of Soviet ties with India, China became slightly more acquiescent in recognizing Indian interests, particularly within South Asia.

Offsetting these new developments and perceptions externally has been the growing Indian internal crisis. Power struggles involving a major realignment of forces making up the ruling power alliance is one manifestation of such crises. Kulak farmers, as well as businessmen with interests abroad, are making their power increasingly felt. Rising consciousness among many people in rural areas is leading to increasing violence, putting pressure on the system as a whole. In addition, this may be coupled with fissiparous tendencies on India's peripheries.

India's quest for some sort of great power status has not been determined by the superpowers alone. Indeed, the primary force remains the aspirations and perceptions of the ruling classes within India itself. No matter how far-fetched the idea may seem, their dream has been to build an India which is an equal to the superpowers, a position many feel was usurped by China.

It is important to remember, however, that the aspirations and perceptions of the Indian ruling classes occur against a background of economic forces, which are the very underpinnings of their position. In other words, if the Indian ruling classes have imperial aspirations, these are not based on some vague craving for power on which Schumpeter's theory of imperialism was based, but on the economic forces which cause India to go abroad. The aim to dominate is not a cause in itself but a manifestation of these underlying forces.

It may be that this self-perception by India's ruling classes is nevertheless at least partially derived from India's sub-imperial role during the colonial period, in which Indian soldiers and officers were sent overseas to battle-fields in Asia and Africa;[15] Indian clerks, and later administrators, were sent to foreign countries; and Indian traders were to be found playing a key intermediary economic role in most parts of the world. In this way many world-wide economic and political links were formed in the pre-independence period, when Indians acted as agents of a European colonial power and an imperialist capitalist system. In pursuit of its wider aims, India has acted to assert itself in the political and economic fields abroad since 1947 in areas where it has had the capacity to act. Where it has lacked this capacity, it has assiduously sought to develop the institutions and infrastructure necessary for it to act, despite the enormous internal constraints placed on these efforts.

It is against this background that we must view India's relations with other developing countries, and it is in this context that the concept of sub-imperialism may have some application. India can be loosely classified as a sub-imperialist power, with the proviso that its case is complex. Because of its policies, India cannot be said to be totally beholden to a Western imperialist centre, for it is simultaneously dependent on two centres, one of which, the Soviet Union, is not directly a part of the world capitalist economy. This alone makes the term difficult to sustain in India's case. Bearing in mind the Indian ruling classes' aspirations, autonomy, not total subordination, has been the real position of India since 1947. This is not to suggest that India has been able to transcend its dependent status, but that this autonomy has influenced the conduct of India's external relations [9b]. The Indian capitalist class has never been a pure comprador class; rather it is a genuine national bourgeoisie. Indian investments abroad in developing countries are in many cases from Indian resources, and international capital is sometimes completely absent. Indian aid is extended to a wide range of states according to Indian interests and not according to Western capitalist or Soviet economic wishes, although these interests may sometimes coincide. Indian banking and insurance abroad, which were once purely service industries for overseas Indian populations, are now increasingly concerned both with servicing Indian investments and external economic relations, as well as direct intervention in local capital markets. The capital used in such banks is Indian national capital, not foreign. The growth in the Indian arms trade and military aid, and other economic activities in developing countries, all suggest a different, if related phenomenon, to sub-imperialism.

Here it is suggested that a more apt and accurate description of India and similar Third World states would be in terms of words like 'proto-imperialist' and 'second-tier imperialist'. These are philological refinements of the term 'sub-imperialist', but important ones. What they do is emphasize the differences between those states which simply play a subordinate agent role on behalf of a fully fledged imperialist power, and those states which have some autonomy and whose foreign policies may sometimes even conflict with imperial centres although, at the same time, they remain basically dependent.

Proto-imperialism indicates a power which is gradually developing all the trappings of imperialism but whose tendencies are not yet fully manifest in an active sense. This precedes a further stage: second-tier imperialism. A second-tier imperialist power acts partially on its own, but only within a theatre with circumscribed limits i.e. the second tier of the international economic and political system, namely relations within the Third World.

Deciding whether India is a proto-imperialist or already a second-tier imperialist power is made difficult by one fact. While in most areas of the Third World, India's present economic activities do not justify such charges, and at most could be characterized as being in the 'proto' stage, in other regions closer to hand, notably within South Asia itself, where the Indian economy is all pervasive, it may be possible to sustain a description of India as a second-tier imperialist state. Sub-imperialism, on the other hand, suggests vertical, organic links to an imperialist power, with consequently very sharp limits on a state's room to manoeuvre autonomously. Second-tier imperialism puts less stress on the limitations, and more stress on the horizontal relationships fostered between the second-tier imperialist power and the developing state it dominates. Superpower centres remain, of course, above this. The proto- and the second-tier imperialist states both act beneath them, exploiting whatever divisions that occur at the top in order to extend their own imperial aspirations at the lower levels. This, no doubt, is a fine distinction from sub-imperialism but one which is absolutely necessary for describing a case such as India, a state which is increasingly involved on its own behalf in other developing countries.[15]

As a proto- and second-tier imperialist state, India shares features with some other developing states. For example, parallels can be found in Brazilian involvement with other developing countries in Latin America and Africa. The smaller economically and technologically weaker developing countries are today facing new fortes in the guise of developing proto- and second-tier imperialist powers, who may contribute to the continuation of a web of exploitation in international relations.

Notes

1. Neither Lenin nor Hobson first discussed the economic roots of imperialism, but an American, Charles Conant [C22] ; see also Robinson and Gallagher [R17] ; W.L. Lancer [L5] and J.A. Schumpeter [S6].
2. This was not always the case, as the example of the Canary Islands illustrates.
3. To which could be added South Korea and Pakistan. The literature thus far has excluded investigation of possible 'social-imperialist' sub-imperialists.
4. Halliday and McCormack [H2] attempt rather unconvincingly to show Japan's dependent links to US capital to support their sub-imperialism thesis. This view shares weaknesses with other analyses of post-war Japanese reconstruction, which all underrate the impact of unseen war loot for initial post-war investment in rebuilding industrial enterprises damaged by war.
5. Some disagree with this exclusion of sub-contractors from the ranks of sub-imperialists. See S11 and R38a.
6. For a discussion on capital accumulation and reproduction, Karl Marx

Capital Vol. 1, Pt. 7, Moscow, 1977.

7. Even in states such as Brazil which currently have a large private industrial sector, state enterprises have been of crucial importance in building up domestic industry. So, too, in the case of Japan during the Meiji period. In the next chapter this link will be shown more explicitly.

8. Marwah, Onkar, 'India's Nuclear and Space Programs: Intent and Policy', *International Security* Vol. 2, No. 2, Fall 1977. India's second and successful launch of an IROM (SLV-3) took place in July 1980.

9. Henceforth the term 'ruling classes' will be used to indicate in a collective sense all the elements, that is the national bourgeoisie, military, Kulak farmers and the bureaucracy who compose the ruling capitalist alliance in India.

10. Roosevelt and Churchill meetings during the War, and other Allied conferences, seem to have been the genesis for this type of thinking. Ganguli, B.N., *Integration of International Economic Relations*, New Delhi, 1968. This may also help to explain why Stalin viewed India as little more than an Anglo-American puppet.

11. A position it shares with Venezuela which is seeking to impose its own sphere of influence over the Caribbean and Central America. See P5 and M25.

12. San Gupta [S5] puts his own gloss on the Soviet–Indian relationship when he writes that the USSR recognizes that: 'India as a major power capable of playing, destined to play a significant role in World Affairs' (p. 88). Soviet interests in promoting India are in part due to its belief in the progressiveness of the Indian national bourgeoisie, whose interests, once promoted, it is believed, will help erode Western imperialism.

13. This after accusing India of expansionism in 1974 during the absorption of Sikkim. *Hsinhua*, 24 June, 7 September, 12 September 1974. Deng Xiao-ping stated early in 1981 that he regarded India as the 'elder brother' of South Asia, *Times of India*, 9 April 1981.

14. A tradition carried over into the post-independence period, in which Indian soldiers have been despatched all over the world on training missions and as part of the UN's peacekeeping operations.

15. As in the analysis of Soviet 'imperialism', India's external relations many times manifest themselves first in the political field; economic features only follow later. This does not invalidate analysis of Indian second-tier imperialism however; rather, a political–economic analysis must be applied to fully explain the Indian case, and must be based on examining the nature of the state in India.

2. The State Capitalist System in India

An extensive literature exists on the definition of the state. For Marx, it was a committee for managing the affairs of the bourgeoisie, a coercive instrument of a ruling class [M28; P13]. But some of his other definitions of the nation state were unclear. For example, he wrote that it was an organization adopted by the bourgeoisie to guarantee their property and interests and serve their needs [B30; H11]. Lenin made the link between capitalism and the state clearer, when he wrote that the state was a product of irreconcilable class antagonisms, an organ by which one class oppresses another [L76]. Both saw the state as specific to the structure of bourgeois capitalism which, with the advent of socialism, would wither away. Murray [M38a] has elaborated this point, arguing that the state acts to safeguard and guide capitalism in the use of its infrastructure: generating capital and technology and managing its external relations.[1] Murray sees capitalism as developing the state and the state as colluding to protect capitalism. This Marxist view differs from conventional liberal theories that see the state as an independent reality [M28; M38a]. Theirs is a utilitarian conception of the state according to which states are defined as self-determined units. International relations in this view are those relations between these units, with each state seeking to maximize its own interests.

The Marxist view is opposed to the liberal view that sees states as being determined solely by internal political processes. For the Marxist, the state is not an independent reality but is made up of the institutions which comprise it. These institutions in turn are related to the international economy. The world market is not a collection of many national economies, these are structurally linked and integral parts of one another. Thus it is not a question of a specific state's origins but its political structure in relation to the world market which is important. Hence the internal structure of the state has its own importance, because a Marxist interpretation is that a ruling class dominates a particular society in order to safeguard its interests in each state and determine its participation in the existing international capitalist system.[2] Any conventional study of nationalism will show that states can be created and dismantled, although certain political and economic forces must exist in order for a state to emerge or disappear. It is often overlooked, perhaps due to Eurocentrism, that all states have been created,[3] that none is immortal: many modern European states, such as Italy, Finland, Germany, Belgium, and Bulgaria are less than 150 years old. This may be why some European Marxists have diverged from their own theoretical foundations when discussing states in Europe. Poulantzas [P13] saw states in Europe as springing from economic forces, but went on to argue that territorial, linguistic and ideological factors were all motivating forces; he thus confuses state with nation. The latter, a completely different phenomenon, is often invoked to justify a state, but just as often bears little relation to it, as when state and nation do not coincide. As states are created, so — where common linguistic or cultural ties exist — can nations. For these ties to be translated into a 'nation', however, is not necessarily 'inevitable'. Modern nationalism is just one element which capitalism utilized to provide itself with added support. Where 'national' capitals have developed, they have needed the assistance of modern institutions, such as the state, which becomes an institution for the exchange of and division of labour, the basis of the capitalist mode of production.[4] The need for inviolate boundaries (tariff barriers) is linked with the rise of capitalism, and state power can serve that end too. This does not prevent the state becoming obsolete after the stage of national capital, as may occur in advanced capitalist countries due to the activities of multinational companies. The international system is interdependent, linked world wide through imperialism. It has not, however, reached the extent of Kautsky's ultra-imperialism which envisaged transnationals in complete control. International economic institutions, such as the IBRD, IMF and OECD, are more symptomatic of the present trends of a system that is linked through international capital. The difference between the Marxist and the liberal use of the term 'interdependence' is that the latter sees it as essentially equal and natural, while the Marxist sees it as less than equal according to concepts of unequal exchange.[5]

The Transition and the Post-Colonial States

A problem for Marxist and neo-Marxist analyses of the state is the continued existence of socialist states in a long-term condition of transition. A body of literature exists [B17b; B17c] addressing itself to the phenomenon of the failure of the state to wither away after the achievement of socialism. This literature concerns itself with the nature of the state in a transitional social formation, particularly in socialist societies. Marx wrote that it was not enough to transfer control of a bureaucratic military machine after a revolution, but that it had to be smashed.[6] As a result of his practical experience, Lenin envisaged a transition period between capitalism and socialism.[7] In 1923, Pashukanis wrote [H11: 18] that, while in transition it was understandable for the state to use inherited bourgeois forms, such as the law and government institutions. Bettelheim has elaborated on these points, claiming that there are no socialist states, only states in transition to socialism. He also argues that the possibility of a capitalist restoration persists as long as these states continue to use capitalist models and participate in the world capitalist economy.[8] A transitional society can either go forward to a new mode of production, or backwards to its old mode. The transitional social formation is not confined solely to the change from capitalism to socialism but can also be used as a term to describe societies in transition from feudalism, or some other pre-capitalist mode of production, to modern capitalism.[9]

The concept of transition may not be seen as viable on its own, but it is a crucial tool for understanding not only the socialist societies but also the nature of the state in post-colonial societies.[10] This concept has much wider application to those countries which are characterized as state capitalist, post-colonial societies. Transition implies movement from one social formation to another, a process that aptly describes the situation in many developing countries like India. State capitalism is essentially a capitalist strategy in a situation where several modes of production exist and are in the process of transition to capitalism. At the same time, these dying modes are to some degree in contention, with capitalism resisting their onslaught. This in turn generates contradictions in which different classes contend, resulting in conflicts which are reconciled by the over-arching capitalist system [C21].

Kalecki offers another view of the transitional state [K1a; S3b] which he calls the 'intermediate regime' in the Third World. In his view, the present international situation creates autonomy for the native bourgeoisie because of the numerical strength of a lower middle class, the intervention of the state in economic relations, and economic assistance from the socialist world. Internal hostility from big bourgeoisie,[11] foreign capital, feudal land-lords, and the landless, subsistence farmers and workers, confronts such a regime. To counter this, such regimes follow policies of economic autonomy, to gain a measure of independence from foreign capital. They institute land reforms and try to assure continuous growth. For Kalecki, it is a state capitalism devised by a petty-bourgeois ruling class that characterizes the transitional regime, led by 'tycoons with a lot to lose'.

Those who control the transitional state are most important to our analysis as it is they who guide the direction taken by the state. Again, it is the study of the socialist states and their bureaucratic elites, particularly in the Soviet Union, which has furnished models for understanding the nature of transitional states in post-colonial societies. The starting point is what Lenin called the 'workers' state with bureaucratic distortion' [C4b] wherein a state bourgeoisie was formed out of state functionaries. These agents grow out of the transitional social formation and gain their power and autonomy through their control over state property. They become the collective owners, maintaining a state for their own interests. Such bureaucratic elites are not unique to socialist countries but exist in capitalist societies as well [M28]. They are not servants or instruments of state policy but policy formulators ensuring the continuity and preservation of the capitalist (or ostensibly socialist) system. Deutscher [D16] has analysed the tendency towards bureaucratization throughout the world — the 'managerial' approach to the running of states. Bureaucracy thrives under certain conditions, its strengths being only the reflection of a society's weaknesses. Bureaucracy grows and is stimulated through the breakdown of feudalism and the rise of capitalism, which elevates bureaucracy in its own interests. When feudal and bourgeois interests conflict, bureaucracy is the arbiter and power ultimately passes to it.

This account sums up the condition of transitional post-colonial states. Deutscher describes a stalemate of contending forces, as in post-1921 USSR in which only bureaucracy gains and creates its own special elite. If this deadlock should be broken, as eventually it must in any transitional social formation, then this bureaucratic elite should disappear, since because it does not constitute a unique social class it lacks the ability to reproduce itself.[12] It is only a reflection of a society's class content and can either merge into the bourgeoisie of a capitalist society or dissolve through socialist development [S34].

Role of the Bureaucracy in Post-Colonial States

In the post-colonial society at independence the state is integral to its identity. The residue of colonial rule remaining in most Third World states has been a large service sector or government bureaucracy; an intermediary stratum formed to administer and help extract resources. This sector is deliberately permitted to emerge faster than the local industrial sector. The superstructure is so overdeveloped at independence that it dominates all social classes. Bureaucrats, military officers, professionals, academics, commercial and banking personnel comprise this intermediary stratum. Bureaucratic order presides over the state machinery in the absence of any single coherently organized and more powerful social class, such as peasants and workers or an industrial bourgeoisie.[13] The bureaucratic elite, in fact, wish to perpetuate a stalemate between private business and the working class so as to maintain their control. This necessitates a strategy of land reforms, labour laws, rhetorical socialism, restrictions on foreign capital and some control over private business. To maintain their state power, the services sector must foster development, and accumulate more power so as to distribute the benefits to the constituent portions making up the state capitalist alliance [J7]. For this reason, after independence, the bureaucratic elites launch public sector growth and use it to destroy the old feudal aristocracy. They never own but only control the public sector [M24; K8: 30–1].

Alavi [A9b: 59–81] has defined the bureaucratic elite in post-colonial states as a 'military-bureaucratic oligarchy' playing a semi-autonomous role determined by those classes directly engaged in the production process. This oligarchy in turn acts to safeguard the interests of those who are the owners of production. This analysis differs from neo-colonial dependency theories that view bureaucrats, along with the national bourgeoisie, as compradors and agents of a metropolitan centre.

The gradual trend toward increasing economic nationalism in Third World states is an indication of the autonomy of bureaucratic elites in transitional post-colonial states. This autonomy is determined by internal class structures, and the fact that other social forces are undergoing formation or disintegration. An additional factor is the external environment which does allow for a limited variety of choices in meeting the state's technological and financial needs. The bureaucratic elites mediate between these forces by utilizing the state capitalist system.

Dependency and Development

Development (or its absence) in Third World countries has been extensively studied. The economic and political structure of the post-colonial state is an integral part of dependency theories, as it is of the development of underdevelopment and the neo-colonial perspectives.[14]

In all examinations of post-colonial states, the question of relative autonomy arises. The neo-colonial perspective [F2; N12; F1] concedes little autonomy to the decolonized state, propounds the view that the nominally 'independent' state is totally dependent. Thus, primarily, the present system is a sophisticated continuation of the old colonial system. Such analysis, however, involves several simplifications. The different social formations within each post-colonial state are overlooked, as well as the achievement of various stages of growth. Additionally, their differing degree of integration in the world economy is disregarded. The types of social structure in each state at the time of colonization, the degree to which an economic transformation took place, and the resulting nature of these social structures at independence all vary. The comprador view ignores the existence in some post-colonial states of a national bourgeoisie that helped determine the present dominant mode of production. Whilst this view is not wholly incorrect – indeed it describes the condition of many Third World states – nevertheless, in some cases, due to thě scale of internal class development, and more importantly, the degree of independent industrialization, the state in these cases has achieved autonomy.

Independent industrialization was the direct result of independence for many post-colonial states, even while they remained dependent in many respects. In India, the quality of dependence changes with the response to changes in the international environment: for example, the availability of alternative sources of aid. Alavi [A9c] sees the dependency theory as inadequate because it denies the fundamental structural differences between the post-colonial and the colonial situation, in that, instead of native capital being subordinated to imperialism, there is a post-colonial convergence of interests. Dependence continues in the areas of technology and finance, but under the leadership of the bureaucratic capitalist elite, indigenous industrialization can take place on a much larger scale. 'As a consequence of indigenous capitalist development, an increasing proportion of surplus value is appropriated internally, by the capitalist class' [A9c : 193]. Issa Shivji[15] divides the possible structures in post-colonial states into three, here transposed into two.[16] First, there is the neo-colony, in which a large private sector dependent on international capitalism predominates; states of this kind are characterized by uneven internal development. Secondly, there is the state capitalist regime, with a large public sector run by bureaucrats and a national bourgeoisie, who have 'non-antagonistic contradictions with the international bourgeoisie'. It is this last case, with its degree of relative autonomy, with which we are most concerned.

The claim that state capitalist regimes enjoy a measure of autonomy does not mean that independent industrialization results in the elimination of dependence, as Warren argued [W4]. A distinction must be drawn between autonomy and total independence, because technological dependence remains even under state capitalism. Nevertheless, some Third World industrialization has led to the formation of some autonomous finance capital [M9: 374]. It is important to bear in mind, however, that state capitalism remains firmly capitalist and an integral part of the world capitalist system. Its exploitative relations abroad are maintained as part of its imperialist nature.

In most post-colonial societies since 1945, a hegemonic position by a single dominant social class has not yet been achieved. This position must be created in order for capitalism to flourish effectively on native soil. Just as classic imperialism needs a secure territory of its own and legitimacy of state power at home, so does the peripheral capitalism of the Third World states. This was the historical experience of Meiji Japan when it was placed on the periphery of an imperial system. It utilized state investment and the modern state itself to lay the foundations for the growth of industrial capitalism [H1].

State Capitalism

State capitalism is determined by the class nature of a state, and 'state ownership' is the 'seizure of the means of production in the name of society' [B17b]. Szentes has defined state capitalism as 'nothing else but the restriction and regulation by the state of economic spontaneity stemming from the existence of private capital.'[17]

The Soviet state, in which the planning process, the power of the state and the collective private property of a state bourgeoisie comprise its major features, has been described as state capitalism [B17b]. The important fact to be drawn from an analysis of the USSR, and applied to the post-colonial state, is that such a regime is specific to a transitional social structure.

Chattopadhyay [C4b] claims that any transitional social formation can move towards state capitalism. Thus, a colonial experience is not essential as long as a state can be said to be in transition from one mode of production to another. State capitalism fuels this transition, as was the case in Japan where the bureaucracy eventually relinquished its control to the private sector; an example repeated in Brazil in the late 1960s. Turkey, Mexico and Bolivia, all state capitalist countries, sought to industrialize independently and tried to create internal markets through land reforms, and proposed nationalization of their natural resources.[18] [P11b].

There are, however, differences between the state capitalist regimes of the 'new' states and the pre-war examples. One difference is that 'new' states now gain more support for their policies from the socialist states. While Western imperialism weakens as a result of its own divisions, the 'new' states are becoming strengthened. This has enabled the post-1945 state capitalist regimes in the Third World to seek alternative sources of technology and finance instead of relying on one centre. State capitalism in the Third World is, then, a response to the present international system in which dependent states seek to lessen this dependence by asserting their autonomy in fields where they have room to manoeuvre. State capitalism in Third World countries is based on a different internal class composition, which distinguishes it from the parallel phenomenon in advanced capitalist and socialist countries. The 'new' states are fighting foreign capital and domestic feudal interests — both essential tasks if their own productive forces are to be developed.

The definition of state capitalism is too loose for contemporary Third World states. A provisional distinction must be made between those regimes with a bureaucratic bourgeoisie that mediates between and acts collectively on behalf of all the capitalist interests within a country, and those regimes whose bureaucrats use state capitalism to discriminate against and erode the power of a particular capitalist sector in the national economy. It is this factor which differentiates states like Malaysia and Kenya, led by Malay and African (especially Kikuyu) bureaucratic capitalists only, from India and Tanzania led by truly 'national' bureaucratic capitalists.[19] In the former case, this imperfection in the mediating role of the bureaucracy over national capital leads to far more metropolitan dependence and reliance on Western capital. In the latter case, national capital is represented and managed more equitably, leading to greater unity and autonomous strength in these state capitalist systems.

As capitalism has suffered shocks, the state in all parts of the capitalist world has increased its intervention in the economic process, in many cases by adopting Keynesian solutions. As a result, some authors have labelled all capitalism state capitalism. Lenin saw the intervention of the state as the result of capitalist development which was itself leading to state capitalism [C4a: 17]. The intervention of the state under state capitalism in post-colonial societies differs from the intervention of the state under liberal capitalism. Under the latter it is always undertaken in the direct interest of the private sector. In state capitalism, this is also true but, additionally, the state itself is the owner and substitute for a private sector. State intervention in such cases is designed to eliminate underdevelopment and unleash productive forces, a function quite different from liberal interventionism which is designed to serve and not create private capital.

Second-Tier Imperialism

Once the productive sectors of the economy have begun to function and classes and social forces within a state have coalesced, the bureaucratic elite cannot develop further on its own and state capitalism reaches an impasse. At this point it is postulated that new formations may be either in the direction of private capitalism or of socialism. In the short term a solution to this capitalist crisis must be sought.

This crisis of internal forces and limited opportunities for bureaucratic state expansion may lead the post-colonial state capitalist regime to seek external outlets. By this means, the state can continue to expand the powers and influence of bureaucratic elites, postpone the battle of forces within the post-colonial society and thus prolong their power *and* the transitional phase of state development. This is what this book designates as second-tier imperialism. Bearing in mind the relative autonomy of the state capitalist regime, sub-imperialism, as suggested in chapter 1, seems inappropriate to describe a situation that indicates a neo-colonial agent role for the post-colonial state. Second-tier imperialism, on the other hand, stresses the horizontal stratification of the international system and the opportunities provided by such a structure for state capitalist regimes to penetrate other developing countries. At the same time second-tier imperialist countries continue to be dependent upon the advanced capitalist world.

State Capitalism in India

India shares many of the characteristics of other post-colonial state capitalist nations.[20] India's state capitalism is led by a bureaucratic elite, even though the regime embraces several other elements comprising a ruling coalition, including: the national bourgeoisie (large private business), the army, Kulaks (wealthy farmers), small traders and moneylenders. This view of India's political economy diverges from others both from the left and the right of the political spectrum. Without this basic definition as state capitalist, it is difficult to account for India's economic and political drive in respect of other developing countries.

The conservative view is that India is a democracy with strong socialist tendencies; the liberal view modifies this by pointing out that since independence India has been a democracy with a 'mixed' economy. On the left, the most popular view of India is that of a bourgeois comprador regime headed by native big business: an oligarchy in alliance with foreign capital. According to Ajit Roy 'The State is not an independent social force but a coordinate of private business',[21] an argument that received part of its main thrust from M. Kidron's study of foreign investment in India.[22] After the early 1960s, foreign capital regained and resubjugated India through its control of capital supported by Indian big business. This viewpoint, however, is not supported by the data. As Kidron shows, in 1963, of 2,000 collaboration agreements, 1,750 were technical and not equity capital agreements [H9a]. Assigning a key role to big business (foreign as well as indigenous) in India has become almost a doctrine in left-wing Indian politics. It has also been conveniently adopted by some bureaucrats playing the role of controllers of the public sector. Focussing on private big business alone is also consistent with the neo-colonial perspective, which stresses the role of a native ruling class, in this case the Indian bourgeoisie, who collaborate and act as lackeys of international capital.[23] This point of view, however, overlooks the historical and present reality of India; from India's industrial beginnings, native capitalists have sought to build a national capitalism. Another shortcoming of the neo-colonial perspective is its assignment of a primary place to Indian big business, neglecting the other ruling class groups which also help determine the state's economic and political policies, and indeed, compose part of the state's power.

In the early 1970s a debate — influenced by Andre Gundar Franks writings — raged in India's *Economic and Political Weekly*[24] about India's mode of production. The only conclusion to emerge was that capitalism had established itself in India and was in the process of destroying a pre-capitalist mode of production. But the debate did illustrate that Indian society was undergoing a sharp transition; the consequence of capitalism which was still conquering remote areas.[25] Native capitalism in India was late in developing due to the depredations and deliberate policies of the colonial regime [D24, J6]. Full-scale colonization in India saw no shortage of capital, and incipient industrial enterprises existed in the form of native merchant capital and imperial Mughal enterprises [P8; I8]. A vast literature exists concerned with the drain on Indian capital to fuel Britain's industrial revolution and the destruction of Indian weaving in order to create a market for British cloth factories. Later in the 19th Century, colonial policy was deliberately designed to stifle any native industrial growth so as to safeguard British industry, already increasingly threatened by German and American competition.

The colonial period in India in many ways laid the foundation for India's post-independence system. The public sector — railways and ordnance factories — was created by the British. Deliberately or not, colonialist India was singled out to serve a sub-imperial role. Movement of Indian labour to other colonies and the dispatch of soldiers was a common feature, and, by the late 19th Century, Indian traders were playing a key intermediary role in opening new areas for the British as they penetrated the hinterland of colonies in East Africa and South-east Asia. With independence, this role as mere colonial agent was supplanted or supplemented by Indian national aims; sub-imperialism giving way to second-tier imperialism.

Although the end of the 19th Century saw the rise of the first native capitalists in India (notably the Tatas), political events in 1905 and during the First World War really sowed the seeds of India's rise to industrial capitalism. A consequence of the Swadeshi movement (resulting from the 1905 partitioning of Bengal) was attempts (often abortive) by Indian businessmen to set up light industries and to capitalize on nationalist feeling by boycotting foreign goods.

During the First World War, the British out of necessity dictated that India must manufacture more of its own goods as well as contribute to the war effort. This change, once conceded, was irreversible and, between the World Wars, India's industrialists continued to build up their enterprises. What is striking about this second oldest (after Japan) industrial bourgeoisie in Asia is that its nationalist aims were manifested from its earliest days [C3]. Operating within a colonial framework, Indian industrialists were constantly fighting against restrictions designed to preserve their market for British industry. This is of cardinal importance to the understanding of subsequent post-independence events and government policies, as well as Indian state capitalism. In frustration, many Indian capitalists turned towards the politics of nationalism in order to further their interests. For example, India's foremost capitalist, G.D. Birla, began funding the Congress Party from the 1930s, and Gandhi's alliance with the Ahmedabad textile industrialists was an important factor in the nationalist movement. It is not surprising, then, that the most influential section of Indian big business sought to shape post-independence industrial policy along national lines. Their aims thus coincided with the interests of India's rising professionals, petty-bourgeois and medium-sized rural land-owners. A broad consensus on the issue of extensive state involvement in industry was therefore accepted and in 1938, when the National Planning Committee of the Indian National Congress decided that post-independent India would have a large public sector, representatives of Indian big business concurred [C4a].

The most important document from the pre-independence period establishing the state capitalist path for India was the Bombay Plan of 1944, issued from a conference led by the two largest Indian capitalists, J.R.D. Tata and G.D. Birla and including political leaders such as Nehru [J6]. It openly called for increased state intervention in the Indian economy and was the precursor of the 1948 Industrial Policy Resolution.[26] This Resolution envisaged state and private sectors working in tandem and the role of the state as one of opening up new, high technology and heavy industry. A public sector would be established to augment, assist and complement a private sector. The Indian state capitalist system was designed to build a cost-free infrastructure for the Indian bourgeoisie.[27]

While the main concern of the system is to maintain state power and foster industrial growth the private sector of the economy is still the largest, its size maintained not only by private industry but by private agriculture too, which, in 1971, contributed over 40% of the GDP.[28] Therefore, as long as agriculture and small trading remain in the private sector, a state capitalist system will continue to be maintained in India.

Since Independence, India's agricultural policy has been two-pronged. While the government has sought to 'rationalize' agriculture by abolishing large feudal landholdings, hence the land reform legislation of the early 1950s, simultaneously land reform policy has been approached with extreme caution to avoid upsetting the rural landed class, which is part of the existing ruling alliance. The aim has been to widen this class by gradually removing the biggest landlords, and replacing them with a Kulak class of smaller land-owners or 'farmer-cultivators'. In the early 1960s when (due to non-implementation of land reforms), this 'rationalization' by legislation in agriculture was making slow progress, Western technology resulted in new farming techniques that necessitated a switch from labour to capital inten-sive agriculture. Medium-sized farmers were ideally suited to these new processes (the 'Green Revolution' [F3a]) which hastened the capitalization of the countryside, destroyed feudal vestiges in many areas, and created a new independent class of kulak farmers who, in the colonial period, had formed an intermediate stratum beneath the feudal landlords. Today they comprise one of the constituent parts of Indian state capitalism. The Green Revolution, while raising production, also increased the impoverished rural population by adding to the pool of landless peasants. As feudal ties gave way to modern capitalist wage relations, the population driven off the land has nowhere to go as India's industrial development is ill-equipped to absorb a labour force of such magnitude. Another result of the Green Revolution in India has been·a growing regional disparity as prosperous agricultural areas gain at the expense of other areas. Thus, rather than 'neglecting' agriculture, Indian state bureaucracy and the government have been equally concerned to develop capitalism in both agriculture and industry. This has involved sizeable investment in irrigation projects, chemical fertilizer plants and rural electri-fication in some areas.[29]

India's Defence Industries
The defence industries are one manifestation of India's state capitalism, with implications not only for analysing the Indian state itself but also its long term relationships with other developing countries which sometimes take the form of military aid and assistance (see chapter 4) in turn generating arms exports on a commercial basis. By the 1970s, India had an important, growing arms industry, largely ignored by analysts of India's economy and foreign policy. Since 1947 India has sought to develop all its productive forces for the benefit of the ruling classes, and central to this process is the defence industry. In this context, Japan provides an important model.[30]

From the early Meiji period there was an awareness of the dangers of over-reliance on foreign capital for development, and the threat then posed to Japan's independence by the imperialist powers. To safeguard this independence, Japan's Meiji leaders sought to build a modern industrial state by the fastest means available. This led to what has been characterized as the 'unique features of Japanese industrialization' [N13: 224], namely, monopolistic state control over 'strategic' industries. The aim was to establish industry not simply for its own sake but also for strategic reasons, laying the foundation of a modern army and navy. This led to the creation of heavy industries and forced the Japanese state to undertake the development of an armaments industry. Special attention was paid by the Japanese imperial state to industries such as shipbuilding, mines, steel and communications.[31] In Japan, therefore, industrialization can be equated with militarization, and the 'normal', classical order for capitalist development was reversed. Japan rapidly equalled Western technology in the field of armaments and some key industrial sectors. This emphasis on heavy industry, however, did facilitate the continued existence of a traditional small trader and handicrafts sector. The early importance of military industries and their continued expansion resulted in an overall stimulation of industry, boosting self-sufficiency in all fields of industrial production, and, in some defence industry areas, the state transferred its powers to the private sector. Concomitantly, state-owned strategic industries conferred strength on the bureaucrats who eventually largely controlled both public and private sectors of the economy. The Japanese defence industry continued to play a central role in the economy up to 1945, accounting for 25% of annual public expenditure and numerous loans to underwrite the cost. One result of this was high inflation, since industries required increasing rates of taxation to finance them [K7a; K7b; O1]. Another, more disturbing, feature of Japanese defence related industrial development was the inherent crisis in the expansion of production necessary for modern arms industries. The Japanese imperial state had to expand and engage in imperialistic wars in order to absorb the tremendous output of arms; an almost classic example of the Luxemburg imperialism thesis [L15].

These features of Japanese development led to analyses of the arms production sectors of all developed economies in those states which have not only developed defence industries but a fairly broad industrial base. In 1957, Michal Kalecki — a foremost analyst and proponent of the view that arms production is a key to the understanding of advanced capitalist economies — wrote[32] that in the post-war period the US became dependent on the continuous production of armaments; which helps to explain the entire structure of the American 'military-industrial complex'. Kalecki's analysis was based on Rosa Luxemburg's contention that capitalist development is dependent on constant expansion into external markets, and one way of reaching these markets is through 'wasteful' expenditure on armaments. This may be an extreme conclusion but nevertheless, it is essential to recognize the importance of arms industries to the viability of capitalism in most industrialized countries, and possibly to some newly industrializing countries such as India. Defence industrial development and expenditure are vital to many national economies in maintaining profitability, a healthy rate of reinvestment, and generating exports. Arguments about the 'wasteful' aspect of arms industry have, in the past, perhaps been misguided,[33] in so far as defence industries generate long-term gains in technology through research and development that eventually boosts the overall level of production. Whether these confer any great gains to the population is debatable, but some have argued that, eventually, they do.

Today, arms industries and the exports generated are necessary to the economic health of the USA, USSR, France, UK, West Germany and, in the future, increasingly so to Israel, Japan, South Korea, India, Brazil, Singapore and perhaps China.[34] The superpowers participate in the world arms trade for strategic reasons, nevertheless economic determinants play a key role. The USA is the largest arms supplier in the world, although this accounts for only a small part of its total exports, defence industries are an essential part of US domestic economy. This was particularly striking in the post-1979 period when a 'new cold war economy' was launched. The second largest arms supplier in the world market is the USSR. Arms exports constitute more than 10% of total Soviet exports. France is the third largest followed by Britain and then West Germany; in these three countries, exporting arms is seen in terms of commercial motives.

In order to survive modern defence industries must exploit economies of scale, and this generates massive excess capacity. Today such industries cannot be suddenly keyed-up, modern wars of short duration require vast stockpiles and continuous production. Such industries can hope to survive only through exports. These economic compulsions manifest themselves in two ways: in their importance to the country's overall economic health through the generation of employment and demand on all other sectors of the economy; and the needs of defence industries to maintain large scale production for guaranteed markets. As India develops its defence industries along with its overall level of industrial production, many of these features may present themselves. This could have far reaching effects on India's external relations.

Whilst possessing its own unique features, the context in which the arms and defence-related industries in India have developed is similar to that of other countries. The foundations of India's defence industries were laid during the colonial period to service British imperial armies, with the first modern ordnance factory opened in 1793. By the end of the 19th Century, the British-led Indian army was used increasingly for a variety of colonial missions. In the 20th Century, as a consequence of the Indian army's involvement in two world wars, there was greater demand for India to use her resources to equip and arm her own troops. The defence industries introduced and built by the British played a vital role in India's industrial development as the precursor of the heavy industrial base for the public sector developed after 1947.

In 1979 there were over 32 ordnance factories plus nine other defence industries in the public sector and 32 defence research establishments for a total of at least 75 military units. These employed at least 280,000 workers with 1.5 million others indirectly benefiting from defence related employment. These units were under the overall control of a Minister of State for Defence Production although ordnance factories had their own Director-General. Illustrative of India's tremendous capacity in its defence industries was a 400% rise in production between 1971 and 1972 alone, due to Indo-Pakistan hostilities.[35] Production between 1968 and 1969 was worth Rs.450 million, reaching Rs.6,000 million by 1977 (see Table 2.1). In the past 35 years India has become self-sufficient in many areas of defence (see Chapter 4, Table 4.8) with defence industries producing a full range of

Table 2.1
Indian Arms Exports

Year	Value of Exports (Rs. Million)	Value of Total Production (Rs. Million)
1967	25.5	450 (1968–69)
1971–72	22.70	3,140
	70.5	
	100	
1972–73	35	–
1973–74	44	4,174
	54	
1974–75	196.40	3,000
1975–76	93.80	3,620
	146.50	
1976–77	125.80 (first half)	6,000 (full year)
1977–78	–	4,250

Source: *Economic and Commercial News, Hindu, Indian Economic Diary, BBC Summary of World Broadcasts, Times of India, Christian Science Monitor, Financial Times*

hardware and software, from sophisticated electronics and heavy arms to a full range of ancillaries. But despite efforts to develop indigenous models of heavy weaponry, a substantial part of India's defence industry is still in production under licence. In an attempt to remedy this, from 1978 India raised its defence research and development expenditure to 20% of the total defence budget.[36]

India's annual defence expenditure accounts for only 3.5% of its GDP, but this does not include all defence expenditures [T1]. More importantly, such figures cannot give a true indication of the importance of the defence industry to the overall economy. Marwah [M11] has claimed that defence is the second largest industrial sector in India. The effect of defence on growth is, then, a concealed area of the Indian economy. Benoit [B14] in his study of defence and development in India found that in the 1960s defence had stimulated economic growth and financial investment. The National Defence Council, formed in 1962, targetted key sectors, such as machine tools, steel, minerals, power and scientific development, for expansion and development in the civilian sphere. One of the most important effects of defence industry lies in the field of procurements it generates. In the late 1960s these comprised 58% of the defence budget; in 1964–65, 7% of India's total production. By the 1970s the spin-off effects became increasingly apparent and important. In 1971–72, private sector sub-contracts from the government for such items as bomb bodies, tail units, and other ancillaries were worth Rs.279 million, excluding software contracts. The private sector has been well aware of the importance of defence industries to its own growth. A favourite ploy of Indian businessmen in the past was to seek industrial licences for items to be used in defence during times of 'national' crisis. Such production, although licensed for defence, was subsequently used for the civilian market bringing windfall profits. This kind of private public sector link-up of defence production is a general characteristic of India's state capitalism but must not be overstated.[37] In 1979 the Indian Defence Minister announced that ancillary production in the private sector would be encouraged by the signing of long-term contracts involving 28 defence projects worth Rs.3,200 million. In 1977, in South India alone, over 250 private industries were involved in defence contracts, with 125 sustained orders on their books. Integration remains incomplete and defence experts [S32] have advocated a deeper understanding of defence production as an integral part of overall industrial growth.

As in Japan in an earlier period, India's industrial sector, including defence, co-exists with small industry and traditional handicrafts. Vast areas of the domestic economy remain outside the modern industrial sector without any purchasing power. India's defence industry shares many of the problems of all Indian industry, particularly under-utilization of capacity. This problem has become particularly acute since 1965 when arms projects began to produce results [T3]. Indian arms industries, therefore, face a classic dilemma of maintaining their standard and participating in modern economies of scale. They must keep production going at a high optimum level or stagnate; in short, expand or perish.

India's Arms Exports

Against this background it is essential that a medium-sized industrial economy such as India's, with sizable arms production, take certain steps in order to maintain itself. The answer has been to export its arms, irrespective of long-term political implications — a familiar pattern in other industrial arms economies, but a new phenomenon for India. In 1967, the government hinted that excess production could be exported to other developing countries. In the same year, automatic weapons worth Rs.25.5 million were exported, mostly to Sri Lanka. In January 1970, the government confirmed that India was exporting arms, involving five defence factories. A government decision to export arms on a large scale, setting a target of £5 million worth of arms exports per year was taken in 1972. In that year between Rs.70.5 million and Rs.100 million worth of arms (see Table 2.1) were exported to countries in Africa and West Asia, including Kenya, Egypt and Malaysia. In addition military software worth Rs.40 million was exported to Nigeria, Lebanon, Jordan and Saudi Arabia. A special cell for arms exports was established by the Ministry of Defence.

In 1974, requests from friendly countries for arms supplies were also met, with substantial orders then coming from Singapore, Iran and elsewhere, according to government statements. By 1975 the Indian defence industry's

export quota was said to be 20% of all production, and software worth
Rs.174.9 million was exported in the same year. India's exports of arms had
grown steadily by 1977–78, as Table 2.1 shows.

Exports of Indian defence products fall into two categories: commercial
sales, and arms transfers based on informal aid agreements. In the latter
category only a few countries have received arms. The former has consisted
of two types of sales: government to government, without recourse to agents
or commissions, and sales by private agents licensed by the Defence Ministry.
In the late 1970s, this last category led to complications and embarrassments
that had political repercussions for the Indian government. These included
reports (later denied) of sales of Hunter aircraft to Pinochet's Chile, of tanks
to South Africa and of tank spares to Israel (cancelled in late 1980). In
1979, seven private entrepreneurs were licensed to sell arms to Nigeria,
Uganda, Iraq, Singapore, Bangladesh, Kuwait, United Arab Emirates, Hongkong, Ghana, Togo, Tanzania, Ethiopia, Indonesia, Spain, Czechoslovakia,
Italy and Yugoslavia. Over 450 exportable items were on their lists, including
guns, ammunition, small arms, tanks, aircraft, armoured vehicles and
electronic equipment.

Brazil, a developing country with similar economic motivations provides
a parallel. $500 million worth of arms, including missiles, tanks, aircraft and
naval frigates, was exported by Brazil in 1979, to 33 countries in Latin
America, the Middle East and Africa [R5]. More markedly than in India, a
huge arms segment of the Brazilian economy has emerged, with almost 500
companies directly participating in the arms trade. Much of Brazil's arms
industry is produced under licence to West Germany, but this has not acted
as a constraint on its exports, whereas the licence agreements between India
and the Soviet Union have inhibited India's planned exports of MIG 21
spares to Egypt.

Despite official denials India was still involved in arms transfers in 1981.
This is a natural outcome of its aim to establish an independent arms industry
which, to sustain itself, needs enormous scale and constant output. Despite
pious declarations that Indian arms are exported only to 'friendly countries
and those who would not misuse them', commercial considerations have
proved to outweigh political consequences in the long term. Today's friend
may become tomorrow's enemy, and Indian arms transfers may antagonize
those states unfriendly to the recipient of Indian arms. The sale, by private
Indian arms traders, of arms via transfers through third countries is another
manifestation of these trends. On the constructive side India gives material
rather than simply moral support to liberation struggles such as in
Palestine and in Southern Africa. Like South Korea, Taiwan, China, Brazil,
Libya and Israel, India is now employing some of its arms exports as an
instrument of foreign policy. The arms export industry is one of the prime
new indicators of the Indian state capitalist economy and the new relationships being forged abroad.

Conclusion

In 1956 the Indian government strengthened its state capitalism with a Second Industrial Policy Resolution which classified certain industries as the target for increased government control and nationalization. Even then, what was perceived as an onslaught against the private sector was aimed only against a few individuals and foreign companies. In the long run Indian private capital as well as state capital have benefited. Special capital lending institutions were established to aid private industry, and high tariff barriers, maintaining a captive home market for their goods, sheltered Indian firms. Kochanek [K8] reports that private investment in India's protected market has shown 12-14% return on capital invested.

The captains of the Indian state capitalist system are its bureaucrats, who represent an increasingly swollen administration inherited at India's independence[38] and created during the colonial period to expedite the extraction of resources and the governance of populations; a role that is still maintained. As a sector, services (defence, law and order, bureaucracy, banking and insurance) have had the fastest growth in the Indian economy, even faster than the commodity producing sector.[39] Private capital has a voice in the state capitalist system through organizations like FICCI; the rural rich have a voice through the politicians and kulaks; the army, through its generals and small traders and professionals through their shared links with bureaucrats and politicians from the same urban base.[40]

The Indian experience then, has all the ingredients that compose a state capitalist system: 1) land reforms to erode a feudal pre-capitalist mode once prevalent in the countryside; 2) introduction of capitalist farming; 3) building modern industry through massive state investment and nationalizations; 4) restrictions on the activities of foreign capital; and 5) furthering the interests of national capital, as well as the bureaucratic service segment of the ruling class.

Being in a transitional period of social formation, Indian state capitalism has one great fear; economic stagnation; this could result in an ensuing political crisis through a rising level of mass consciousness among different groups. State capitalism, like any other form of capitalism, wishes to preserve itself and the ruling classes. Like any other form of capitalism there are built-in contradictions in the Indian system, for example economic growth has been sluggish or has remained stagnant [S15]. This has led to political convulsions, such as rural violence and the imposition of a State of Emergency. One weakness in the system comes from the continued existence of pre-capitalist social formations in the countryside which have inhibited capital formation and prevented capital accumulation on a broad scale. The government has tried to modernise the rural areas regardless of social costs; the Green Revolution and the extension of rural banking-credit were both intended for this purpose. The main effect of the contradiction is that the domestic market is too small for India's public and private industries, largely because they remain oriented towards the consumer-based desires of an urban and service sector bourgeoisie. These problems have created the endemic qualities of Indian capitalist growth; lack of demand, under-utilization of capacity and lack of new investment. The attempted resolution of this dilemma is basic to the history of capitalism but may appear novel when applied to the Indian case. As Ranjit Sau [S3b: 146] put it: 'A Third World country does not have a colony to dispose of its industrial output.' It is precisely these colonies that India is attempting to find; looking for a solution to its internal capitalist crisis by actively seeking markets abroad with new fields to invest in and conquer and ultimately, influence and control politically.[46] Thus is the link between the nature of the Indian system and India's relations with other developing countries provided.

In the literature, India's total dependence on foreign powers is exaggerated. Much of this is derived from 1960s data, when Western aid poured into India, obscuring other features. India does have some measure of autonomy, and the fact that multinational companies have been so restricted in India is further evidence of a national capital at work endeavouring to lessen its dependence.[42] In the late 1970s India had over 107 joint equity investments in over 25 countries overseas both in the developing and the developed world (see Chapter 6). It had bank branches in over 34 countries engaged not only in commerce and trade but in local capital markets and industrial financing (see Chapter 8). Detailed analyses of these investments and banking reveal that in the majority of cases, particularly public sector investments overseas, Indian, not foreign capital is involved. This refutes the notion that Indian joint ventures are merely sub-agents for international capital. Since 1950 India has given aid to over 65 developing countries (see Chapter 4) including over 54 tied loans to 13 of them. In addition, India's commercial presence in the developing world is precipitating related phenomenon: the rise of Indian transnational and multinational firms[43] (see Chapter 9).

Thus, India's development of a form of state capitalism contains inherent contradictions which it seeks to resolve by expanding abroad. This external thrust by India may, in future, find it acting as a proto- and second-tier imperialist power in other countries.

Notes

1. This definition suggests that all capitalism is state capitalism, but there is a difference between liberal interventionism and state capitalism, in the latter the state itself owns important parts of the means of production.
2. What determines whether a state in a capitalist society remains capitalist is not its internal class composition alone but the position it occupies in the capitalist mode of production worldwide.
3. A state being a society of political economy, that is containing economic and political institutions. Therefore there is nothing primordial or reified about a state.
4. For a discussion of the two predominant views of the state: 1) that it is

based on social inequality; 2) that it is a form of social contract, see C17.

5. In M12a, Labour input in a commodity determines its value; labour and exchange value are themselves rooted in the production process. Where the method of production is relatively advanced, an advantage in capital and technology will accrue. Hence international relations of exploitation will result between societies with more developed and those with less developed methods of production. This theory does not support Emmanuel's theory of unequal exchange which sees international trade and wage rates as a mechanism of exploiting 'backward' countries, the key being the rising wage rates of the West. For a critique see K6a.

6. L7b: 313; B35. According to Buick Marx never spoke of a transitional society but only of a political transition period between capitalism and socialism.

7. L7b: 326–7. The term was used particularly during the NEP period in early Soviet development, and in China to describe the first five year plan period.

8. B17b and B17c. Any regression would, however, be extremely temporary. See C4b. Elliot [E2] calls it the 'Transilient moment'.

9. It is important to remember that this is why the modern state itself has often been a colonial creation, imposed on a pre-capitalist social formation and states in the Third World. Thus beginning life in many of them as a minority institution.

10. 'Post-colonial' means here, states which have achieved independence since 1945. There are still unresolved difficulties in applying concepts of transition which have been used to describe socialist states to post-colonial societies. While similar, they are quite distinct types of social formations. Particularly important is that in socialist states a single party is a *raison d'etat* and in post-colonial states, while single party dominance may be the rule, ideologically it is not always a major *raison d'etat*.

11. K1a. This is questionable, for the most part the big bourgeoisie get along well with the government of such a system.

12. Although this point is debatable as for example Djilas' 'new class' in the socialist world happily reproduces itself long after the first generation of cadres have died.

13. There is a powerful industrial bourgeoisie in India, but it finds itself ranged against a rising rural landed interest, kulaks who have some quite separate interests, nevertheless, a coalition between the two is in the best interest of both. Whether or not it materializes itself in a coherent and stable fashion is the pressing question of the next few years.

14. L9. Terms such as 'dependency', 'underdevelopment', and 'neo-colonial', used by these theorists, are grouped together as dependency theories here.

15. In C21 and E2 David Elliot declares that while Thailand was state capitalist before 1945, afterwards it was subjugated, becoming a fully neo-colonial dependency.

16. Here Shivji's [in C21] last two categories are combined. He distinguishes between 'bureaucratic capitalism' and state capitalism, the former (in the author's view) is a permutation of the latter. Shivji's division of neo-colonial and state capitalist neatly resolves the problem of defining

states, such as India, where neo-colonial concepts do not accurately apply.

17. S34. This relation between state capitalism and the existence of a private sector is very important to its definition.

18. It can be argued that such control is never relinquished. For example, Carlos F. Diaz-Alejandro in A6 states that despite its image as a private capital paradise, Brazil continues to shelter a large public sector.

19. Several post-colonial states have unsuccessfully attempted to emulate the Meiji model of development. D19 states this lack of success is because 'enthusiasm for international equality is stronger than their sense of history.' Meiji leaders were able to disregard the conditions of the people as they built a modern state. Jomo [J7] calls the Malay elites 'administocrats'.

20. India has been described as state capitalist by Soviet scholars such as Levkovsky in 1958, see C20. Later these Soviet analyses were taken up by other scholars such as Bettelheim [B17a] ; Chattopadhya [C4a] ; Prabhat Patnaik 'Imperialism and the Growth of Indian Capitalism' [in O4] and Ranjit Sau [S3]. All agree on the general use of the term but none have analysed its long term implications and effects on India's external relations.

21. Roy [R20] sees the Indian state playing only a supporting role, a view consistent with liberal interventionist definitions of the state. But the ruling classes in India have no particular long term commitment to parliamentary democracy. Its sole purpose is to mediate between the various forces composing the ruling alliance. In 1969 J.R.D. Tata called for an end to democracy; retired generals have also voiced such views from time to time.

22. K6a and P8. In the latter India is defined as state capitalist but stresses the structural limits to state power which allow for its resubjugation.

23. For a summary of this view see L9, Chapter 1.

24. A summary of the debate is found in D8.

25. Author's unpublished paper 'Chotanagpur moneylenders' (1975). In the mid-1960s hill peoples in India were still being drawn into the money economy for the first time.

26. In 1948 49% of India's national income came from agriculture, 17.1% from industry, 18.5% from transport and services, and 15.7% from other services, bureaucracy etc. These figures illustrate the foundations for India's subsequent state capitalism.[B17a]

27. D13. This raises questions over a future handover of state industries to private capital in India, a real possibility after 1976 in some political circles. See C20, Chapters 4, 5.

28. C7a. Industry was only 13% of GDP in 1965. Kochanek [K8: 4], using GNP instead of GDP puts the total private sector's contribution in the late 1960s to the economy as 80%.

29. As an example of capitalist development, imperatives overriding stated aims of equitable development can be found in some of India's irrigation projects, which have followed a philosophy of commercial, short-term gain. Water goes only to those who can afford it (kulaks) and often, due to short-sighted planning, no provision made for proper drainage, resulting in raised water ground tables leading to widespread

salinization rendering large tracts of land useless.

30. N13 and H1, also Gautam Sen, forthcoming thesis, Department of International Relations, London School of Economics analysing the role of defence and economic growth.

31. This 'strategic' motive was evident in the building of railroads which also occurred in colonial India. After 1962, the massive road-building activities of the Border Roads Organization has had far-reaching economic, political and social effects in the border areas. Strategic motives are also manifest in the setting-up of specialized state defence factories such as Mishra Dhatu Nigam for the manufacture of high grade alloys and metals, such as titanium.

32. K1b and B14.found that defence spending stimulates growth.

33. The 'wasteful' expenditure of the US and Soviet space programmes have been tied to defence industries: in turn these have generated tremendous technological advances which have been converted into wider fields of commercial production, and brought benefits to all industry in these countries and elsewhere.

34. China's arms transfers have hitherto (1980) been mostly on a grant basis.

35. In 1979, Indian defence industries had a turnover of $1.33 thousand million [P14].

36. In 1975, 7,700 scientists and staff were involved in defence research in India. *Economic and Commercial News* 11 November 1978.

37. The wider impact of defence industries on the Indian economy can be seen in the procurements generated from Indian steel plants such as Rourkela, Bokaro and Salem. *Hindu* 28 June 1967, 27 January 1978.

38. This accounts for the Indian 'upper middle classes' popular choice of government service for their sons. The recent trend for young men to seek jobs in business and commerce attests to the growth of the system in these areas.

39. S15. This underlies the fact that governmental structures in India are important to understanding the system. It is through them that the bureaucratic captains plan, mediate and ultimately head India's state capitalism.

40. It is common to find a bureaucrat, a businessman, and a military officer in the same extended family. K9: 267, 338, calls the network of contacts 'subterranean'.

41. Part of India's present thrust abroad in developing countries has an added benefit besides general economic gain. Turn-key contracts in the Gulf require large amounts of labour. By exporting Indian labour from an explosive countryside, a labour aristocracy can be created. Not all of India's landless can be exported, but it is no coincidence that those areas experiencing a high degree of capitalization in agriculture are exporting large quantities of semi-skilled and unskilled labour.

42. In one way India differs from many states in that its dependence is simultaneous toward two centres, which allow it a larger field from which to attract technology and capital.

43. H8. Such firms in India include BHEL, the Steel Authority of India, Indian Oil and Engineers India Ltd. In the private sector the Birlas and the Tatas may comprise Indian multinationals. This is a much more

strictly defined listing than occurs in some other analyses. *Business India* 20 August–2 September 1979; *Frontier* 19 April 1980.

3. Economic Co-operation: India and the Third World

The process of development creates disequilibrium, pre-existing economic sectors are disrupted and ultimately destroyed to enable new sectors to be formed. The type of development widely extant at present is based on pillage [J1]. Differing levels of production within and between states are based on these inequalities and their perpetuation in order to draw on a continual flow of resources to sustain development. The paradox arises when we have the spectacle of an incompletely and disparately developed state with an increasing burden of mass poverty, establishing unequal relations with other states from a position of relative superiority. With its insatiable drive the capitalist development process is no respecter of boundaries or distributive justice within state boundaries, but constantly seeks to expand where opportunity arises. Patterns of inequality are perpetuated where one set of productive forces is too weak to protect itself from the onslaught of another stronger set. India's ability to supply aid, technology, skills and capital allow it to occupy this position vis-à-vis many other developing states, even those relatively well endowed in terms of finance or resources but lacking technology, infrastructure and a developed skills base.

Discussion, in the past, about contemporary development tended to focus on relations between the less-developed and the developed industrialized countries. This obscured the fact that the developing world is not an undifferentiated whole but includes states in process of becoming economic powers in their own right. The new international economic order allegedly aims to foster growth in economic relations among developing countries, whether such rhetoric has dealt realistically with certain factors remains to be seen.

The phrases, Technological Co-operation among Developing Countries (TCDC) and Economic Co-operation among Developing Countries (ECDC) have been used, at non-aligned meetings since 1955 and UNCTAD meetings since 1964, to indicate a commitment by developing countries to foster mutual co-operation. The stress on the phrases TCDC and ECDC has been relatively more recent [C13]. It is suggested here that examination of this growing phenomenon already shows disturbing parallels with the relations maintained between the fully industrialized world and the lesser developed states. In other words, while attention is focussed on the established relations

37

of inequality between the Third and the fully-industrialized worlds, possibly new forms of inequality are forming between several developing states, adding to the general web of inequality in international relations. Because the environment in which these relations operate focusses on the major international inequalities, conditions are created in which developing states are not fully aware of the potential dangers to their independence. As a result, they unreservedly welcome intra-developing world co-operation and fail to examine the full implications. With some justice nevertheless, Third World governments see co-operation as a means of breaking away from well established dependent relations with metropolitan centres. But do such (South-South) relations really build economic independence? May they not in fact be simply perpetuating dependency patterns? An outcome more likely when, for example, increased oil prices by producer developing states severely penalize non-producer developing states. In addition the interests of relatively industrialized developing states are diverging from those of weaker less-industrialized commodity producers.[1]

This differentiation is, however, relative. In India, industrialization occurs against a background of massive dependence on the developed world. According to the Reserve Bank of India [Gov.16d], in 1977 India was Rs.170,000 million in debt to industrialized countries and international lending agencies. Debt servicing of this magnitude is an immense problem, necessitating a constant generation of foreign exchange. While India is contributing to a growing pattern of 'South–South' economic relations, however, its economic dependency relationship with the developed world persists.

The importance of expanding international economic relations is rapidly becoming recognized and economic diplomacy plays an increasingly prominent role in all states. Some writers [C18: 143-54] have suggested that diplomats have merely become salesmen and buyers, though this role has been resisted by some countries. Where reluctance toward or procrastination in adopting this new role exist, there has been a tendency to bypass the established channel of unresponsive institutions. Most strikingly in Japan – a local business representative with expert knowledge of his home office, in conjunction with Ministry of International Trade and Industry officials, knows and often decides upon Japan's international relations and links, rather than the Foreign Ministry.

Economic diplomacy in India has not reached this stage of sophistication. Foreign policy – particularly foreign economic policy and relations – is diffused, with only sporadic attempts at integration. The overall importance of India's international economic ties are still insufficiently understood in ruling circles.[2] Many in government and business point to the fact that quantitatively, India's foreign trade sector accounts for only 12% of national income, without appreciating the qualitative importance of this. India has a large domestic economy, but without foreign economic ties in addition to those of foreign aid it cannot exist. More pertinently, these external economic ties help us to understand India's relations with developing countries and provide an insight into the foreign policy role played by interests not generally articulated through government channels in the conventional, diplomatic sense.

Fostering economic co-operation among developing countries has been basic to Indian policy since independence. In earlier years this arose from India's desire to play an influential world role as leader of a group of developing and non-aligned states. As part of this role, Indian policy-makers envisaged forging strong economic links with other developing states.[3] The first chairman of the Colombo Plan wrote in 1948 that: 'India has a special responsibility to regional co-operation in Asia' [L13a]. One observer [L13b] claimed that the Colombo Plan itself was the idea of another Indian official, K.M. Pannikkar, who thought that regional economic co-operation could be built on the basis of the finance and resources of the old Commonwealth, together with the development aspirations of the newly-independent states of Asia. Another organization in which India sought to gain an audience for its plans of economic co-operation was ECAFE (now ESCAP) which, it was hoped, would promote economic links in Asia, by the use of US money along the lines of the Marshall Plan.

Addressing the third meeting of ECAFE held in India in June 1948, Prime Minister Nehru expressed India's desire for economic co-operation with other developing countries when he said: 'People vaguely talk of India's leadership in Asia. I deprecate such talk . . . rather in a spirit of co-operation among all countries of Asia, big and small.'[4] Nehru later said that: 'India's role of leadership may not be so welcome to others although it may satisfy our vanity. But it is something we cannot escape, the various responsibility [sic] that arise out of our geography and history.' [B31]. The spirit of economic co-operation to which India became committed in the immediate post-independence period was based on the belief that; 'Fate has marked us out for a leading role in Asia and international affairs.'[5]

Thus, economic co-operation was conceived by Indian policy-makers as part of its global political role, which, as the 1950s progressed, aroused suspicions among many developing countries. It has been incorrectly concluded that India never greatly supported multilateral economic co-operation. Encountering opposition to its wider economic co-operation schemes, India reduced them to more manageable regional schemes, and ultimately, when even this failed, to bilateral economic co-operation. This last form is currently most important for India; not because of opposition to wider schemes of economic co-operation, but because of obstacles created by political and economic hostility, particularly from small neighbouring South Asian states. As a result, since the 1960s India has been forced to adopt a diminished strategy. Despite these limitations, however, India has never relinquished its aim of fostering multilateral economic co-operation among developing countries in which it would be an important, if not pre-eminent member.

In rationalizing India's desire for co-operation with other developing countries, one Indian ex-foreign policy-maker [K4] has written that such co-operation is an 'integral part of India's foreign policy' in which mutual

co-operation helps to build a new world order. The Indian government
sees itself as having a 'responsibility' to share its own development experience
and, through practical schemes, to help other developing countries.[6] To
pursue this aim; 'some limited sacrifice of our short-term economic interests
may thus even be necessary in the larger and long-term interest of stable
political relationships and overall national interest.' [K4]. Yet even the
practitioners of this rhetoric do not deny that through economic co-
operation India is furthering its own economic and political interests and
seeking an advantageous position over other states.[7] This is the underlying
contention of this study.

Despite setbacks, India has continued to be a keen supporter of international institutions and groups that advocate economic co-operation among
developing states. As part of a more generalized commitment to the UN,
Indian participation in the UN's economic agencies has been a notable
feature; its highest aid contribution is channelled through UNDP and India
has constantly sought to strengthen the work of other UN agencies, such as
UNIDO, which foster economic co-operation. The formation of UNCTAD in
1963[8] found key support from India, both in its foundation and subsequent
operations. At the policy level, India has never wavered from: the adoption
of a common South approach to North–South negotiations; the formation
of commodity-producer associations; gaining equitable pricing arrangements;
increasing the transfer of technology, and generally encouraging trade in
the developing world. By 1975, India's constant championing of economic
co-operation was set in a new context. Like several other medium-sized
developing countries India is increasingly cast in the role of a donor of
finance, technology and aid. Beneath a rhetoric of co-operation, therefore,
India has formed a complex of tangible economic relationships which illustrates the nature of this co-operation.

Co-operation Projects

Apart from participation in ESCAP, many observers have been surprised
how little India has been active in co-operation schemes in Asia. On either
side economic co-operation groupings exist, to which India does not belong;
to the west, the Regional Co-operation for Development (RCD), to the east,
the Association of South-east Asian Nations (ASEAN). While, throughout
its existence RCD (Pakistan, Iran and Turkey) has been a failure, India has
always viewed it not as an economic, but as a politically hostile grouping.
India could not publicly oppose any economic co-operation scheme, but
privately she opposed RCD because it was seen as designed to provide help
from Turkey and Iran to Pakistan, at a time when it was in conflict with
India. Publicly, India must support ASEAN, but privately expresses
misgivings that ASEAN could exclude India's developing trade and investment in the region.

There are, none the less, two examples of India's participation in regional economic co-operation in Asia. The first was participation in the formation of the Asian Clearing Union (sometimes called Asian Payments Union) in Kabul in 1971. This Union was the result of ideas put forward in 1948 and subsequently adopted by an ECAFE meeting in 1960 and again in 1964. In 1969 the idea was revived and received support from Iran, Afghanistan, Nepal, Sri Lanka, South Vietnam, South Korea and India, while Japan strongly opposed it. The scheme envisaged participants depositing 5–10% of their total foreign exchange reserves in a central clearing house to facilitate payments for trading transactions between themselves. In practice this percentage has never been met and the time span of deposits has been only two months. In 1974 the inaugural meeting was held with only India, Iran, Sri Lanka, Pakistan, Nepal, Bangladesh, and later Burma (1976) joining. Headquarters were set up in Tehran and, in operation, only 1–2% of the total bilateral trade between the participants was channelled through the system, but India emerged as the main creditor with Sri Lanka and Pakistan as the main users.

The second and more important co-operation venture in which India participated is the Asian Development Bank (ADB), inaugurated in Tokyo in 1966. This commitment is important in illustrating India's desire to be a leader of economic co-operation in Asia. A refusal to accept ADB channelled aid and loans, and an insistence upon classification as a donor, is an indication of India's desire to adopt a 'superior' position from which to acquire economic gains from developing countries; in short behaving as if it was a fully industrialized country. For political and economic reasons this strategy has failed: most ADB aid has gone towards developing industrial capitalism in South Korea, Taiwan and Singapore and not to states with possible markets for Indian goods and services. As a result procurements or 'pick-ups' generated through ADB activities have gone to Japan and the West.

The ADB was established as a lending institution based on contributions from member states, with the intention that loans would be extended for specific projects to developing countries in Asia. Japan, in particular, gained the advantage by making the largest capital contribution, thereby controlling the institution and is thus in a position to determine the direction of ADB aid. With its sophisticated economy, this enables Japan to gain an advantageous position vis-a-vis procurements generated by ADB projects; these are then fed into Japanese industry. In essence, all ADB aid is tied to the economic and political interests of the big donors, and Japan and the Western powers have favoured their friends in Asia, rather than the poorer non-aligned Asian states, as special targets for ADB aid. Based on agreement, members of the ADB are represented according to the size of their yearly donations. The largest donors thus have the right to nominate their own executive director to sit on the ten member Board of Directors, and even though one Governor is elected by all members, the major donors dominate the Board. India, as a major donor was, until recently, able to keep an Indian Vice-President while Japan monopolized the post of President. To attempt to secure a dominant position in ADB's structure India had to donate an increasing amount of capital.

In 1967, when the Bank started, India's contribution was $9,290,072 which was third less than Japan and the US. In 1975, India was in third place in voting strength, just ahead of West Germany with a contribution of $48,168,696. In 1976 India abandoned the race and fell to fifth place, behind Canada and West Germany. While endeavouring to gain voting power by massive donations, India's contribution to the ADB's Technical Assistance Programme has increased as follows:

Year	Contribution
1970	US$ 26,667
1971	66,667
1972	121,617
1973	241,499

In spite of this increase, Indian participation has remained comparatively low: for example, in 1973, Japan contributed $8.1 million as against India's $241,499. In July 1975, when the ADB formed the Asian Development Fund as a soft loan agency, India did not join with developed countries in donating capital for its operations.[9]

Despite Japan's insinuations that India wanted a dominant position in the Bank in order to monopolize funds for its own purposes she never took any ADB loans for herself. There are pragmatic reasons for this: in the first place, to do so would possibly have meant that agencies such as the International Development Agency and the World Bank would reduce their aid to her. But the more important reason is that of India's prestige and economic objectives. India would like to see herself as a significant Asian power, and the role of donor in the ADB helps support this image. Nevertheless, India has failed to influence Bank policies into aiding countries close to her instead of those such as Taiwan. In 1975, in response to criticism, the ADB provided a list of the most needy countries in Asia: Pakistan, Bangladesh and South Vietnam; a list hardly calculated to satisfy India. The Japanese argue that, in any case, most member countries cannot afford the ADB's high interest rates on its loans (7½% in 1974). A few Indian aid experts have been sent abroad under ADB's auspices; between 1970 and 1974 India sent specialists to Sri Lanka, Western Samoa, Indonesia, Laos, Thailand, Afghanistan, Nepal, Philippines, Bangladesh and South Korea.

In 1972 the procurement of Indian goods and services for ADB projects was 1.5%,[10] dismally low against Japan's 60% in the same year. One explanation offered to account for this was that Asian countries have a poor opinion of Indian goods and services. India's attempts to increase its procurement levels have thus been largely ineffective. In March 1977 the Indian government redoubled its efforts, and a co-ordinated plan was drawn up by the Engineering Export Promotion Council; but despite publicity given to sub-contracts gained through the ADB connection, Indian procurements remained at only 2.4% against Japan's 45%.

Clearly, India's participation in the ADB failed to fulfil hopes of political and economic advantages, despite a large annual donation and gains in voting power. Even in the matter of staff, Indians were not as important as Japanese, Americans, Australians and Sri Lankans. The outcome of India's participation in the ADB demonstrates how ineffectively she is placed to obtain a role as a leader of economic co-operation in Asia. But this does not preclude future attempts to secure a larger voice in the ADB's affairs. If this is successful it will be as a consequence of India's new levels of technology, expertize and finance rather than as, in the past, a result of voting strength and capital subscription.

Trilateral Co-operation

In the late 1940s, trilateral economic co-operation took place among three developing countries in Latin America when Colombia, Venezuela and Ecuador set up a joint shipping line.[11] The possibility of trilateral economic co-operation, in the context of the non-aligned movement, was first raised by the then leading three non-aligned states: Egypt, India and Yugoslavia at meetings in 1956 and 1961. In late 1966, the economic ministers of these three countries met in Delhi, and made arrangements for operating the scheme. The following year a mutual automobile project was announced, and in 1968 a Tripartite Pact was signed in which the three states agreed to 50% tariff reductions on 500 goods for five years. In addition the agreement was held open to any other members of the group of 77 non-aligned countries. In 1969 and 1970 more meetings were held and further projects were announced. By 1971, however, not a single project had taken off. The conclusion seems inescapable, India's participation was concerned more with political rhetoric than co-operation.

In 1977, after the Janata Party came to power, interest in trilateralism was renewed, as was the agreement, but there were few tangible results. Overall, Indian efforts in the field of trilateral economic co-operation have been a failure, due to an absence of complementarity and the political will to translate aims into practice. Trilateralism affords a glimpse of the problems India faces when attempting co-operation with developing economies of a similar size and scale. They are competitors among whom India cannot easily play a superior role. Economic imperatives then seem to deny success to economic co-operation schemes such as trilateralism. But these same imperatives are leading India to economic ventures among the smaller and weaker states of the developing world.

Bilateral Co-operation and Trade

Up to 1960 import substitution was of prime importance in Indian government policy. This required the erection of tariff barriers and the building of India's own industrial capacity within the confines of the domestic economy [N10]. Exports and their promotion received little attention until 1960-65. In 1965, acting under the influence of the World Bank and the IMF, export promotion became a fixed policy of the Indian government [C14b]. Fundamental to this was changing the composition of exports from traditional to non-traditional goods. Although the rising proportion of engineering goods exported, from the 1960s, has gradually eroded traditional commodity exports such as jute and tea, it has not displaced them. The value of engineering goods exported grew from $14.1 million in 1960–61 to $155.5 million in 1970–71, 7.6% of total exports in that year [N10]. Increasingly during the 1960s, Indian goods found new markets in Africa and Asia in addition to traditional markets in Europe and America, a trend which was intensified in the 1970s. To promote exports, the government provided a number of assistance schemes and institutions to give cash subsidies to exporters; in 1977 these were worth Rs. 3,900 million [C14b]. Other measures included tax holidays, monetary incentives, infrastructural support and import concessions, directly linked to subsequent exports or re-exports.

Another important facet of India's foreign trade was the role played by the Soviet Union and Eastern European countries in trade expansion. In the early 1960s these countries helped to expand India's non-traditional as well as traditional exports made when she was severely short of foreign exchange: arrangements were made for the USSR and the Socialist bloc countries to make payments in rupees. By 1977 most of this trade had gradually become converted to foreign exchange dealings, but by then a constant proportion of India's export trade (20%) was directed towards Eastern Europe. The increase in India's exports is a consequence of her development of traditional sectors. Exports of engineering goods fuel Indian foreign investments. Supply and export of new Indian goods and services provides the basis for increased Indian contracts, the expansion of Indian banking, and technical aid and loan activity abroad. No one activity necessarily precedes any other but all are interlinked, and trade expansion is a clear manifestation of this process. These are all linked to the domestic industrial context which, facing stagnation at home, seeks external outlets to boost production and provide increased employment. Whatever the government's policy, as Indian industry has developed so too has its search for overseas markets.

Joint Commissions and Committees

The Indian government has sought to encourage bilateral economic co-operation by way of Joint Commissions, Committees and, more recently, Business Councils. Bilateral Joint Commissions to promote and regulate economic exchanges between India and other countries were first suggested in the late 1950s. In 1959, according to one participant, a prototype was set up between India and the USA after joint trade promotion talks. Three distinct types of Joint Commission were envisaged: 1) Those with Western developed states, to implement signed agreements. 2) Those with Eastern Europe, to regulate the particular type of trade (in rupees) India was then developing with them. 3) Those with developing countries, set up to promote generalized economic co-operation, particularly with states where trade and other ties were relatively undeveloped. This third type is of relevance to this study. A distinction must first be drawn between a Joint Commission and a Joint Committee: both are bilateral bodies constituted between governments but the essential difference is one of level. A Joint Commission is chaired by ministers of the respective governments; Joint Committees are at the official level, chaired by government bureaucrats in various ministries. The work done by Joint Commissions and Joint Committees is identical but confusion sometimes exists, particularly at the level of sub-committees: for example, both a Commission and a Committee exist with Sri Lanka. Some maintain that Joint Committees are an outgrowth of Commissions as the parent institution.

As can be seen from Table 3.1 India's earliest Joint Commission/ Committee with other developing countries was with Morocco and Iran in 1962.[12] These early examples as outgrowths of trade agreements set the pattern for subsequent Commissions/Committees. By devoting specific clauses in these agreements to the formation of Joint Commissions/ Committees, India attempted to promote economic contacts with other developing countries, and occasionally, to encourage educational scientific and cultural exchanges. Most actual operations of Joint Commissions have been a failure and there is some question as to whether they really have promoted bilateral exchanges. One reason for failure has been total confusion in respect of which government departments should have administrative jurisdiction over a particular Joint Commission/Committee. It has been claimed that this confusion is deliberate, and intended to distribute responsibility among several ministries to ensure that one man/one department does not monopolize India's external economic co-operation (see Table 3.1). During the 1960s Joint Commissions/Committees were primarily the responsibility of the Commerce Ministry; it has been suggested that the confusion is a result of 'ad hocism': each time an economic minister goes abroad a Joint Commission/Committee is formed. The situation until 1976 was that most of the Commissions/Committees were hastily set up (and moribund in 1980) to serve as excuses for foreign travel by bureaucrats and ministers. Some think incorrectly that the Economic Division of the External Affairs Ministry has responsibility, but in fact it is in charge of Commissions with Nigeria, Mauritius and Tanzania only; others marked 'External Affairs' are administered by the territorial divisions within the Ministry. The result, obviously, is lack of co-ordination and sustained interest in building bilateral co-operation. The role of Joint Commissions/Committees in promoting economic co-operation has been very limited, and most links India has formed with other developing countries have been irrespective of the activities of these bodies.

Joint Commissions/Committees entail regular, bi-annual or annual meetings. Most became defunct almost immediately after their formation, but there are some notable exceptions, where Commissions have at least served as a forum to air ideas for co-operation. In 1969 an Indo-Iran Joint Commission was formed and at its second meeting, in 1970, 'turn-key' and

Table 3.1
Joint Commissions/Committees: India/Developing States

Joint Commission/Committees and Status		*Date and Government Department*
Indo-Morocco	x	1962
Indo-Iraq	x	1962, 1971
Indo-Sudan	x	1965, 1974
Indo-Kuwait	x	1966, 1974
Indo-Cameroon	x	1968
Indo-Sri Lanka	*	1969 (MEA)
Indo-Iran	x	1969
Indo-Afghanistan	*	1969 (MEA)
Indo-Turkish	x	1973
Indo-UAE	x	1974
Indo-Senegal	x	1974
Indo-Tanzania	*	1975 (MEA)
Indo-Pakistan	x	1975
Indo-Saudi Arabia	x	1975
Indo-Libya	x	1976? (DHI)
Indo-Tunisia	x	1976 (MC)
Indo-Jordan	x	1976
Indo-Algeria	x	1976
Indo-Guyana	x	1977
Indo-Mauritius	*	1978 (MEA)
Indo-Nigeria	*	1978 (MEA)
Indo-Zaire	x	1978
Indo-Malaysia	x	?
Indo-Nepal	x	? (MEA & DHI)

Notes: * = active; x = moribund. (MEA) = Ministry of External Affairs,
(DHI) = Department of Heavy Industry; (MC) = Ministry of Commerce

Sources: Ministry of Commerce, *Indian Economic Diary, Indian and Foreign Review, Foreign Affairs Reports, Times of India, Hindu, BBC Summary of World Broadcasts.*

Third World projects were discussed. The Commission's third meeting took place in 1974, when the Shah of Iran urged the formation of an Indian Ocean Common Market. Subsequently, the Indo-Iran Joint Commission put forward plans for several joint projects including irrigation projects in Rajasthan and in Karnataka, the Kudremukh iron ore project, a paper plant in Tripura, and in Iran, aluminium and steel plants. All these were delayed indefinitely after the fall of the Shah.

Joint Business Councils

The Indian government has also utilized Joint Commissions/Committees
to encourage co-operative activities of both private and public Indian business.
The Federation of Indian Chambers of Commerce and Industry (FICCI)
[K8] is a member of the International Chambers of Commerce Association
and as such regularly liaises with the national chambers of several countries.
The idea of more formal contact, in the form of Joint Business Councils,
first emerged in 1966 during a Japanese business delegation visit when it was
suggested that a regular Joint Business co-operation committee be set up.[13]
This became the first Joint Business Council (JBC) between FICCI and a
foreign business group. The rationale behind such councils is the expansion
and promotion of business contacts (joint ventures, technology transfers,
etc). By 1980 India was a partner in 15 Joint Business Councils: with the
USA and Japan; USSR, Hungary, East Germany, Bulgaria and Yugoslavia
in the Eastern bloc, and Arab League countries, Sri Lanka, South Korea,
Iran, Nigeria, Thailand, Indonesia and Bangladesh in the developing world.

There is a fundamental difference between Joint Business Councils with
developed countries, which have been moderately successful, and developing
countries, which have so far been unsuccessful. With the USA and Japan
Indian business attends meetings as a supplicant for capital, technology and
links with the private business community. Much of this negotiating involves
US based multinationals and the Joint Indo-US Business Council. This latter
council deliberately created itself as a forum for discussion on the role of
multinationals in India. In negotiations with developing countries, where
Indian business is a potential donor of capital and services, there has been
less success in following up opportunities that JBCs are intended to reveal.
While JBCs are lodged within the FICCI, a grouping of private business and
public sector firms also participate in them.

These Councils are relatively new, particularly those with developing
countries — and their success in contributing to the expansion of Indian
bilateral economic links with other developing countries has been extremely
limited. Nevertheless, they indicate the close connection between government and business in India, where both constituent parts of Indian state
capital agree on the need to expand economic links abroad.

Indian Economic Policy

It was emphasised at the outset that Indian economic co-operation with
other developing countries occurs at two levels; one directed by the economic
imperatives of its own internal development, the other by the mechanisms of
foreign economic policy. We have seen how the Indian government's commitment to multilateral co-operation became diffused into schemes of bilateral
co-operation, but there have been opportunities to expand economic ties
with other developing countries, which the government has failed to pursue.

To seek for coherence in the daily operations of India's external economic ties is to seek in vain. No single authority in the bureaucracy for foreign economic relations exists, and as a result, overall direction at the policy level is absent. Paradoxically, India's growing economic links with developing countries have grown through their own initiative and volition, irrespective of the government machinery, which, given the mechanisms and infrastructure at its disposal, has been disappointing. In fact the bureaucracy has often stifled the full potential for India's economic growth abroad. As we shall see (in chapter 8) concerning operations of the Life Insurance Corporation abroad, bureaucratic immobility can be a severe handicap.

Three major Ministries are involved in India's foreign economic relations, although virtually every government department is involved in some way. For example [V5], in one case Indian aid to developing countries was channelled through 13 government departments, at least half of which were operating aid programmes unknown to the supposed apex aid-giving section (Economic Division of the External Affairs Ministry). On paper, however, the major ministries are External Affairs, Commerce and Finance. In 1964 the External Affairs Ministry set up a special Economic Division in an attempt to tie together all India's external economic relations. Within the bureaucracy the work of this Division has been criticized; it employs some technically trained staff, but also, at the senior level, generalists of the Indian Foreign Service. By trying to monopolize the administration of all India's overseas economic links, the Division over-burdens itself with work that its small staff cannot handle. Beyond repeating clichés regarding India's potential position in regard to economic co-operation, the Division apparently works on an *ad hoc* basis, preparing papers for meetings at short notice without appreciating their long term policy implications. All forms of economic ties with developing countries are lumped together as a form of 'co-operation' irrespective of the different kinds of links that have arisen, or assessing India's potential gains and losses in pursuing this widely defined 'co-operation'. As a system of formalized economic diplomacy, the Economic Division maintains a network of commercial attachés in Indian embassies who are supposed to file monthly reports of the countries to which they are posted, informing the government of the economic prospects. With a few exceptions the quality of these reports is extremely low, as few commercial attachés possess even elementary knowledge of economic affairs. One bureaucrat told of an attaché asking the difference between the State Bank and the Reserve Bank.[15]

According to the Economic Division of External Affairs, its task is to implement India's commitment to TCDC and ECDC to co-ordinate the work of the various ministries specializing in one particular area of international economic links. However, other ministries frequently fail to inform the Economic Division of their activities. Within the Division, entire geographic areas are assigned to various officers, in rotation. For example all of West Africa is assigned to one man. By excluding other government departments the Division tries to monopolize policy-making on international economic

issues, as well as by attending international economic conferences. Despite
this the Division has neither been very successful in controlling nor being
aware of the full extent of Indian economic ties abroad. In 1980, for example,
the activities of the Industrial Development Bank of India and its credit
activities to other developing countries was largely unknown to the Division.
Furthermore, the Division was totally uninformed of the activities of Indian
multinationals or of overseas Indian firms as they affected India, or, in a
more generalized sense, what other Ministries were specifically doing in the
field of international economic relations. While trying to set itself up as the
apex body for international economic relations, the External Affairs Ministry
and its Economic Division in practice overlaps and duplicates the work of
other Ministries, such as Commerce. Although officially concerned only with
trade matters the Commerce Ministry is also the head of the Inter-ministerial
Committee concerned with approving Indian investments overseas. In the
Ministry of Finance, its own Economic Division is responsible for an important portion of Indian economic co-operation with developing countries,
administering government loans and credits, some aid programmes, and
monitoring banking and insurance abroad.

According to some bureaucrats, integrated thinking on international
economic issues in the Indian government is still non-existent. The coming
together of the diplomatic-political-economic aspects of external relations
still has not taken place in India despite the real and growing importance of
economic interests in India's relations with other developing countries. The
closest the bureaucracy has thus far come to an integrated policy plan was in
the Cabinet Secretariat during 1977-78, when the Committee of Secretaries,
the highest bureaucratic body under the Cabinet Secretary, initiated steps
to regularly consider international economic policy. This body tried to
formulate long-range international economic policies for India, but political
changes aborted the process.

We can conclude, then, that in its bureaucratic institutions, the Indian
state's policy in operation on international economic issues has been one of
'*ad hocism*'; short range responses to growing economic imperatives only
broadly articulated in the government's policies of export promotion and
commitment to co-operation. Even in 1979, alone among countries of a
similar size, the Indian government was not formulating long-range plans to
secure future oil supplies.[16] Such matters continued to be handled by
individual government departments placing their orders for external supplies
of raw materials on a case-by-case basis. India needs to secure raw materials
and must go to many developing countries to secure them, but so far the
process has lacked over-all direction. Immediate needs have dictated the
pattern of actual relations.

As will be seen (chapters 4-8) a whole host of phenomena has arisen in
India's relationships with developing countries, mostly developing according
to their own imperatives and those of the Indian economy, not at the bidding
of the Indian state machinery alone. This serves to show that underlying
forces at work in India's growing economic ties abroad operate more rapidly

than official measures taken to promote them. This is the paradox underlying some of India's relations with developing countries. Sometimes the bureaucracy has stifled these growing ties, and at others helped them. It may be no accident that India's contract and sub-contract activity growth has been very fast because bureaucratic interference has been minimal, approvals being given by professional bankers in Bombay not by bureaucrats in Delhi. Based on our knowledge of the Indian political economy it appears that India's new relationships with developing countries will continue to grow with, at times, only partial reference to Indian bureaucracy or government policy.

Notes

1. The World Bank is well aware of these growing differences, reflected in categories in one of its recent reports (*World Development Report* Washington, 1979) in which the terms 'low-income' states, 'middle-income' and 'capital surplus oil exporters' are used.
2. In the past a few tentative steps have been taken to integrate India's diplomacy with her economic policy. In 1972 the Prime Minister sent a letter to all Indian diplomatic missions abroad urging them to promote Indian economic interests, (*Indian Economic Diary* 1–17 March 1972). In some of the periodic diplomatic envoy conferences held in Delhi the importance of economic diplomacy has been discussed, (*Commerce* 3 September 1977).
3. This was related to an early policy of the US to treat India as a 'key nation'. See Chapter 1.
4. *Speeches of Prime Minister Nehru, 1946–1963* New Delhi, 1964, p. 260.
5. *United Asia*, Vol. I, 1948.
6. Interview, External Affairs Ministry, New Delhi, 16 February 1980. An official gave the example of the Senegalese Finance Minister who, on a visit to Delhi, demanded the services of Indian agricultural experts free of charge, based on what he characterized as India's 'responsibility'.
7. Interview, Economic Division Ministry of External Affairs, New Delhi, 16 February 1980, and C12.
8. While certain Indian officials are said to have played an influential role in setting up UNCTAD, the follow-up by India, aside from broad policy commitments, has been neither coherent nor systematic.
9. A fund which ran into serious difficulties in early 1980 through a lack of liquidity.
10. *Commerce* 11 May 1974. In Commercial attachés reports, one of the set headings reads: 'aid and credit facilities provided by developed countries and international organizations such as ADB which may open up export opportunities for India'.
11. Diaz-Alejandro, Carlos F. 'Foreign Direct Investment by Latin Americans' in A6.
12. *India's Trade Agreements* in force as of 1 May 1976, Government of India, Ministry of Commerce, New Delhi, 1977.
13. Interview, FICCI, New Delhi, 31 March 1980. These Councils are

separate from the private activities of certain Indian traders, mostly based in Bombay, who have set up various bilateral friendship associations as fronts to promote their commercial interests. Some examples include; the Indo-Southeast Asian Friendship Society, the Bharat-Mauritius Friendship Society, the Indo-Fiji Cultural Association, Indo-Malaysia Society, Indo-Mauritius Society, Bharat-Nepal Friendship Society, and others.

14. Interview, Ministry of External Affairs, New Delhi, 16 February 1980.
15. As above (14).
16. Interview, Ministry of Commerce, New Delhi, 16 January 1980. Pre-1973, in the ONGC, there was some awareness of the need to secure long term supplies of oil (see Chapter 6). This earlier failure may have influenced policy-makers in the 1970s to adhere to a *laissez-faire* policy.

4. Civil and Military Aid to Other Developing Countries

India's aid and assistance programmes are perhaps the most striking illustration of her 'co-operation' policy, and help to demonstrate how India's political economy is manifested in her external relations. While quantitatively small, Indian aid is far more influential than is generally known. Influence is achieved in two ways: one, by the economic gains to be made in opening up export markets for Indian goods, preparing the ground for Indian investments, gaining procurements for goods and services, and facilitating the penetration of Indian financial and other economic institutions in developing countries. The other — less easy to measure but no less important — springs from the more broadly political and economic motivations underlying Indian aid giving. For example, the political gains made through military aid programmes are a little known aspect of Indian foreign relations and, in particular, are an indication of the importance of relationships being established with other developing countries. Military aid programmes also have inherent economic advantages, such as subsequent orders for military equipment.

Non-military Indian aid is set in two contexts: one, as part of the UNCTAD 'spirit' referred to earlier, that is as a consequence of a group of developing states seeking to build economic and other forms of co-operation amongst themselves. The other as part of underlying imperatives in the nature of the Indian state. Short of scrutinizing the motives of every aid-giving developing state, political interpretations must be ascribed for some of this aid. In addition to India are many other Third World aid donors. Cuba, Singapore, South Korea, Taiwan, Pakistan, Indonesia, Malaysia, Egypt, Kuwait, Libya, Iraq, Saudi Arabia, Brazil, Venezuela and the United Arab Emirates all have aid programmes, and are amongst the least developed countries. But Indian aid should be equated with that of states such as Venezuela, Brazil or Indonesia, which are seeking to exercise influence in their immediate regions and aspire to a bigger role on the world stage; though not with such oil and capital surplus states as Kuwait, Saudi Arabia, UAE, Libya, Iraq and pre-revolutionary Iran, that, through oil wealth, seek to gain influence in other developing countries. Such states, however, still lack the skill and infrastructural base to exercise influence beyond capital aid giving. Other Third World donors (such as South Korea, Pakistan, Malaysia, Taiwan, Singapore and Cuba) have similarities with the Scandinavian countries or Israel, whose aid programmes are for limited aims. Such states seek to gain a modicum of political influence from a position of relative weakness, help their own industries and act purely as sub-imperial agents supplementing the activities of a superpower with little autonomy in their foreign policies.[1]

India's aid activities are those of an aspiring middle-power whose economy is sufficiently developed, and whose leaders have ambitions to play an influential role in the world. Despite constraints on its bilateral aid programmes, India's underlying motives are the same as those suggested for aid programmes of the big powers [H6], whose primary objective is to gain economic and political advantages and perpetuate patterns of dependence. Aid opens markets, creates situations resulting in procurements for the donor's industries and employment of its expertize. China's aid programme, which began when China itself was the recipient of massive external aid, is analogous to India [M26: 286]. Indian aid is a reminder that the Indian state is not as weak as its international image suggests, and is designed to strengthen its relationships and procure a measure of influence with other developing countries. The economic and political success of foreign policy is partly dependent on readiness to aid. Economic imperatives force the Indian state to adopt measures designed to augment its economic presence in other developing countries; political implications arising from this are well known. India's massive aid to Bangladesh, Nepal, Bhutan and, to a lesser extent, the Maldives and Mauritius underscore this point.

A sizable literature exists on the phenomenon of aid, particularly the activities of institutions and programmes such as IBRD and USAID, that are now generally accepted as the principal means whereby the industrialized world perpetuates its domination over the Third World. Domination via aid-giving is not confined to Western capitalist countries, as the case of China has demonstrated. In 1964, when it dissociated itself from the USSR, China accused the Soviet Union of deliberately attempting to create a relationship of dependence through aid. Ironically after breaking with Beijing, Albania and Vietnam made identical charges against China. In this context of virtual universal suspicion India's aid activities have taken place, and already charges of seeking to exploit other countries, notably in Bhutan, Bangladesh and Nepal, have been made against her.

Government officials have estimated that the total Indian aid from 1947 to 1980 was around Rs.12,000 million,[2] though considering that credits and grants given by India total Rs.9,500 million, this is probably an underestimate. According to the author's own computations of officially known figures, Indian aid up to 1979 totals Rs.11,796.48 million (see Table 4.1). Clearly, however, these figures exclude military aid expenditures, and an estimated total of Rs.20,000 million would seem reasonable if these programmes were included. The overall figure for Indian aid has been put even higher [V5], at Rs.25.400 million up to 1979. Compared to the government of India's overall public sector plan outlays of Rs.699,310 million[3] on five 5-year plans between 1951 and 1979, aid commitments have been minimal. The actual amounts spent fluctuates around these figures, amounts

Table 4.1
India's Total Aid Contributions

Multilateral Programmes

Up to:	Programme	Amount (Rs. million)
1974	UNDP	357.25
	SCAAP	8.90
	CFTC	1.50
	ESCAP	4.99
1970-73	ADB	483.51
1959-73	IAFA-TAP	(US$ 482,000)
1979	Colombo Plan	900.00
—	IBRD-TASF	?
	Total:	*1,276.05*

Rupee Variant* total up to 1979: 1,710.00 million

Bilateral Programme

1978	ITEC	216.54
1978	*Total Bilateral Loans/Credits*	*4,631.575*
1978	*Total Bilateral Grants*	*5,234.86*
Total Indian aid through all programmes:		*11,359.025*
		*(11,796.485)**

Note: Total aid to India up to 1976 Rs.196,040.0 million

* Variant figure from *Financial Express* 17 September 1979.

Sources: *Financial Express*; D.C. Vohra, *India's Aid Diplomacy to the Third World,* New Delhi, 1980; Government of India, *Ministry of External Affairs, Annual Reports;* Indian Embassy; Washington DC, USA; *Colombo Plan Reports;* Government of India, *Dept. of Atomic Energy Reports*; *ADB Annual Reports*; *SCAAP Annual Reports*; *Indian Economic Diary*; *BBC Summary of World Broadcasts*; *Economic and Commercial News*; *RBI Reports on Currenc Currency and Finance*; *Times of India*

utilized in the case of aid commitments have always been less than the outlay, thus further reducing their quantitative significance. More significant is India's aid expenditure compared to receipts, these totalled Rs.196,040 million up to 1976 (Table 3.1 Note). Irrespective of this disparity, however, the amount that India has spent on aid indicates her commitment despite internal political and economic constraints.

Aid Policy

Central government bureaucrats tend to understate the dynamic role that
India plays in aid programmes, preferring to stress her 'responsibility' towards
other developing countries. They see aid only as a response to requests from
developing countries.[4] As evidence, and with some justification, they point
out that more than half of Indian aid is tied up in multilateral programmes
(see Table 4.1) whilst the bilateral programme, Indian Technical Economic
Co-operation (ITEC), is comparatively minor (see Table 4.2). This does not
take into account bilateral loans, credits and grants, or the growing importance of other bilateral forms of co-operation outlined earlier, particularly
in the formation of Joint Commissions/Committees. Increasingly, in fact,
Indian aid operates under mutual co-operation agreements, modelled on that

Table 4.2
Indian Aid via ITEC, 1973 and 1974

Date	Country	Value (Rs.)
1973:	12 Countries	16,689,100
	Afghanistan	26,000
	Burma	50,000
	Cambodia	586,000
	Fiji	50,000
	Guinea	100,000
	Iraq	25,000
	Laos	16,500
	Malaysia	355,000
	Mauritius	2,600,000
1974:		4,400,000
		100,000
	Oman	100,000
	Peru	373,000
	Somalia	85,000
	Sudan	10,000
	Tanzania	1,050,000
	N. Yemen	800,000
	Zambia	374,000
	Total	11,269,500

Source: *Ministry of External Affairs, Annual Reports*

signed with Nepal in 1951. Such agreements exist with Zambia, Zaire,
Mauritius, Tanzania, Fiji, Nigeria, Senegal, Sri Lanka, and the Solomon
Islands. Yet even in the majority of cases where such agreements do not exist,

this has not inhibited India from aiding over 65 countries up to 1980. Much of this aid is on a small scale particularly in states outside the immediate South Asian region, but it has grown in significance, particularly in places with large Indian expatriate populations, or countries with important political and, increasingly, economic ties with India.

Table 4.3
Indian Loans and Credits (Some overlap with IDBI credits after 1973, grants excluded).

Key to abbreviations:

C	=	Credit
Bc	=	Buyers' Credit
Cc	=	Commercial Credit
L	=	Loan
Lc	=	Commodity Loans

Year	*Country and Type of Loan/Credit*	*Amount (Rs million, unless indicated otherwise)*
1978	Afghanistan	
	L (wheat: 80,000 metric tonnes)	
1971	Bangladesh	
	Ls	190
1972-3	Lc	600 (value)
	Bc (banking)	150
	Bc (railway)	100
	Bc (transport)	60
	C (commodity purchase)	100
	C (oil supply)	80.10
	L (foreign exchange)	£ 5 million
	Bc	10.33
1974	Bc	100
	Bc	60
	C (Commercial bank)	250
	L (project)	BD taka 38 million
	Bc	100
	L (relief)	100
1978	C	120
1979	Lc (rice?)	?
	Total:	*2,270.43*
	(excluding BD taka and £)	
1958	Bhutan	
	L (roadbuilding)	150
	L (development)	220 (thousand rupees)

Table 4.3 (continued)

Year	Country and Type of Loan/Credit	Amount (Rs million unless indicated otherwise)
	Bhutan	
1969-70	L	6
1970-71	L	2.5
1971-72	L	6.8
1972-73	L	6.8
	Total to 1976	*22.47*
	Burma	
1959	Bc	200
1975	Lc	70.5
	Total:	*270.5*
	Indonesia	
1948	L (government)	75 (thousand rupees)
1966	Bc	100
1975	Bc	50
1976	Bc	250
	Total:	*400.075*
	Kenya	
1976-77	Bc	?
	Mauritius	
1972	Bc	32.10
1975	L (development)	50
	Cc	100
1977	Bc	100
1978	C (IDBI)	50
1979	Lc (rice: 24,000 metric tonnes)	
	Total:	*332.10*
	Nepal	
1964	Bc	10
1974	Bc	50
1975	Bc	100
1976	Bc	100
1978	L (request)	1
	Total:	*261*
	Sudan	
1965	Bc	50

Table 4.3 (continued)

Year	Country and Type of Loan/Credit	Amount (Rs million unless indicated otherwise)
	Sri Lanka	
1966	Bc	20
1967	Bc	50
1969	Bc	50
1971	L	50
	Bc	4
1973	Bc	50
1975	C (project)	10
1976	Bc	50
	Bc	1
1977	Bc	70
1978	Bc	100
	Lc (wheat: 50,000 metric tonnes)	
	Total:	455
	Tanzania	
1972	Bc	50
1975	Bc (Sch.)	100
	L (development)	20
	Total (excluding Tanzanian Sch.)	70
	Vietnam	
1977	L (wheat: 100,000 metric tonnes)	
1978	Bc	100
	Cc	300
	L (wheat: 300,000 metric tonnes)	
	Total:	400
	Total wheat: 400,000 metric tonnes	
	Zambia	
1978	Bc	100

Total of all Indian loans and credits: Rs.4,631,575 million

Sources: *BBC Summary of World Broadcasts*; *Indian Economic Diary*; *Economic and Commercial News*; *Commerce*; *Eastern Economist*; *RBI Report on Currency and Finance*; *Capital*; *Ministry of Finance, Annual Reports*; *Ministry of External Affairs, Annual Reports*; *Foreign Affairs Record*.

Multilateral Aid Programmes

The Colombo Plan: This was founded, in 1950, at a Commonwealth conference in Colombo. An Indian diplomat, K.M. Pannikkar, as already noted, was one of its principal architects. It was hoped that the Plan would draw upon the capital and skills of Commonwealth countries outside as well as within Asia. India's contributions have been mainly limited to technical aid, providing experts (1,379 up to 1980) and training foreign nationals, with a total of 5,305 foreign students trained up to 1972 (see Table 4.4). At least half of India's activities in the Colombo Plan were directed toward Nepal, and half of the students trained have been Nepalese. Malaysia, Sri Lanka, Afghanistan, Philippines and Thailand were other major recipients; South Vietnam, Burma, Pakistan, Indonesia, Singapore, Iran, Maldives, Laos, Cambodia, Bhutan, and South Korea, have also benefited by Indian aid under the Colombo Plan in the past.

Because of its size, India has usually been fifth among the donor states included in the Plan, and has itself been one of the Plan's major recipients. India has given technical aid in statistics, engineering, forestry, power, agriculture, finance and administration. India's participation in the Colombo Plan has been the second highest in a multilateral programme, after UNDP, higher than its own bilateral aid programme (see Tables 4.1, 4.4, 4.5 and 4.6). Most disbursements are for technical aid and training, but occasionally India spent small amounts of Colombo Plan aid on equipment, in 1972 for example, it supplied $2,000 worth of machinery to Burma.

Table 4.4
Indian Participation in the Colombo Plan

Year	Amount (in $)
1972	656,600
1973	668,100
1974	917,200
1975	739,500
1976	897,500

Total Amounts spent (Rs. million) up to:

1973	58.0
(1974	52.8)*
1979	900

Total number of experts provided by India under the Plan:

1950–70:	1,379

Total number of students trained:

1950–72:	5,305

Sources: *Colombo Plan Annual Reports;* Indian Embassy, Washington; *External Affairs, Annual Reports; Indian and Foreign Review*

Table 4.5
Indian Technical Co-operation Programmes: Annual Budget Allocations

Year	Amount (Rs. million)
1964–65	0.446
1965–66	1.0
1966–67	3.76
1967–68	4.0
1968–69	4.0
1969–70	4.5
1970–71	6.0
1971–72	10.0
1972–73	8.0
1973–74	12.0 (12.67)
1974–75	37.5 (30.63)
1975–76	46.16 (40.70)
1977 (data missing)	–
1978	80.18
Total:	*216.54*
(Total:	400 up to 1979 according to Indian Government figures).

Sources: *Ministry of External Affairs, Annual Reports, Times of India Financial Express,* D.C. Vohra, *India's Aid Diplomacy to the Third World*, New Delhi, 1980.

Because the Colombo Plan was the first organized aid programme[5] in which India became involved as a donor, it set the tone for participation in other programmes. The emphasis on technical aid and training has been referred to as the 'sheet-anchor of India's economic assistance programmes.' [M27]. India's own strictly bilateral programme, ITEC (Indian Technical Economic Co-operation) is also modelled on the Colombo Plan, and provides the rationale for expanding participation in other programmes whereby potential economic and political gains may accrue through aid. *Special Commonwealth Africa Assistance Plan* (SCAAP): This was set up in 1961 to aid African Commonwealth countries, many of whom were just attaining independence. Major donor participants were the UK, Canada, Australia, New Zealand, India and Pakistan. As for the Colombo Plan, India participated mainly in the provision of technical assistance and training. In co-ordination with SCAAP, India has also operated a General Scholarship Scheme in which Africans have been given training in many fields at Indian institutions. Indian participation in SCAAP was quite small, only Rs.8.90 million up until 1974.
Commonwealth Fund for Technical Co-operation (CFTC): Established in

Table 4.6
United Nations Development Programme: Indian Participation

Year	Amount ($ million)
1973	3.75
1974	3.75
1975	3.75
1976	3.70
Total:	14.95

Total Amount spent (Rs. million) in UNDP up to:

1974	357.25 (Govt. of India estimate).
1976	306.22 (D.C. Vohra estimate).

Number of experts deputed:

1977	408
1978	453

Number of fellowships given under UNDP by India:

1977	138
1978	349

Sources: *UNDP The Administrator Reports*, cyclostyled document, Planning Commission (G. of India), D.C. Vohra, *India's Aid Diplomacy to the Third World*, New Delhi, 1980.

in 1971, with the aim of pooling the technical skills of Commonwealth countries, Indian participation has again been quite small,[6] confined to supplying technical experts in such fields as small industries, sugar, planning, logging, teaching and handicrafts. India has sent aid under CFTC to Tanzania, Sri Lanka, St. Kitts, Barbados, Ghana, Swaziland and, although not a Commonwealth member, Mozambique. Due to its capital resources Nigeria has displaced India as the largest developing country donor. CFTC performs an explicit role in export market development,[7] and CFTC members in developed countries are able to use it to open up new markets in small developing countries. Gains for such developing countries as Barbados are that, for example, handicraft industries are set up and export markets identified. Whether this builds genuine development equitably is debatable, but as a relatively developed country, India stands to gain in the same way as do participants from developed countries.

Economic and Social Council for Asia and the Pacific (ESCAP): As outlined earlier India has been a strong supporter (from its formation as ECAFE) of the activities of ESCAP and other UN sponsored plans for Asian economic co-operation. As part of this commitment India became involved as a donor country in the ESCAP administered Tonle-Sap project in Cambodia, as well as the wider Mekong project encompassing Laos, Thailand and the then

South Vietnam. Due to the Indo-China war neither project came to fruition but India gave grants worth Rs.0.35 million and aid worth Rs.4.99 million for these projects.

International Bank for Reconstruction and Development – Technical Assistance Special Fund (IBRD – TASF): India itself is a foremost recipient of World Bank financial aid, and the extent of its participation as a donor in the TASF is minimal. The Fund acts mainly as an executive agency for projects that utilize UNDP finance, the World Bank simply supplements UNDP contributions up to $200,000. Occasionally, however, the Bank has granted technical assistance unilaterally, mostly as a pre-investment ground-breaking exercise, in the form of surveys and reports.[8]

India's participation in the multilateral aid programme of the Asian Development Bank (ADB) and its technical assistance programme has already been outlined (Chapter 3) where it was noted that her contribution was overshadowed by that of countries such as Japan and Australia (see Table 4.1).

United Nations Development Programme (UNDP): This programme and agencies under its aegis comprise the largest single channel for Indian aid. In keeping with her strong commitment to the UN system generally, India has remained amongst the top 20 contributors. In 1974 this was $3.75 million; $1 million more than a comparable country, such as China (see Table 4.6). Similarly to other aid programmes, India's activities are primarily in the form of technical aid: providing experts for most developing countries, particularly in Africa and South-east Asia, and offering numerous training programmes in India.

A common factor in India's participation in multilateral aid programmes to date, is that neither her expectations nor any potential advantages have materialized. With the possible exception of the Colombo Plan,[9] India has been dwarfed by the Western industrialized countries, which have monopolized all the gains to be obtained, to such an extent as to render almost specious the claim that such aid programmes are truly multilateral. The largest procurements and sub-contracts generated by UNDP go to France, UK, USA, and West Germany – a business worth millions of dollars annually.[10] It has already been seen (Chapter 3) how Japan takes the largest share of business generated by the ADBs.

Bilateral Aid

The government of India has claimed that, up to 1961, economic co-operation and aid to other developing countries was not generally perceived in the light of anticipated foreign policy implications.[11] In that year the Economic and Co-ordination Division of the External Affairs Ministry was formed to 'advise on economic matters and diplomacy'. Initially this role was confined to trade, but, in 1962, in the aftermath of India's defeat by China, a closer examination of Indian aid was made in order to counter what was seen as China's successful aid diplomacy in the Third World [V5]. A conference of Indian emissaries was held in 1963, and in the following year, based on their deliberations, a decision was taken 'to provide technical and economic assistance to other developing countries' [V5: 282]. Up to 1964, India's aid programmes, all multinational, were administered by the Finance Ministry, but it was then decided to form India's own bilateral aid programme, Indian Technical Economic Co-operation (ITEC), to be supervised by the Economic Division of the External Affairs Ministry, with five functions: 1) training foreign nationals in India; 2) sending Indian experts abroad; 3) aid gifts; 4) economic and technical surveys abroad; 5) undertaking aid projects. According to the government, ITEC was designed to generate political goodwill for India, and procure mutual economic benefits. It is seen as part of India's commitment to the concept of collective self-reliance and, as such, the government prefers to perceive its activities as 'co-operation' rather than 'aid'. It is said that, officially, ITEC 'is non-ideological and non-political in motivation' [D2]. ITEC aid is extended to over 50 countries.

Despite denials, it is evident that ITEC was designed as a means whereby India could obtain unjustifiable economic advantages in developing countries [D2]. Government officials are understandably sensitive on this issue, realizing that should ITEC's activities become too widely known and understood, the tenability of India's position on many international economic issues could be questioned. The government's attempts to disguise its real motive have been unsuccessful. Unlike China, India has given little aid on a grant basis, but has chosen far more explicit aid-tying patterns.

The clearest examples of this are: techno-economic surveys, undertaken in South Yemen, Laos, Mauritius, Malaysia, Iraq, Iran, Trinidad-Tobago and Fiji; industrial surveys have been conducted in Guyana, Surinam, Liberia, Nigeria, Oman, Dubai and Libya. In addition, India has established, or sought to establish, industrial estates in Afghanistan, Kenya, Tanzania, Bangladesh and Laos, in the hope of finding a ready market for its machinery, goods and services. While a cost-benefit analysis on this programme has yet to be done, Vohra [V5: 313-14] suggests a link between ITEC and the expansion of exports, particularly in the case of techno-economic surveys, with follow-up in the form of Indian joint industrial project investments. For example, the techno-economic survey compiled for the Fijian government in 1969 aimed to improve handicraft industries, and identify the potential for new industries. The cost of expanding Fiji's existing industries was calculated on the basis of machinery made in India rather than either the best, or the cheapest available. Among the suggestions made by the Indian team was the opening of a free trade zone, at a time when India's own attitude towards foreign investment was becoming less open. The Indian team utilized the local services of the Bank of Baroda and of Air India, who offered India an entry point.

Another activity of ITEC, designed to gain immediate goodwill rather than short term economic gain, is the aid gifts India donates each year (see Table

4.2), costing an annual total of under Rs.20 million. Gifts are often part of a wider aid package, and as an added bonus. One gift of 1,000 milch buffaloes to Sri Lanka in the mid-1960s was later discovered to have been eaten! Other gifts under ITEC are for humanitarian reasons, such as disaster relief in the Philippines, or Yugoslavia, or the emergency rice given to Hang Samrin's government in Kampuchea.

As in multilateral aid programmes, most ITEC aid is in the technical field. Thousands, indeed, if aid to Nepal is included, tens of thousands of experts have been sent abroad under technical assistance programmes.[12] Selection is carried out by the Department of Personnel and Administrative Reforms which has a foreign assignment section and maintains a registered pool of experts. This department covers 21 different fields of specialization and places advertisements for posts abroad. In 1975, out of thousands of applicants, 2,341 persons were selected for 3–12 month assignments abroad. This sytem is seen by the government as a means of employing India's idle technical manpower.

An allied activity is training developing country personnel under ITEC in India. As earlier noted, since the late 1950s India has operated its own General Scholarship Scheme for Asian and African students in many fields. This Scheme not only encompasses ITEC but the Colombo Plan, UNDP and SCAAP too. In the mid-1960s India also initiated a scholarship scheme under UNESCO auspices for overseas Indians, called the General Cultural scholarships. By 1980 foreign students of Third World origin studying in India numbered in their thousands. Simultaneously with the increase in the numbers of Indian government sponsored students was an increase in self-financing or foreign government financed students, particularly from Nigeria, Libya, Iran, Iraq, Thailand and Zambia. The highest Indian government expenditure was for Afghan students and the lowest for Somalis, Cubans, Burmese and Maldivians.

This last activity may be the most significant for India'a bid for long term influence in the Third World. Paradoxically, because domestic poverty cannot be concealed, Third World students, once in India, see India as less of a threat than perhaps they had supposed, but her achievements do leave some impression. Many of India's foreign ex-students go on to influential positions. For example, Prime Minister Lisulo of Zambia, and Tun Abdul Razak's son, a graduate of an Indian military academy. The benefits for India as a result of this are difficult to assess. Nevertheless, the Third World's awareness of India, its strengths as well as weaknesses, is growing due to the many foreign students graduating from Indian institutions each year.

Loans, Credits and Grants
Loans, credits and grants are also provided on a bilateral basis outside the purview of any particular aid programme and of the External Affairs Ministry. Such bilateral aid at times includes transfer of capital resources — a further indication of India using its new, enhanced status as a basis upon which to build new relationships with developing countries. Such aid,

naturally, is provided in the hope of some gain, notably where credits are tied to purchases of Indian goods. In a few cases, where development loans and commodity loans, as well as grants are given, India anticipates longer term gains.

Discussions on development in the past have focused on capital flows and the resulting problems of international indebtedness.[13] Conventionally, the roles of creditor and debtor are thought to be at the heart of most contemporary international inequalities, yet this has not always been so. For example, before the First World War the US was a major debtor state only to become the greatest creditor later [A1]. From the 1920s international credits became more overtly political in nature and, following the Second World War, were used unreservedly as a major foreign policy weapon in international diplomacy. Developing countries' international indebtedness became a marked feature in the 1960s and a major manifestation of their dependence on the industrialized world. The problem of debt-servicing has been a cardinal preoccupation of many Third World states and international institutions. Indian debts have been rescheduled three times: in 1968, 1971 and 1973. The ominous history of the crippling war debts imposed on Germany in the 1920s has led to warnings from some quarters that the present situation might lead to serious political upheavals [A1].

Against this background, India, itself a chronic debtor state, has emerged as a creditor to other developing countries (see Table 4.5). The nearest analogy to India is China, which in 1973 alone gave grants of $529 million, making Indian efforts seem small in comparison. Compared to India's overall budgetary expenditures, the amount extended in loans and grants is small, but their political and economic effect is by no means inconsiderable.

The Indian government describes its loans, credits and grants as co-operation, a form of aid it has extended since 1948.[14] The terms 'loans' and 'credits' are distinguished because the former indicates Indian monetary aid, usually in rupees, not tied to specific purchases of itemized Indian goods, though still linked to overall purchases of Indian goods and services. It is also used here to indicate foreign exchange and non-monetary loans, such as those in the form of commodities. Indian 'credits' have been a far more common phenomenon, more accurately described as 'buyers credits' tied to the purchase of Indian goods. These are straight commercially motivated transfers, while 'loans' are provided with more long-term political as well as economic gains in mind — thought to come through helping underwrite another state's development. The Economic Division of the Finance Ministry categorized loans and credits three ways: 1) Government to government credits, for example to Zambia and Vietnam, with a validity of 15 years at 5% interest and a three year repayment holiday. 2) Government to government commodity loans, no interest imposed, to be repaid in kind, usually after three years.[15] 3) 'Suppliers or buyers credits' within an international trade environment in which incentives are offered to foreign importers. This activity comes increasingly under the IDBI rather than the economic ministries.

India has also given grants or straight monetary transfers to nine foreign states. Usually grants are administered by the Economic Division of the External Affairs Ministry. The rationale for Indian activity here is slightly different from that for loans and credits; grants are aimed at procuring long term influence in other countries. Grants are usually a manifestation of India's special interest in a particular state and its stability; they are, of course, also intended to gain economic advantages for India. No grant, particularly if made in rupees (and there are few exceptions) can escape this implication; rupees can only be used to purchase Indian goods and services. The number of grants given to other countries has remained steady over the years (see Table 4.7), mostly to states such as Bhutan, Nepal, Bangladesh and Mauritius, where India has long term interests. Some have also gone to states such as Cambodia, Laos, Mozambique, Somalia and North Yemen

Table 4.7
Indian Grants to Developing Countries

Country and Year of Grant	*Amount (Rs. million) (unless indicated otherwise)*
Bangladesh	
1971–72	250.00
refugee relief	180.58
1972–73	1650.17
1973–74	120.47
1974–75	30.41
1975–76	90.22
Total:	*2321.85*
RBI reported total up to 1977:	*1454.00*
Bhutan	
1960–80 Annual grant Rs.700 thousand	
Total:	*14.00*
1961–62 1st Plan	172.20
1966–71 2nd Plan	200.00
1971–76 3rd Plan	350.00
1976–81 4th Plan	722.20
Total	*1458.40*
RBI reported total up to 1977:	*1109.00*
Khmer Republic	
(Lon Nol) 1970s in foreign exchange	0.30
Kampuchea	
(Heng Samrin)	
1979 commodity grant: rice 1,004 tonnes	

Table 4.7 (continued)

Country and Year of Grant		*Amount (Rs. million)* *(unless indicated otherwise)*
Laos		
1972 through ESCAP		0.05
1975 for development		0.20
	Total:	*0.25*
Mauritius		
1972 (up to)		13.10
1977		36.00
	Total:	*49.1*
Nepal		
1960–80 Annual grant:		1.00
	Total:	*20.00*
1950–77 RBI	*Total:*	*1382.00*
Mozambique		
1976 Ease shortages following closure of border with Zimbabwe		$100,000
Somalia		
1964–65		.260 thousand
Sri Lanka		
1976 For Non-aligned Summit		1.00
North Yemen		
1964–65		1.00
1965–66		.600 thousand
	Total:	*1.60*
Total Grants given by India:		*5234.86*

Sources: *BBC Summary of World Broadcasts; Indian Economic Diary;*
D.C. Vohra, *India's Aid Diplomacy to the Third World,* New Delhi, 1980;
RBI Report of Currency and Finance; Economist Intelligence Unit-Report on Kampuchea; Ministry of External Affairs, Annual Reports

and can be explained partly in terms of seeking future advantages. In 1966 and 1967 India offered grants to Sudan, Kenya, Uganda, Tanzania and Ghana but none were accepted. A particular type of grant given annually is a hang-over from colonial days when the British gave grants to native rulers. Under the terms of the 1949 Treaty with Bhutan for example, the king receives an annual grant of Rs.700,000 (Rs.1 million). A special budget exists in the External Affairs Ministry for these 'Diplomatic Expenditures' which also includes Nepal and, until 1975, Sikkim [V5: 261].

To maintain the paradox of why India, itself a debtor country, should extend loans and credits to other developing countries, it is necessary to again consider the nature of Indian political economy. The phenomenon (beginning in the late 1970s) of large foreign exchange reserves accumulating in India was the result of a massive inflow of remittances from Indians overseas. But this was only temporary and as such cannot provide an adequate rationale for Indian loans and credits to other countries. The pattern was established in the 1960s, when India was extremely short of capital and itself dependent on Western and Soviet loans. Yet, as early as 1948, Indonesia received a grant from India as did Bhutan and Nepal from at least 1950. Why did India extend monetary aid to other countries when facing acute financial distress itself? In one way, by extending these loans and credits in rupees, India lost very little. Perhaps, also, it was an attempt to replicate India's own dependency pattern by building a similar relationship with other states less developed than itself — particularly in the case of Nepal and Bhutan — and is part of the explicit aim of many loans, credits and grants extended to these countries by India. Loans and credits have not been confined to South Asia but extended also to countries such as: Sudan, Tanzania, Indonesia, Zambia, Afghanistan, Burma, Vietnam and Kenya.

As seen earlier, loans and credits are part of a more generalized Indian projection abroad involving aid and investments, and as the capability of the Indian economy grows, probably more loans and credits will be given to developing countries. Nevertheless, the Indian government is defensive about this activity. In conversation, officials stress that such aid does not constitute any sizable export of capital (Rs.400 million in 1979) compared to the annual net inflow of capital — Rs.2–4,000 million a year in 1979. Nevertheless, there are strong economic motives for India's aid, the strongest being the need, inherent in Indian state capitalism, to export Indian manufactured goods, and now capital [B7]. Salient features of many Indian loans, credits and grants is that they serve both to promote Indian exports and to involve India in the financial structures of other developing countries.

Indian monetary aid has taken several forms since 1959 [16] (see Table 4.3). Credit in Indian rupees tied to the purchase of goods or to specific trade deals being the most prevalent. There are at least 34 credits in this category, including stand-by arrangements, totalling at least Rs.4,631,575 million. Another type is direct bank credits and foreign exchange lines of credit, which were given to Bangladesh, to bolster the liquidity and purchasing power of that country and enable it to buy more Indian goods. A third type of credit is tied to a specific development project for procurements of Indian goods. In addition to foreign exchange, loans have been extended for generalized development in Bhutan, Mauritius and Tanzania. A more recent form of non-monetary loan is that of commodities, such as rice and wheat. This last may appear to be motivated by overtly political rather than economic considerations, but lack of storage space for bumper harvests may be partially solved by 'storing' grain abroad that returns after three years.

Until 1972 loan and credit activities were directed and administered either by the Finance, or External Affairs Ministries. From 1972 a third institution (the Industrial Development Bank of India (IDBI)) entered the field, on a more commercial basis. This institution runs two schemes, one offering credit to Indian exporters and the other extending lines of credit to foreign governments and overseas buyers. This has led to some overlap in activities of the IDBI and the economic Ministries in Delhi, IDBI being only indirectly under the Ministry of Finance. Under the IDBI schemes credits are extended to Indian suppliers/exporters either directly or via commercial banks. Under the second scheme, buyers credits are given either directly to foreign financial institutions, or to the foreign buyer himself. Until 1980 no buyers credits had been given to foreign private importers, but only to foreign public sector concerns. Users of buyers credits have been bodies such as the New Zealand Electricity Board, or governments. IDBI offers credits at commercial rates, rather than on soft terms which, it claims, the government usually does for political reasons. Yet government sometimes imposes pressure on the IDBI to lower its rates to 'cost breaking points' fixed at a 'low' 7½%, 8½% or 10%. It is claimed that this occurred in the case of credits to Bangladesh. IDBI wished for higher interest rates in 1980, but this was frustrated by the government. While it tries to adhere strictly to economic criteria in its credit activity to foreign countries, the utilization rate of IDBI credits has been quite low and time limits have frequently been extended. So far, according to the IDBI itself, it has been most active in Mauritius (to a bank), Zambia (to the government), Indonesia (to a public sector company), Kenya (to the government) and Bangladesh (to banks). The IDBI credit system is an illustration of the increasing sophistication of the Indian economy, manifesting itself in overseas relations of a 'commercial' character divorced from overt government direction. These IDBI credits and their character have wide-ranging implications for India's deepening relationships with other developing countries.

As can be seen in Tables 4.3 and 4.7, since 1959 India has extended loans, credits and grants to numerous countries for the purchase of goods and the supply of commodities. The terms under which the loans and credits operated have varied, but were mostly liberal, with a three year grace period and low interest rates, varying from 3% to 5.5%. After 1972, India began to extend food grain loans and other credits to a larger number of countries. Credits were not given on such liberal terms in all cases, as the case of Bangladesh shows. Bangladesh has the dubious distinction of being the recipient of the largest number of Indian loans, credits, and massive grants which, in total value, also make it the largest single recipient of Indian financial aid; even prior to Bangladesh's independence India gave loans to the provisional government. After the war, in 1972, three agreements were signed, tied to purchases of Indian rail equipment, aircraft, ships and oil. Repayment was to be after 25 years with a grace period of seven years. In 1973, these loans were followed by the offer of a Rs.600 million commodity loan. Two bank credits (Rs.250 and Rs.150 million) were extended for the purchase of textiles; a Rs.100 million interest free loan to Bangladesh railways; a credit for the purchase of aircraft and ships; a Rs.100 million loan for the supply of commodities; a Rs.80.10 million loan for importing oil at 6¼% interest; a foreign exchange loan of £5 million, at 2% interest; and a loan for purchasing Indian buses, were also extended in 1973. In 1974 more Indian credits and loans were given: one for 90% of the purchase value of Indian manufactured goods c.i.f. to the Bangladesh border, with repayment terms of 24 repayments over 15 years at 5% interest.

The terms of many of these credits required repayments in Indian rupees to come from the sale of foreign currencies to specified foreign exchange banks in India. In essence, therefore, India demanded foreign exchange for a rupee credit. Other terms imposed by India on Bangladesh included a penalty charge of 2% for any overdue payments, while defaults on payments after three months allowed India to call in the entire debt. Furthermore, the rupee value of a 1974 credit had its value fixed to the gold value at the time of signature. Another Indian credit to Bangladesh of Rs.60 million was spread over a 20 year period, with repayments scheduled for every 6 months, at 4% interest with a 2% penalty charge. The stipulation that repayments had to come through the sale of hard currencies to India was also imposed.

Other credits were given in the same year to Bangladesh banks for a cement project, and to encourage Bangladesh to buy from India to 'save foreign exchange', as well as a loan to help overcome flood damage. As political relations became increasingly tense as a result of domestic pressure inside Bangladesh, India and Bangladesh discarded rupee trade and, in late 1974, switched to hard currency payments. At the same time some technical credits were converted into inter-governmental loans, with repayment of 50% within a year, the rest falling due after 3 years. The severity of Indian lending terms could be said to have contributed to the breakdown of Indo-Bangladesh relations, in that it supported popular views in Bangladesh that India sought to exploit it. A period when no Indian credits were given to Bangladesh ended in 1977, and in 1978 a new IDBI credit was provided.

Since the early 1970s India has increasingly extended monetary credits, loans and grants to a growing number of states in an increasing variety of forms and under widely varied terms that, in some cases, have been less than equitable. In an earlier period Indian credits were partially tied to bulk purchases of Indian commodities such as jute and cement, but by the 1970s they had become totally tied to purchases of Indian manufactures and services. That not all Indian loans and credits have had a high utilization rate may be because foreign buyers have been reluctant to buy non-competitive Indian goods which, without the crutch of a rupee credit, would not attract a market. Whether India is able to impose harsh terms or is forced to lend on liberal terms depends on the degree of leverage over the recipient, which may arise from non-economic factors. Whatever the terms, the primary motivation remains, to sell Indian goods which cannot find a market at home, or which the ruling classes decline to sell domestically, preferring to reap higher profits by selling abroad.

As seen at the outset, the total cost of Indian aid through all programmes, including loans, credits and grants, is far outweighed by that received by India, and her own overall budgetary expenditure. The varying utilization rates of Indian aid outlays have been particularly important. In 1974 over 82% of aid authorized was utilized; in 1975-76 this fell to 40%. The total number of countries aided by India is impressive, but the bulk has remained with neighbouring countries, with 87% of the total to Bangladesh (46%), Nepal (27%) and Bhutan (14%).

India operates two other aid programmes. One in the field of nuclear technology, a subject dealt with in the next chapter. The other, ostensibly part of the ITEC programme, but because of its military aspects is under the Defence Ministry and the Cabinet Secretariat, is military and other aid to armed liberation movements.

Despite certain anomalies (e.g. the Life Insurance Corporation's investments in South Africa, see Chapter 6) Indian policy has constantly supported Southern African liberation from white racist regimes. As a natural outcome of this India has aided several movements dedicated to change in Southern Africa: civilian aid to Angolan refugees in Lusaka as well as training its nationals, and aid to SWAPO in Namibia. India has had longstanding ties with Zimbabwean nationalist leaders and by 1978 she was aiding ZAPU as well as ZANU. Officially, such aid was confined to sewing machines, boots, clothes, medicines, blankets and food. In 1975, a delegation from the OAU's Liberation Committee visited Delhi and asked for know-how and technical staff. Given the close military ties India has developed with Tanzania, Zambia and Botswana, 'technical staff and know-how' probably included arms and training.[17]

In early 1980 India gave full diplomatic recognition to the PLO and reports emerged shortly after of Indian military and civilian aid to the Palestinians, channelled through Iraq.

In both Southern Africa and Palestine, as well as substantiating its diplomatic support, India has assessed the future gains to be made by aiding these struggles.

India's military aid must be seen in two contexts: the strategic and political context within which the government seeks to influence other Third World states, and the economic, as discussed in Chapter 2. Indian military aid performs a dual function: it cements relationships abroad, and it helps generate exports for some of India's most important industries, namely armaments. In this area of aid activity, India has been extremely secretive, particularly in more recent years as her military aid has grown in scale and importance. Until more facts emerge this discussion will remain incomplete, serving only as a tentative introduction to a hitherto unknown aspect of India's foreign relations.

India's defence forces, the third largest in the world, are well suited for an aid role (see Table 4.8). Their level of expertize, battle experience and

Table 4.8
Indian Defence Forces and Arms Production

Armed Forces: 1977
Army:	913,000
Navy:	42,500
Air Force:	100,000
Total:	*1,055,500*

Military Budget: 1978–79:
Rs.29,450 million

Weapons Manufactured Under Licence in India:
Soviet: MIG-21M aircraft; Missiles; Tanks (T-72); MIG-23 aircraft? Transport aircraft?
French: Alouette-3 helicopters; Cheetah helicopters; Naval frigate; Mirage 5 aircraft?
British: ASW frigates; Tank (Vijayanta); HS-748 Avro aircraft; Jaguar aircraft (cancelled 1980?); Ajit aircraft (Gnat)
Swiss: Avionics
West Germany: Submarines

Indigenous Arms Production:
Small Arms: Pistols; Rifles; Machine guns; mortars; grenades; anti-tank weapons; anti-aircraft guns; artillery; most ammunition
Aircraft: HAL HJT 16 MK 1 & MK 2 Kiran fighter/trainer; HF-24 MK1, MK 2 & MK 3 Marut fighter; HAC-33 Stol; HPT-32 Trainer; Target Drone; Aero jet engines
Naval: Landing craft; Ship to ship missile; Patrol boats; Frigates; Naval tenders; Submarine (under development); Torpedoes
Infantry: Main battle tank (under development); Armoured Personnel Carrier; Anti-tank missiles; Ground to air missiles
Advanced Weapons Systems: Electronics; Avionics; Radars; Rockets; Missile (IRBM) SLV-3; SLV-5 (improved MRBM planned); Satellites

Sources: *SIPRI Yearbooks*, IISS Annual *Strategic Surveys*

equipment, their familiarity with the Soviet designed arms – and Chinese copies – found widely in many developing countries, and perhaps above all their record of non-involvement in domestic politics make them especially welcome in Third World countries.

According to the government 'requests from friendly countries for the supply of defence stores are complied with'[18] and 'friendly-country military personnel receive Indian training and instruction.' Foreign armies not only receive training, but occasionally, Indian weaponry too. Before. independence, Indian military aid was extended to: Indonesia (1946, and the early 1950s); Nepal (1952, including manning Tibetan border-crossings until 1969); Burma (1948 to early 1950s), and Sri Lanka (early 1950s).

Military aid decisions apparently remain almost solely in the hands of the Prime Minister and hardly involve the bureaucracy or Parliament. Between 1947 and 1979, according to government sources,[19] more than 30 developing countries received military assistance and more than half of them were supplied with Indian arms – either as aid or on a sale basis – additionally, military aid has been extended to at least two liberation movements.

Naval aid has mostly been confined to training, although Bangladesh was supplied with patrol boats and a ship. Up to 1964 the Indian navy had trained over 600 Indonesians and 50 Sri Lankan naval officers and men; by 1971, 750 Sri Lankans had received training, and in the same year Singapore also benefited. Whilst training is usually given on board Indian naval vessels, officers are occasionally seconded to foreign navies; for example in 1971, ten naval officers were seconded to the Nigerian navy. Repair facilities have also been made available to other Third World navies – in 1970, Egyptian and Ethiopian vessels were refitted at Vishakapatnam naval base.

Indian military aid to Indonesia in 1946 was by way of Dakota aircraft and pilots, but participation in aid programmes by the air force was minimal in the 1950s. In the early 1960s, however, Indian manufactured planes were given to Ghana, Indonesia, Singapore and Malaysia, usually along with training programmes and occasionally with maintenance technicians. A joint jet-engine and MIG manufacturing project with Egypt in 1964 was terminated in 1969 owing to technical difficulties. In the late 1960s and early 1970s, Iraq and Bangladesh received aid in the form of aircraft, and India reportedly undertook the training of Iraqi and Afghan pilots.

As a colonially created force the Indian army has experienced substantial foreign service, and after independence played an active part in UN peace-keeping missions. The experience and background thus provided enabled the Indian army to undertake a variety of roles in military aid programmes. The cases of Burma and Nepal have already been mentioned. In 1961, India sent a military training mission (IMTRAT) to Bhutan both to build a Bhutanese army and to perform a reconnaissance role for Indian defence. By 1976 the Bhutanese army numbered over 5,000 and, with the addition of an Indian army Engineer and Military Border Roads Organization mission (DANTAK), numbered approximately 15,000. In 1961 the Malaysian army began to receive Indian help, as did the Ethiopian army, including the setting-up of a military academy at Harar at the Emperor's request. Training of the Afghan army by India started in the same year, and in 1962 India was requested to set up a military academy in Nigeria; Nigerian cadets also began to come to India for training. This laid the foundations of a firm and long-standing relationship between India and the Nigerian military, and, in late 1979, an entire Indian training brigade was sent to Nigeria.

In addition, by 1967 South Yemen, Uganda, Iraq, Sudan, Ghana, Egypt and Somalia were also receiving military aid. India subsequently built up strong military ties with both Egypt and Iraq, although in the 1970s this relationship with Egypt was sharply curtailed. Military aid to Iraq has involved all three services, and included armaments, advisers and large scale training programmes, with an Indian military training brigade in Iraq in late 1979. Iraq is probably the most important Indian military aid recipient outside South Asia, and for this reason it is via Iraq that India aids the PLO.

Tanzania and Zambia were involved in Indian military aid programmes in the late 1960s; Tanzanian cadets were training in India in 1971, and co-operation extended to most fields of military science. In 1970, an Algerian delegation visited India to seek military help, and in 1971 Guyana's Prime Minister requested arms, aircraft and training for his country's para-military and police. In Bhutan (until 1976), Oman, and Botswana, Indian army personnel have been on secondment or recruited into their armies. Like Guyana, Oman has received para-military aid from India's Border Security Force.

While much Indian military aid takes the form of training, some has been in arms, although to what extent it is difficult to measure. Despite claims that Indian arms are exported on a commercial basis only, statements were made in Parliament, in 1967, that aircraft had been given to other countries.[20] Apart from the special case of Bangladesh during 1971–72, India has given few arms to other countries, though where this has been on a strictly aid and where on a sale basis is difficult to discern.

In South Asia particularly, India's military aid serves a strategic purpose aside from the broadly political and economic roles mentioned earlier. India has naval bases in its Indian Ocean islands of Andaman and Nicobar and in the Laccadives [O2]. During 1971 the Maldives allowed Pakistan to use the former RAF base at Gan as a refuelling base. Against this background India offered military aid to the Maldives and in 1978 sought unsuccessfully to secure the use of naval facilities at Gan.[21] In Nepal and Bhutan, military aid was clearly designed to meet Indian strategic interests, as well as to maintain those states dependent; for a time its military aid to Bangladesh served a similar purpose.

India's military aid is a little-known aspect of her growing relationships with other developing countries, but given the nature of her own development one likely to parallel non-military aid programmes in its extent.

Notes

1. These generalizations are difficult. For example, they cannot illustrate the problems for any model which tries to distinguish between big power and middle-power aid programmes.
2. Interview, Ministry of External Affairs, New Delhi, 16 February 1980.
3. *Plan Documents 1st–6th Plan* (1950–1976), Government of India, Planning Commission.
4. Interview, Ministry of External Affairs, New Delhi, 16 February 1980. An official stated that 99% of all Indian aid is given in response to requests.
5. In the 1930s, an Indian medical team, under Dr Kotnis, went to aid China, and the Indian National Congress voted relief aid to Spain. See D2.

6. £15,000 in 1971–72; £60,000 in 1975. Total spent to 1974: Rs.1.50 million. See Ministry of External Affairs Annual Reports and V5.
7. CFTC pamphlet, Commonwealth Secretariat, London, June 1974.
8. *World Bank Annual Reports* 1968–1978.
9. It is no accident that it was India which constantly sponsored new members of the Colombo Plan; countries such as Bhutan, Maldives and Bangladesh which it felt would be under its influence.
10. *UNDP: The Administrator Reports*, 1973.
11. *Government of India, Ministry of External Affairs, Annual Report*, 1970–71.
12. It is reported [V5] that between 60,000 and 100,000 Indians are working on aid projects in Nepal at any one time. This, added to the Indian aid presence in Bhutan of roughly 15,000, gives a total figure of around 90,000 Indians on government sponsored aid missions all over the world.
13. *World Development* Issue on Debt, February 1979, and P11.
14. *Reserve Bank of India: Report on Currency and Banking* 1976–77, p. 234, Tables X-8 and Statement 105.
15. According to bureaucrats these loans are given for 'purely humanitarian reasons'. That repayment is required is because India cannot afford to run down its buffer stocks of food-grains.
16. The Economic Division of the Ministry of Finance administers all loans and credits except those to Nepal, Bhutan and Bangladesh which are kept with the Economic Division of the External Affairs Ministry. This attests to the special status these enjoy in the Government of India. Interview, Ministry of Commerce, New Delhi, 16 January 1980. Cyclostyled document, Functions of Different Departments in the Government of India.
17. On a visit to Delhi in 1978 the Prime Minister of Zambia requested Indian military aid to liberation struggles. *BBC Summary of World Broadcasts* FE/5991/A5/1, 11 December 1978.
18. *Annual Report*, Ministry of Defence, Home Affairs and External Affairs, and author's interviews, New Delhi and London.
19. *India Office Records* L/P&S/12/2267 Coll.9/44. With unconfirmed reports of other Southern African liberation movements receiving military help. Ironically, India also gave counter-insurgency training to Sri Lanka, Malaysia, Iraq and Kenya. *Statesman*, 31 December 1980.
20. *Indian and Foreign Review*, 15 July 1967, quoting Surendra Pal Singh, Deputy Minister for External Affairs.
21. There was a precedent for this; in 1957 the Indian army assisted Sri Lanka with flood relief, see B14.

5. India's Investments

Transfer of Technology

India's commitment to economic co-operation with other developing countries has been strengthened in recent years by a related commitment to expand the transfer of technology amongst developing countries themselves [B23], under the Technological Co-operation among Developing Countries (TCDC) organization. This commitment is, however, presenting India with a dilemma. On the one hand, on the basis of its own experience India adheres to a position that no single country should have a monopoly of technology; on the other, because India has developed its own technological base, commercial imperatives are leading Indian companies, and the government, to have a less than open attitude to the unrestricted flow of certain of its own technologies. There is, then, a conflict, centred upon whether India should see technology as an intellectual quality to be freely transferred,[1] or a tool whereby India can demonstrate technical and financial superiority over other countries and thus benefit from royalties, payments and so on. This conflict is still unresolved and is likely to become more acute as India builds up its technological base.

At a symposium on the use of science, held in New Delhi in 1964, a resolution was passed condemning the developed world's monopoly of technology. The original UNCTAD agenda included the question of the transfer of technology as one of its main items [R15]. Following these initiatives, an Afro-Asia conference on the use of science and technology was held in Delhi in 1966, at which a committee was formed with the object of encouraging the interflow of technology among developing countries. Subsequently, under the auspices of ESCAP, a further conference was held in New Delhi directed towards implementing this goal. In 1977, these early steps culminated with an Indian commitment of $1 million to set up a regional centre for technology transfer under ESCAP and located in Bangalore. Its task is to document available information on technology and facilitate its dissemination.[2] Up to 1979, little work had been done at the Centre, largely because it was under the control of bureaucrats with minimal understanding of technical matters, rather than to any shortage of expertize.[3]

In India, the state — and to a lesser extent private industry — has invested heavily in building up research and development facilities. In 1979, between 45 and 50 laboratories were under government control in all fields of industry, defence and medicine. In one government research organization alone there were 15,000 scientists, and today India has the third largest pool of skilled scientific manpower in the world. A decision was taken at Cabinet level in 1953 that indigenous Indian technology should be generated as an import substitution measure and that the government would then transfer applied (not basic) technology to existing industries able to absorb it, with the aim of boosting production and the general technological base in the country. Problems arose and were replicated in India's own international transfers, when it was found that scientists were ill-equipped to market technology or to adopt an acceptable commercial manner. Thus a marketing body — the National Research and Development Corporation — was set up to collate and disseminate information on technological development, and market India's technology abroad.

Despite these measures, investment in research and development, both in the public and private sectors of Indian industry, is at a very low level. Many Indian industries still prefer to import foreign technology, reflecting an international pattern and their own continuing dependence on the industrialized world.

Against the background the Indian government speaks of the technology it can offer other developing countries as 'intermediate technology' appropriate to the needs of these countries. It is true that 'intermediate technology', which is low cost, small scale, basic in quality and sophistication (as in handicrafts) make it well suited to the conditions of other developing countries, but in other cases 'intermediate technology' means machinery and equipment which, in India, is considered antiquated and subject to frequent breakdowns due to low quality.

This points to a major problem India has faced in its technological transfer. Indigenous Indian technology is regarded as inferior in the outside world. At best, most developing countries suspect that Indian technology is recycled second-rate developed country technology (particularly from Eastern Europe). Not only that, but even in basic technologies, such as village industries, where India could make an impact, developing countries' elites prefer to buy inappropriate technology rather than old-fashioned and, in their eyes, 'second-rate' Indian technology.[4] Thus, despite efforts, there has been minimal transfer of Indian technology (see Table 5.1).

India's own experience led it to condemn technology transfers based on royalties and continuing fees as opposed to outright sales, which it has always preferred. The change from technology sales to the demand for royalties by Eastern European countries was thus condemned by India. Official Indian policy is that its technology transfers should be on a straight sale basis. Some transfers have followed this pattern, but, especially when India has high technology for sale, high costs may have to be offset through royalties or other payments. In the transfer of processes to Argentina,

Table 5.1
Technology Transfers: India/Developing Countries

Year	Company/Organization/Country	Process
1971	Ahmedabad Textile; Industry Research Association (ATIRA): Egypt	Durable Press
1973	JK Industries; Gwalior Rayon: S. Korea, Turkey, Thailand	Ethylene Glycol recovery
1969	Regional Research Lab. Jorhat Assam: Malaysia	Bamboo cardboard
1975	Projects and Equipment Corp: Argentina	Reactive dyes; whiteners
1978	Development Consultants: Syria, Venezuela	Cement; Steel plant techniques
1972	Chemicals and Fibres of India Ltd: Sudan	Polyester fibre
1975	Khadi & Village Industries Commission: Tanzania	Gobar gas units; kilns; handmade paper
1975–80	Sri Lanka, Nepal, Somalia, Brazil, Iran, Uganda, Upper Volta	Gobar gas techniques
to 1979	Nepal, Sri Lanka, Bangladesh	Beekeeping
1974	National Research Development Corp: Philippines	Erection of plant
to 1979	Burma, Thailand, Sri Lanka, Nepal	12 transfers; various fields
1971	Amar Dye Chemicals:	Reactive Dyes
1971	Argentina,	
1978	Indonesia,	
1979	Brazil	
	Atlas Cycle Industries:	Bicycle manufacture
1974	Iran	
1978	Bangladesh	
1978	Tanzania	
1979	Guyana, Sudan, Zambia	

Sources: Letters to author from ATIRA; Khadi & Village Industries Commission; Interviews, New Delhi, 1980; *Indian Economic Diary, Commerce; FICCI Report, Workshop on Joint Ventures 1979.*

Indonesia and Brazil by Amar Dye Chemicals (Table 5.1) the terms were
5% royalties for 5 years, plus a $25,000 flat payment. In another instance,
equity participation was demanded, plus 2% royalties and $14,000.

Nuclear technology

Most transfers of Indian technology, particularly at the intermediate level,
have been minimal with limited impact, but in one high technology area,
transfer has been a qualified success with profound political implications.
Despite India's poverty, modern and sophisticated sectors of science and
technology — most notably in the nuclear field — have been developed there.

Whilst the nuclear powers are concerned by what they see as nuclear
proliferation (witness the formation of the London Club) India takes the
opposite view and actively seeks to disseminate the knowledge it has acquired
in the nuclear field to other developing countries.

India embarked on an atomic development programme in 1948, which,
in 1954, led to the formation of the Department of Atomic Energy [J1
and M11]. In 1958, India built the first (after the USSR) nuclear reactor in
Asia (Apsara). This headstart gained India a unique place in the developing
world and by 1974, with the exception of China, India's nuclear programme
was the most highly developed outside the industrialized world. In that year
India's nuclear explosion focused world attention on its development programme and drew foreign (primarily Western) criticism of Indian nuclear
policy.

The cornerstone of nuclear policy in India was a desire to develop an
independent nuclear technology free from enforced constraints by the
existing nuclear powers. The Indian government considers the development
of nuclear technology to be a measure of what it adjudges as India's true
place in the world, which has thus far been unattainable. From the establishment of the International Atomic Energy Agency (IAEA), in 1954 [J1],
India has maintained that there cannot be a monopoly of the knowledge of
nuclear processes, and that superpowers have no superior moral right to
restrict dissemination of such knowledge. Thus, India has seen its role as that
of monopoly breaker (a position shared with China) pursuing nuclear development, not for itself alone but, at least in so far as official rhetoric is concerned, for all nuclear have-not states.

Initially, India signed nuclear co-operation agreements with such countries
as the UK (1956), Canada, USA, USSR, Hungary and Sweden, with a view
to furthering development of its own programme. Countries with which
India subsequently concluded nuclear collaboration agreements included:
Spain, Belgium, Czechoslovakia, East and West Germany, Italy and Rumania;
some of these agreements were later allowed to lapse.

In 1959, India began to train personnel from other countries in nuclear
technology. Two Indonesians (uranium prospecting and health physics),
three Burmese, two Poles and two Yugoslavs (nuclear chemistry and reactor
engineering) were trained that year at India's main nuclear research centre
in Trombay, near Bombay.[5] Two Hungarians also began training in India

in 1968.

In 1962, India signed the first co-operation agreement in nuclear technology with another developing country — Egypt; and by 1964, a Joint Scientific Board had been set up for co-operation in atomic research. In the same
year, under the auspices of the IAEA India signed an agreement with the
Philippines to supply a neutron crystal spectrometer laboratory, a training
programme and technicians; this agreement included a clause banning any
military use of the laboratory [J1: 427]. The Treaty was left open for other
regional member states who might wish to co-operate in the nuclear field,
but none seem to have taken advantage of the offer. In 1965, India signed
an agreement with Yugoslavia for the exchange of unclassified information
in atomic energy. In the same year India entered into an agreement with
Afghanistan on atomic energy, and set up an isotope centre there in 1966.
During Mrs. Gandhi's visit to Brazil in 1968 an agreement was signed for
nuclear collaboration and the exchange of unclassified information; this
was ratified in 1970. India signed subsequent agreements with the
Philippines (1969), Egypt (1970) and Bangladesh (1973).[6] In Bangladesh,
India agreed to provide a reactor, and the project was being implemented up
to July 1975. By the 1970s India was dispatching 2,000 radio isotopes for
medical, agricultural and other purposes to Argentina, Colombia, Australia,
Indonesia, Kenya and Mexico. In 1972, a team was sent to Burma to advise
on a nuclear science programme.

After 1966 the Department of Atomic Energy ceased reporting which
countries' personnel were being trained in nuclear technology in India,
although it was noted that: 'A number of foreign trainees came to different
units of the Department for training in India in the nuclear field.'[7] The
early 1970s saw an increasing number of foreign delegations from other
developing countries visiting India with an interest in collaboration in the
nuclear field. In March 1971, the Director of Science and Technology of the
Arab League visited India for talks with the Department of Atomic Energy,
and in 1972 the Libyans came to discuss possible collaboration in the nuclear
field, a visit reciprocated by India in the following year.[8] India entered into
a secret agreement with the Soviet Union in 1977 to build a nuclear reactor
in Libya.

Alerted by India's nuclear explosion, from the mid-1970s other states,
notably Iran, Indonesia, Peru and Iraq, sought help for their own nuclear
programmes. After signing an agreement with Argentina in 1974 India offered
to build their third nuclear power plant. In the same year the 'basis' for
nuclear co-operation was laid with Iran, leading to announcements by the
Iranian Director of Atomic Energy that joint ventures in this field were
possible. By 1978 nine countries had sought or were already in the process
of receiving Indian nuclear help: Algeria, Colombia, Guyana, Madagascar,
Peru, Mexico, Venezuela, Indonesia and Vietnam.[9] In 1978, agreements
with developing countries were in operation with Afghanistan, Argentina,
Bangladesh, Egypt, Iran and Iraq.

Demonstrably India prefers to channel its nuclear aid bilaterally rather than through international agencies. Nevertheless, India has contributed to the IAEA's Technical Assistance Programme as is shown by the following: (see also Table 4.1)

1959 - 1964	each year	$25,000 x 5
1965 - 1970	each year	$35,000 x 5
1971	–	$40,000
1972	–	$42,000
1973	–	$42,000
Total 1959–73:		*$482,000*[J1: App.B: 180]

India's nuclear co-operation initially took the form of radio isotope supply, research laboratories and other simple uses of nuclear technology. With increasing sophistication and achievement in its own nuclear development programmes, the level of sophistication in assistance has also risen. In the 1970s, India entered the world market, offering its own designs and expertize for nuclear reactors. Simultaneously, however, India began to write safeguards into the agreements it entered into. India itself, however, has been unwilling to accept such provisos in collaboration ventures with existing nuclear powers. India's nuclear ties have been with developed countries with which it has had particularly good relations or with those that offer no threat to her interests or relations with other states (miscalculated in the case of Libya).

India's co-operation with Bangladesh, Afghanistan, Iran and Libya raises interesting questions. It is evident that nuclear aid to Bangladesh was a manifestation of India's good faith and demonstrated the extent of the relationship. It is not coincidental that after the events of 1975 and the assassination of Mujib, Bangladesh's nuclear reactor programme was suspended, to be revived only with other outside help in 1979. Nuclear technology aid to Afghanistan has been symbolic rather than substantive (confined to the medical field) but perhaps designed to show Pakistan and other regional neighbours the extent to which India goes to help its friends in the region. This is also true of nuclear aid to Burma. Indian nuclear aid to Iran illustrates the strength of the ties that both governments sought to foster, particularly after 1973. Despite being then seen as India's potential rival in the military and political fields, Iran was clearly a recipient vis-a-vis India in nuclear technology, a situation balanced by India's role as an oil importer.

Indo-Libyan nuclear co-operation is an interesting illustration of India's miscalculation in its nuclear aid programmes. No doubt the Indian government hoped to obtain oil supplies by aiding Libya, but the result was unwittingly to aid Pakistan's nuclear development (see note 8).

In high, intermediate or basic technology, technology transfers have become closely associated with Indian aid and investment abroad. The natural market for India's technology lies in developing countries. As the productive capacity of the economy grows, and as Indian industry seeks outlets, these countries will increasingly become the target for transfers at all levels.

Export of Capital

As we have seen, the total capital resources India has 'transferred' abroad through its government administered loans, credits and grants, totals some Rs.9,866.455 million. There are several other avenues for the movement of Indian capital abroad. It must be stressed that these capital movements occur simultaneously with a movement of foreign capital *into* India. The outward flows include the investments of institutions such as the Life Insurance Corporation of India, banks and private investment companies with interests abroad, plus joint ventures in other developing countries. In assessing the quantitative importance of India's export of capital its increasing qualitative impact on relationships with developing countries must not be overlooked.

The inflow of foreign aid (see Table 4.1) has consistently outweighed India's total aid expenditures. In the same way India's export of capital has usually been outweighed by foreign capital inflow. After 1960 this was no longer true, because much of the outflow of Indian capital went towards servicing debts and interest payments, as well as on royalties and dividends of foreign investments in India. Much of the annual inflow of capital is, therefore, represented by foreign aid and investment which maintain India's dependence, and the outflow represents debt servicing and profits for these foreign investors. This is the predominant pattern, but a smaller and increasingly important separate movement of Indian capital is becoming apparent, an indication of the autonomy of Indian state capital, which is illustrated by the following figures.

In 1973–74 an estimated Rs.239 million represented the outflow of independent Indian investments out of a total outflow that year of Rs.5,060 million.[10] This excludes figures for other Indian investments overseas, for example, those of institutions such as the LIC banks or the government's grants and aid. Yet even if these were included, the total would still account for only a small part of India's capital outflow, the rest being debt repayments. In 1973, debts, and payments for foreign profits, totalled Rs.70,500 million, and in 1979 Rs.150,000 million.

The movement of independent Indian finance capital abroad may appear to be of scant importance (except in a few cases such as Mauritius, where an Indian financial institution is almost as large as the Central Bank). It is important, however, to the degree to which part of this capital is beginning to act autonomously vis-a-vis India's ties of dependency, as is vividly demonstrated in its yearly balance of payments. Ultimately, as a state capitalist economy, India is part of the world capitalist market, but when the export of its capital occurs autonomously — as in its unseen transfers of capital investments in the form of machinery or cash — it is derived from Indian capital institutions and production, and its links with international capital are indirect. In its outward movements Indian capital does not always act as an agent for a single centre (ie. Western capitalism) but acts autonomously as India itself is simultaneously in a dependent relationship to two centres. Many financial institutions in India, apart from insurance, play a role in India's export of capital, particularly in its industrial invest-ments abroad. (See Chapter 8).

India's most important financial institution is the Central Bank; the apex regulatory body over the entire country's finance and currency, the Reserve Bank of India. The Reserve Bank in theory and law exercises control over the movement of Indian capital abroad, but this does not always occur in practice due to the illegal and evasive tactics of many Indian companies investing overseas.

The Industrial Policy Resolution of 1948 made clear that India's state capitalist system would put the commanding heights of the economy, includ-ing finance capital, in the public sector [A5]. Every step of the way Indian industry is assisted by state financial institutions, some, such as the Industrial Credit and Investment Corporation of India (ICICI) or Industrial Finance Corporation (IFC) have direct links with the World Bank, others, such as the Industrial Development Bank of India (IDBI), the Industrial Recon-struction Corporation of India, Life Insurance Corporation, 33 nationalized banks, and the Unit Trust of India exist as capital institutions, with greater independence, under the Reserve Bank of India [S30]. This suggests that the immediate source, at least for some of Indian finance capital invested over-seas, is Indian in origin and based on the productive forces built up within the country; that is, the 'surplus' capital extracted at the expense of the majority of its people. Thus, irrespective of India's own dependence, while unused capital is being generated within India — either hoarded or because returns from domestic reinvestment are too low — it will seek quick profits abroad wherever possible. The export of Indian capital will continue to increase even if famine conditions were simultaneously to recur in the country, because such capital movements operate according to the exigencies of a world system.

Conventionally, India's export of capital is seen as a dynamic export promotion device, which relies on the build up of Joint Venture investment overseas; and as an indication that 'the characteristics of a dissolute stagnant economy . . . have given way to a dynamic progressive economy.' [S27] Another view sees it as a dynamic manifestation of India's commitment to furthering the internationalization of capital flow [B21]. Closer to reality, is perhaps the view that the export of Indian capital is a further indication of the sickness of the Indian state capitalist system which, instead of serving the country's further development, siphons off capital funds abroad to earn high profits and perpetuate the wealth of the ruling classes.

'Invisible' Export of Capital: There are other, minor outlets for Indian capital abroad: 'foot-loose' money, particularly the black (unreported) money earned by some Indian businessmen in foreign exchange through contract activities in the Gulf, was seeking outlets in the late 1970s. Such concealed foreign exchange earnings (particularly via under- or over-invoicing of trade) were much sought after in earlier years because of strict government controls on its movement. As a result, it was hoarded in foreign accounts or used to

import luxury consumer goods. Possibilities for using such money greatly increased in the 1970s, so that long term investments abroad were sought, many of them not reported to the authorities. For this reason the actual amounts of Indian capital and its involvement abroad are still relatively unknown.[11] There are further indications that Indian capital is slowly becoming involved in volatile international capital markets, looking for quick profits on short term as well as long term investments, even though the Reserve Bank bans such activities. Associated with this are the earlier activities of institutional investors, such as LIC, or private investment companies which, during the colonial period, began to play the international money market, particularly in London. By 1980 three private investment companies had investments abroad, mostly in London. One company, the Industrial Investment Trust, disinvested itself of its London holdings in 1972-73. Two other companies have old, overseas Indian connections, but only the Investment Corporation of India, owned by the Tatas, is fully productive.

Another concealed export of Indian capital (or more accurately circulation of that capital) may be characterized as occurring within India's 'rupee ambit', where the Indian rupee is an effective currency of exchange and acts as a regional or intermediate 'hard' currency. In several neighbouring South Asian countries Indian rupees are legal or, even where illegal, valid tender. This gives India considerable leverage over these countries' economies. It must be stressed that this is not to be equated with the exchange of Indian rupees — illegally, and well above Reserve Bank exchange rates — in such countries as Singapore or the Gulf, usually in the context of smuggling and currency speculation. While, from 1958, the Reserve Bank banned the export or reimport of Indian rupees to prevent smuggling and currency rackets, it looks the other way or officially lifts such restrictions on the export of rupees to neighbouring countries such as Nepal, Bhutan, Maldives and Mauritius where India gains more from the free circulation of rupees than it loses through smuggling. In Nepal and Bhutan it may, of course, be an explicit strategy of Indian policy to irrevocably tie these states to India by controlling their economies. Nepal has declared Indian rupees illegal, but it is virtually impossible to suppress them, particularly under the terms of the Treaty of Trade and Transport that India has signed with Nepal. In Bhutan, the Royal Government has sought to introduce its own currency, yet despite being a sovereign country its sovereignty is restricted in so far as Bhutan is officially part of the RBI's rupee jurisdiction. While Indian bureaucrats claim that this is quite fortuitous, it is no accident that rupee outflow restrictions have been lifted for travel to the Maldives and Mauritius.[12] Bangladesh, which was also subjected to a flood of Indian rupees, chose to convert to foreign currency trade in its dealings with India. This led to even harsher measures being demanded by India regarding payments, and whilst ultimately it failed to eliminate the free circulation of Indian rupees, it reduced their visibility to some degree.

The rupee ambit does not strictly qualify as 'export' of Indian capital but it is one means whereby with some success India has endeavoured to incorporate neighbouring areas into its own economy.

Joint Ventures

Joint Ventures have been defined as the commitment of funds, facilities and services by two legally separate firms for an enterprise extending beyond the short term [T7]. Confusion has arisen when this definition has also been used to indicate contract arrangements; these differ from joint ventures in having an equity content [F4]. It is, of course, possible that some Joint Venture investments are made on contractual terms with equity participation for certain set time periods. Here, Joint Venture is defined as a business relationship with equity participation, and not a contractual arrangement of a short or long term nature exclusive of equity; these latter are described here as Indian contract ventures.

Joint equity investment, in which Indian companies began to engage only after 1960, and in earnest after 1970, have a long, international history. As post-colonial states have faced foreign investment activity, they have preferred to demand the Joint Venture pattern of foreign investment, in the belief that by diluting ownership control and localizing some ownership of a business concern, negative effects which accompany foreign investment can be minimized to a certain extent. In short, they search for a compromise of interests. The model for post-war Joint Ventures in the Third World was that formulated in the early Western Joint Venture investments in the Soviet Union during the 1920s and 1930s. In these ventures, the USSR retained a 50% share, but invited foreign capital to invest in the remaining 50% to develop productive forces in mining, transport, agriculture and the marketing of goods.

It has often been argued that foreign investment is one strategy whereby old colonial powers and new imperial centres seek to perpetuate their domination over less-developed countries. This, in turn, has increasingly led developing countries to demand Joint Venture investment in which the majority share rests with a local partner. More 'progressive' capitalist countries such as West Germany, France and Japan, have readily adapted and adopted this pattern, eroding the position of more conservative capitalist investors, such as the US and UK, who would have preferred to retain the 100% ownership pattern.

India has been a target for foreign investment, but compared to other Asian countries, such as Indonesia, not a major one. However, 481 foreign companies do operate in India, of which, in 1976, 300 were US based. Indian government policy towards foreign investment aims to ensure the adoption of a Joint Venture pattern, and majority ownership eventually becoming localized in India; this policy, expressed in the 1949–51 equity pattern influences India's own investment policy overseas. The instances of Coca Cola and IBM illustrate this when in 1977 they refused to dilute their majority shares and, as a result, were expelled from India.

Foreign collaborations in India are important for another reason, in that they illustrate the decline of the pattern of straight capital control, which is increasingly being replaced by technical collaboration agreements and technology control. In India many foreign collaborations (at least 481 in 1978) were technical agreements with little equity participation. The government stipulated ten years for a limit of these technical agreements with a ceiling of 3—5% of the net sale value of the goods produced for repatriated fees. Foreign capital control of Indian industry through collaborations has been overstressed in the literature [R13]. Examining the case of Japan, a distinction must be made between foreign capital and technical dependence in order to understand the notion of autonomous capitalist growth. In Japan, technical agreements predominated in the 1950s, in order to gain new technologies without introducing foreign capital control. The result of this has been the economic autonomy attained by Japanese capital and industry while choosing to remain politically dependent. The Indian government has been aware of the desirability for itself of technical over financial collaboration, and its policies have not sought to build the same awareness for its own Joint Ventures. This is important because the degree of control that a technical agreement gives to a foreign collaborator in India will in turn affect whether in their own foreign investments Indian investors are acting as agents for Western or Soviet capital. As already seen in Chapter 5 the degree of foreign capital in India is high, in terms of the amounts remitted each year to service investments and debt. Out of 161 companies (surveyed by the author) who had either proposed or implemented Joint Venture investments, 72 had agreements with a foreign collaborator for their own operations in India. It must be stressed that most of these were technical agreements and not equity capital arrangements and, by the time the Indian companies had made their own decision to invest abroad some had lapsed. As a rule however, a sizeable number of Indian companies investing abroad had foreign partners in some form. Nevertheless observations of the type of Indian companies investing, the targets of their activity, and their mode of operation suggest that Indian foreign investment acts as an agent in only some cases, so to say providing the acceptable Third World face to mask the metropolitan reality [T1].

Analysis of successful Indian Joint Ventures indicate that most are from the largest monopoly business houses in India, some are from the public sector, while still others (very few) are quite small firms utilizing overseas-Indian links to facilitate their investment abroad. Broadly speaking, through the predominance of big Indian capital, Indian Joint Ventures could be characterized as playing an agent role in the sense that these same companies (like the Indian state itself) have good links to metropolitan capital. At the same time, in specific cases, Indian investments abroad act autonomously and in competition with Western and Japanese capital; competition that has often been ferocious and on many occasions has forced Indian capital to surrender, Joint Ventures in question being closed down, abandoned or bought out.[13]

The most important aspect of Indian Joint Ventures is that they have occurred in a different environment from Western capitalism's Joint Ventures. India's state capitalist system seeks outlets abroad but wishes to avoid being seen as exploitative. Thus, it adopts the formula legitimized by UNCTAD of 'co-operation amongst the developing countries'. This formula attempts to stress the difference between co-operative and exploitative investment, and obscure the economic imperatives behind all foreign investment. This rhetoric sees intra-Third World investment as a means to destroy the activities of Western multinationals [S31: 104], indeed, some have gone so far as to label Indian Joint Ventures as a 'mutual aid programme'. The rationale presented is that developing countries can pool their expertize and capital and, by emulating the forms that multinational companies take (division of labour and manufacture of components in several geographically separate areas) can directly challenge Western multinational domination (Tanzania has urged Third World states to adopt such a strategy). This view has two fundamental defects: one is that relatively developed national economies will tend to dominate in any such groupings, the other is that there is no guarantee that such arrangements will not later be taken over by multinationals. It is maintained here that intra-Third World Joint Ventures only reinforce the general pattern of exploitation faced by smaller developing countries, while at the same time middle-sized developing countries, who increasingly share common interests with the developed world, are drawn in to the developed capitalist club.

Investment between developing countries increased in the 1970s, particularly as those with spare capital began investing in lesser developed countries [L6]. As an investor, India is in competition with countries with larger investments, such as Taiwan, South Korea, Malaysia, Singapore, Pakistan, Kuwait, UAE, Saudi Arabia, Venezuela, Argentina, Brazil, Mexico and, until its revolution, Iran. Another source of investment in the Third World is Hongkong and its overseas-Chinese companies. Because of its overseas-Indian links, 41 companies from 18 developing countries were operating in India in 1976, a few under collaboration agreements, others simply company offices.

Whatever the final outcome, resulting from growing intra-Third World investment, there is already a split apparent between the more and the less economically advanced countries; thus negating the complementarity in India's foreign investments in other developing countries stressed in government statements. At UNCTAD's fifth meeting in 1979, Tanzania drew attention to this differentiation.[14] India sought to play down the issue by declaring that, 'It is India's policy to recall any Joint Venture which works contrary to the interests of the host country. I [India] want Joint Ventures between developing countries to operate not as centres of exploitation but as symbols of co-operation.'[15]

Types and Motivation

Indian Joint Ventures take several forms, though some have been with the developed world most have been in other developing countries. Statistics for these may be briefly summarized as: Joint Ventures in production, developed countries, 1976, 4; 1979 6. Developing countries, 1976, 15; 1979, 21. Joint Ventures by region; Middle East, Africa, Southeast Asia, South Asia and industrialized, 1976, 67; 1979, 107. Joint Ventures with developed countries are excluded from the present analysis as falling outside its scope.[16] By far the most prevalent industrial ventures are those in which an Indian and a local partner collaborate to set up an industrial enterprise in another developing country. A second type is in the field of shipping and transport. Indian companies have also attempted to launch jointly owned trading companies operating from bases in foreign countries. A fourth type is an offshoot of joint industrial ventures; these are joint resource ventures in mining and raw materials, sometimes in the form of contracts. Finally, there are Joint Ventures (also on a contract basis) in service industries, such as consultancy, or hotels and restaurants.

While up to December 1979 the government approved 409 applications for Joint Venture investments by public and private Indian companies, only 107 were in operation in January 1980, and over 193 were subsequently abandoned.[17] A variety of reasons have been given for these failures, such as poor project management, poor operations control, and lack of commitment, but the author found that many of the units are designed to fail; in other words, some Indian investors are interested only in the prospect of personal gain and the manipulation of foreign exchange regulations. Those Joint Ventures in operation represented Rs.170.1 million worth of investment with equity worth over Rs.212.50 million. By 1979 these units were earning Rs.70 million in profits and over Rs.480 million were generated by additional exports of machinery. Yet even this rate of profitability is extremely low as a report by Prahlad and Rao (*Business India*, December 1980) showed. Indian Ventures in Malaysia alone were 80% unprofitable.

Indian foreign investment motives, as seen earlier, are two-fold. At the strategic level the Indian state capitalist system and its industries have reached a crisis. In order to seek a partial solution to this crisis Indian industry goes abroad. Even where the export of capital is in the form of machinery, as is the case in the majority of Indian equity participation in Joint Ventures, this too can represent an unseen transfer of capital. Joint Ventures facilitate the expansion of Indian capital into foreign Third World markets, utilize idle capital and skills and finally, make gains for the Indian state capitalist system as a whole.

In a tactical sense, Indian Joint Ventures are designed to enhance the strategic solution. These tactical reasons are frequently employed by many participants in the Joint Venture process, Indian businessmen and government officials who prefer to overlook or ignore the primary reason for investing abroad. Added to the general climate that permits Indian capital to go abroad, there are also the personal selfish motivations of some businessmen who have set up Joint Ventures abroad.

Some analyses have sought to draw a distinction between public and private sector motives in investing abroad, but such an exercise is irrelevant, given the essential unity of the Indian state capitalist system.

Specific economic motivations underlying Indian state capital export in Joint Ventures are: 1) export promotion (generalized); 2) possible high profits; 3) opening new markets; 4) protecting old markets; 5) spreading risks; 6) dumping old equipment; 7) need for raw materials; 8) jumping tariff barriers [A7]. Export promotion of Indian manufactured goods is usually the publicly acknowledged reason given by the private and public sectors for investing in developing countries. Joint Ventures create conditions in which additional exports of capital, goods, spares, components, and services lead to a recurring and continuous flow of Indian manufactures to other developing countries; Joint Ventures also create sub-contract opportunities for other Indian industries.

The prospect of the high profitability of foreign Joint Ventures is uppermost in the minds of many Indian businessmen going abroad. Particularly striking in this regard are the Indian monopoly houses seeking to reproduce their monopoly position in other developing countries. In Ethiopia and Nigeria, through judicious use of influence, the Birlas gained a monopoly in domestic textile production and the marketing of certain goods. In Malaysia, in the 1970s, Birlas had plans to monopolize the entire sugar market by building up the sugar industry from scratch. Also in Malaysia, Tata trucks have gained a sizeable local market share as a domestic producer.

The protection of old markets is a more complex function of Indian Joint Ventures than is the opening of new markets; India has only recently made the partial transition from exporting traditional commodities to manufactured goods. Loosely, old markets may be used to indicate places where overseas–Indian populations are present. In these cases Joint Ventures help to preserve old ties through overseas–Indian orders for goods and services. Spreading risks through Joint Ventures is less of a tactic and more a side benefit for the Indian companies involved. Government assistance, and local involvement, lessens the burden on those Indian companies unwilling to use all their own capital to make gains abroad.

Dumping obsolete machinery and equipment through Joint Ventures is a notable feature of Indian foreign investment. The Government of India likes to designate Indian machinery 'intermediate technology', many of those in industry see it as exporting machinery through Joint Ventures which, in their view, belongs in the museum. Because much Indian equity takes the form of supplying machinery, it is dumped at an inflated value, by being sent abroad.

India's need for raw materials is obvious. Planning by the Indian government has not been systematic in this field, and some companies have been quick to see the advantages in securing raw materials and commodities through Joint Ventures in other developing countries.

Jumping tariff barriers as a benefit of investing abroad has caught the attention of some Indian companies where their investments have taken advantage of special preferences enjoyed by certain developing countries in developed country markets. This is one reason why some Indian companies have expressed interest in Sri Lanka's Free Trade Zone.

Apart from these motives are the fundamentally selfish pre-modern capitalist ones of some Indian companies investing abroad. This raises questions concerning the role played by certain Indian businessmen and the state capitalist system. Some of India's most prominent industrialists act abroad like petty-traders. Theirs is a policy of quick extraction, short term maximization of profits, hoarding and nepotism. Investing abroad for them means setting up dummy companies, industries actually intended to fail (hence a partial explanation for the high failure rate); in this way they can manipulate government assistance, incentives and loans, default on previous loans, and still generate funds to bank in Swiss accounts for their families to spend abroad. Many Indian businessmen in the private sector will confess, in confidence, that their primary motive for investing abroad is to evade the government's foreign exchange regulations and the need to report the amount of capital they siphon off abroad each year. Joint Ventures are one way of turning 'black' money into 'white', of employing capital and making quick profits while reporting the failure of such investments.

A more intangible factor in Joint Venture investments, is the role played by overseas-Indian populations. Like Jewish investment in Israel [A7], or overseas-Chinese investment in China, India's foreign investment may sometimes be motivated by emotional factors. Yet the evidence for this is for the most part lacking despite some explicit appeals by foreign governments inviting Indian investment where Indians are resident. It may be assumed, however, that overseas-Indian populations are an important factor for investment where community ties provide a ready pool of 'local' partners and employees for Indian Joint Ventures.

Policy, Promotion and Targets

The general policy of the Indian government towards Joint Ventures sees them as a means of forging stronger economic and political links with developing countries. In this view, investments play an integral role in building prestige abroad and act as a show-case for India's 'achievement'. This leads bureaucrats, academics and businessmen to speak of 'sharing' India's development experience with other developing countries through Joint Ventures. Government policy towards Joint Ventures can be roughly divided into four periods: 1) 1957–64; 2) 1965–70; 3) 1971–75; and 4) 1976–80. The problem of the export of Indian capital arose for the first time in the 1957–64 period, with the Birlas' investment in a textile mill in Ethiopia. The policy then was that India was short of capital and therefore any equity would have to be in the form of machinery. While the government recognized the potential for export promotion of this type of investment, no consideration was given to the probable long-term effects of Indian investments on her general foreign relations. In 1964, following a trade delegation to Africa that reported there were good prospects for Indian investment in newly-decolonized countries, policy was liberalized. At the same time, fears were voiced that the export of Indian capital would have negative effects on her relations with Africa, although these fears do not seem to have affected government policy.

In 1966, as the belief grew that India had surplus capacity which needed to find an outlet, the government laid down specific guidelines for Joint Venture investments abroad. These were: that Indian investment should be confined to machinery, tools, equipment, structures, spares and not cash; that equity had to be a minority share, and that provision for training local nationals had to be made. In addition, the 1966 Finance Bill gave special tax concessions of 25% cuts on dividends and royalties earned through Joint Ventures abroad [F4; B13: 355]. Despite the government's aim to restrict Indian companies to 49% equity, several companies, in practice, were allowed majority shares (at least 6 in 1969) and some 100% Indian-owned companies (3 in 1971) were allowed to operate abroad. In 1971, a concession was made regarding the export of capital in the form of cash, and some cash remittances were thenceforth allowed for expenses arising in setting up a Joint Venture. Since equity has mostly been in the form of equipment supplied, this has counted as a capital goods export and, as such, has been eligible for Indian government cash assistance; 10% of f.o.b. value in 1971. In this way the state has aided Indian companies in their overseas investment activities. In 1973, shortfalls in equity were allowed to be met by additional exports of structural and construction materials.

Until the mid-1970s government policy towards Joint Ventures was diffused over several departments. Prior to 1970 the Ministry of Industrial Development processed Joint Venture applications, though the Ministries of Finance and Heavy Industries were also intermittently involved. In 1973, the Economic Division of the Ministry of External Affairs, the Joint Venture cell of the Ministry of Commerce, the Indian Investment Centre and the Overseas Investment cell of the Ministry of Foreign Trade were all involved. As proposals for investments overseas rose from 38 in 1966 to over 380 in 1978 alone, this chaotic overlap in government administration began to have its effects, particularly as, simultaneously, Indian contract activity abroad also increased.

After 1976, as India's foreign exchange reserves grew, the government gradually relaxed its restrictions on cash participation in investments abroad, so that export of capital in the form of cash was allowed on a case by case basis. In 1978 revised guidelines were released, and a centralized policy-making body was set up in the Ministry of Commerce. This was the Inter-ministerial committee on Joint Ventures that comprised representatives from other Ministries, such as External Affairs, Finance, Industry, the Director General of Trade Development, the Department of Company Affairs, and the Indian Investment Centre. If necessary, other departments are also admitted. The Committee is responsible for screening applications for all Indian equity investments abroad. Decisions take two months, and local Indian embassies also participate in the decision-making process. After approval, the Committee relinquishes any further supervision over the investment, this is left to the Reserve Bank of India in Bombay, which prescribes that each Indian Joint Venture submit a yearly report of its earnings. There is no facility for checking the veracity of the statements made in these, despite avowals to the contrary.[18] The RBI has no facilities to investigate abroad, despite its powers to approve any additional exports of capital.

The government has taken a number of measures in the field of promotion to encourage Joint Ventures, including the tax relief measures covering Joint Ventures in 1966. Through their business organizations Indian companies have complained that unlike their counterparts in industrialized countries they are not protected by double-taxation agreements. This situation has been gradually rectified, and by 1979 India had entered into double taxation agreements with Egypt, Afghanistan, Malaysia, Singapore, Sri Lanka, Kenya, Tanzania and Bangladesh. India has thus emulated other major investing countries by devising measures with target countries to give tax relief to its own investors.

While the Indian government has yet to supply complete risk cover to its foreign investments (such as the US government scheme, which guarantees its investors insurance in the event of loss through nationalization) it has extended a degree of risk insurance in the form of export credits. While mostly confined to Indian contract activity, the Export Credit and Guarantee Corporation has a programme of risk cover to banks which, in turn, provides finance to Indian exporters, and to some extent applies to companies exporting machinery as part of their foreign equity investment.

Within the government, the most important promotional body is the Indian Investment Centre (IIC). In addition to its role of inviting investment into India, in 1971 it was entrusted with promoting India's own investments. The IIC screens all applications for Joint Ventures, investigates the investment climate of particular countries and examines potential local partners. The IIC compiles lists of industries and identifies areas of mutual interest between Indian investors and recipient states. Information concerning prospects are circulated and IIC attempts to put interested parties in touch with each other; it also takes into account political factors that could influence Indian investment. In 1979, major targets for the Centre's interest were Africa — particularly Nigeria, Kenya and Ghana — and Malaysia, Thailand, Indonesia and Philippines in South-east Asia.

The government's other promotion measures have been allied to its general trade promotion policies, that is, participation in trade fairs, and sending trade delegations. Indian private businessmen have been far more active, increasingly joined by their colleagues in the public sector, and together they have travelled abroad to scout for investment opportunities. In 1963 the India–Africa Development Association was set up, consisting both of government and business, in an effort to build up Indian investments in Africa. The Federation of Indian Chambers of Commerce and Industry (FICCI) has sent many delegations to developing countries, as far afield as Latin America and, in addition, has held seminars and issued several reports on Joint Ventures. Other more specialized manufacturing bodies, such as the All India Rubber Industries Association, and the Indian Vitreous Enamelware Association sometimes hold seminars and send delegations to appropriate countries. During their visits to Southeast Asian countries private businessmen, particularly heads of monopoly houses like G.D. Birla and J.R.D. Tata, have sought to encourage Indian investment through their contacts with Heads of States. Finally, the government has increasingly stepped in at international meetings such as those of UNIDC to advertise India's readiness to invest in other Third World countries.

The entire developing world is now the target for Indian investment, with particular stress on South-east Asia and Africa. The most important factor affecting the direction of Indian investment flows is, of course, the local investment climate. At present this is most conducive in South-east Asia, while in an earlier period it was in Africa. The Middle East has been less attractive; local Arab collaborators have preferred to look to high technology investors from the US, Europe and Japan. Latin America has figured little because of geographical distance and lack of knowledge rather than lack of potential opportunity.

Wherever local governments and business have welcomed Indian investment, it has been for their own benefit and not necessarily for general benefit of their people. This is demonstrable in some operations of Indian investments where 'mutual advantage' for the Indian and the local businessmen, politicians and bureaucrats, has been quite literal. Thus are Joint Ventures links between ruling classes in India and those in other post-colonial states.

In addition, most Indian investments have gone to those countries offering attractive incentives for the foreign investor. Malaysia has been the single largest target for Indian investment, with 38 Indian Joint Ventures planned or in production in 1979 [D4]. In 1968 the Malaysian Minister of Commerce called for Indian investment, and in 1970 the Malaysians were suggesting measures to the Indian government to facilitate investment; in 1971, the Malaysian High Commissioner broadcast a call for Indian investment over All India Radio. Since 1970, Malaysia has continued to send delegations and issue invitations for Indian investment, and Indian companies have been particularly attracted by its laws of foreign investment. For example, foreign investments come under the World Bank's International Arbitration and Conciliation centre in the event of any disputes. Investment Guarantee Agreements and double taxation provisions also exist, and there is little or no restriction on the repatriation of profits and dividends. Most important for Indian investors have been Malaysia's special laws regarding 'pioneer industries', these are new industries which, as such, are eligible for a whole package of concessions.

Probably the most important facet of Malaysia's invitation to India is a domestic political consideration, a desire by the Malay controlled government to erode the economic power of its Chinese population. In this exercise local Indians and those from South Asia are accomplices of the government. By favouring Indian investment, the Malaysian government tries to settle several issues simultaneously. Ths local Indian population receives favours and patronage, Malay bureaucrats are assisted in their efforts to erode Chinese economic power under the new economic policy, and Malaysia strengthens its overall relationship with India in an attempt to diminish any perceived long-term threat from China.

A similar motivation underlies Mauritian invitations for Indian investment. Since independence Mauritius's leaders have sought Indian help partly to erode the economic power of the Franco-Mauritians who have strong links with the West and South Africa. Predominantly, the Mauritian government is composed of members of Indian descent who see Indian investment as important in this process. Mauritius also offers the usual tax holidays and concessions for the foreign investor, including an export processing zone and potential entry into third markets. The Mauritian strategy has, however, miscarried: those Indian companies that have invested, have co-operated with the Franco-Mauritians and so complemented their economic stranglehold.

For economic rather than political reasons the prospect of mutual gain has been present in other countries that have invited Indian investment. In 1964, Kuwait invited Indian investment in iron, caustic soda and other areas. In 1967, Algeria, and in 1969 Indonesia, Syria and Tunisia, also invited investment from India. Simultaneously with moves to expel expatriate Indians, the Kenyan government also invited Indian investment. In 1973–74 Guinea, Libya, Gabon and Philippines extended similar invitations. The Philippines kept the door open for Indian collaboration long after the expiry date for sealing of bids had passed. By the mid-1970s, as the Jamaican Minister of State for External Affairs said, there was a 'growing awareness among many developing nations to look to India for technical and scientific assistance,' and this included investment. Since then Guyana, Papua New Guinea and Tanzania have all called for Indian investment. It remains to be seen whether, as Indian investment grows, local invitations will continue to be forthcoming from developing countries.

Joint Ventures in Industry

As already noted (p. 88) at least 107 Joint Ventures were operating abroad in 1980. Most of these were in the fields of textiles, chemicals, paper, cement, electrical and engineering goods.

The first Indian investment abroad in an industrial enterprise in the post-independence period (in 1920 there were Indian industrial investments in Burma) was in 1957 in Ethiopia. In 1956, a managing agency contract with the government of Ethiopia for a cotton textile plant was signed by the Birlas who received $30,000 plus 10% of the profits of the enterprise. In

1957, the company was incorporated with an initial Birla investment of $45 million, comprising a 20% investment, 35% was invested by the Ethiopian government and 45% raised from the public, mostly overseas-Indians. Most cotton for the mill was imported from India, despite potential local sources which remained unused. During its operations the Birlas remitted approximately $75,000 in profits each year to India. After a series of financial scandals, however, the venture was closed by the Ethiopian government. After the revolution, the plant was nationalized, but due to Indian government influence some compensation was paid.

Some analysts [B2] have extrapolated from this first venture by suggesting that the Monopolies and Restrictive Trade Practices Act of 1956 was the primary motivating force behind Indian Joint Ventures in general. This overlooks the fact that as early as 1964 the Indian public sector had begun to express interest in investing abroad in a sugar project in Uganda which, if it had materialized, would have involved direct Indian government participation. This may indicate that the economic motivations outlined earlier were, from the outset, more important than the impact of a single piece of legislation. This view is further supported by the fact that only as Indian industry has confronted its own development problems has it invested abroad, in other words it is not simply a question of facing domestic restrictions but of Indian business seeing good returns and uses for under-utilized capacity abroad. For this reason, Indian Joint Ventures became prominent in the late 1960s and 1970s, rather than immediately following the enactment of MRCP in 1956. A total of 67 Indian Joint Ventures by 1975 were distributed as follows: 1 each year for 1960, 1962, 1965, 1966 and 1968; 4 each year for 1970 and 1973; 5 in 1967; 6 each year in 1969, 1971 and 1972, and 25 in 1975.[19] Indian investment has predominately involved large business houses but, perhaps due to overseas-Indian ties, small Indian companies have also invested abroad (for example the Mysore Government Soap Factory).[20] On the whole, however, most are large scale companies, many of which belong to monopoly houses.[21]

Business Practices: In contemporary international business, investment companies are often found to be engaged in corrupt practices; Indian companies are no exception. This in itself is not extraordinary, but what concerns us here is how these involvements may lead to wider, political repercussions for India. Such a scandal involving a flour mill investment by an Indian company in Fiji emerged in 1978.

Many Indian businessmen habitually bribe government officials to gain advantages as indeed do many other businessmen. In Nigeria, an Indian firm gave Mercedes Benz cars to six government Ministers, as well as shares of the company, consequently these ministers actively assisted the textile project by imposing protective tariff barriers. In Malaysia, an enormous textile project has also been in operation since 1972, opened by the Malaysian Prime Minister. This company is 40% owned by the Indian investors with other finance raised from public subscriptions, the Malaysian government, loans from Citibank as well as from Malaysian banks. The company developed close liaison with the Malaysian power structure and through this means the Indian investor tried to capture a sizable share of the local textile market. A similar strategy was attempted by the same company in Thailand, Kenya, Mauritius and Indonesia. One Indian company created a sizable market share for itself in Malaysia by utilizing a powerful contact (a brother of a Sultan) who in turn successfully persuaded the Malaysian government to purchase its products exclusively. Another example of the degree of some Indian investment activity in Malaysia is one of India's largest company's projects in sugar and paper. If ever completed these projects might have placed the company in a monopoly position. In addition, the scale of the projects ensures that a consortium of Indian companies would also have a stake. The most important fact concerning the operations of Joint Venture investments is the close political connections the Indian company has built up at the highest level. In Sabah, enormous bribes have been paid to local politicians in return for a 500,000 acre concession in timber. Important links have also been forged between this company and UMND, while election funding has become an important activity for several other Indian companies in Malaysia.

The Menace of Nationalization: The level of Indian investment abroad has grown, so, too, have calls by some Indian companies for government protection against nationalizations and expropriations. Where such confiscations have occurred (Ethiopia, Uganda, Tanzania and South Yemen) compensation has been paid. In Uganda, Indian investments were given token recompense by the government of Idi Amin. In the past, the threat of nationalization of Indian assets overseas has not been so serious; where it has occurred, the number of units has been small and compensation was paid. Whether in future the Indian government will be increasingly drawn into actively defending Indian investments as their numbers, and their values, grow, or whether it will adhere to a policy of respecting the economic nationalism of all developing countries remains to be seen.

Financial Sources: A crucial aspect of Indian Joint industrial ventures is their sources of finance, and by extension the relation this bears to international capital. Of the few firms which responded to the author's inquiries, all had minority shares ranging from 21.8% to 48.33%, for which the capital was remitted from India. Majority capital ranging from 51% to 68% was raised locally either in paid-up capital from local partners or by issuing shares on local capital markets. In one case a 25% equity share with an international company was found. In the larger projects involving the Birlas and Tatas, links to international capital are more explicit as the following examples illustrate. These concern two Joint Ventures seeking foreign, rather than Indian, finance, involving the Birlas and the International Finance Corporation (a subsidiary of the World Bank). The projects were the Pan-African Paper Mills in Kenya and the Indo-Malaysian Textile mill. In the first, the Kenyan government and Orient Paper (Birlas) received a total of $19.4 million in finance from the IFC. In the second project, an initial commitment of $4.5 million was made, although in reality the project received only $1.4 million from the IFC. Additional finance for this project totalling $2.5 million was received from a consortium of banks. Instead of relying on Indian and local financial institutions as occurs in many other smaller Indian Joint Ventures, these big ventures draw upon international capital sources. In fact the aim was to strengthen links with international capital — an express desire of some sections of Indian capital. Therefore, explicit links with Western multinationals do occur in Indian Joint Ventures, and ostensibly 'local' partners are often Western controlled firms. This is an extension of the idea mooted in FICCI seminars, that Joint Ventures can serve as export platforms for entering Third World markets, such as the Raymond garment factory in Mauritius, which markets its products in Europe.

The idea that Indian companies should associate with industrialized partners to strengthen their own investments and defuse any competition, surfaced in 1968 in talks with European countries involving the Indian government and business. It was also suggested that Japan, together with India, could make Third World investments, but this was rejected by the Japanese on the grounds that the standard of Indian industry was not high enough. West Germany expressed interest in the idea, but the idea has only come to fruition with Eastern Europe, with the supply of equipment for Soviet projects in Bulgaria and Cuba. Despite continuing offers by India to France, Japan, Australia and Hungary, joint collaborations with Third World countries has not occurred.

Third World Multinationals

While in most cases the integration of Indian with Western capital remains incomplete, and utilization of India's own state capital is the norm, there are two exceptions. There have been suggestions that, by virtue of their size, scale and sources of finance, Tatas and Birlas have emerged as Third World multinationals.[22] While some Indian public sector firms, currently engaged in contract activity overseas, would qualify due to size (in the top 500 world corporations) at most they can be characterized as Third World transnationals, since they are based solely on Indian state capital. Such firms include: Bharat Heavy Electricals, Indian Oil, and the Steel Authority of India.

In 1979, Birla operations existed in at least nine developing countries involving 33 companies and on a scale which places them quite apart from other Indian investors. A Birla company based in Lausanne (in 1979) was reportedly investing in a textile mill in South Korea; China also invited the Birlas to build a rayon mill there. The Tatas have a long history of international operations and in financial resources, personnel and scale, far outstrip rival Indian companies. Unlike some other Indian investors Tatas are always careful to associate with a Western firm when they invest. They not only invest in industrial ventures but have set up trading companies around the world in a deliberate effort to emulate the Japanese Shoshas. The Singapore Prime Minister has spoken of the Tatas in the same breath as Mitsubishi. Because the Tata overseas network is so profound and diversified, the scope of its global operations is less visible than is that of the Birlas, but in fact it may be larger.

Clearly then, simultaneously with the growth of generalized Indian investment, the conglomerates of two companies have built themselves up to the extent of becoming nascent Third World multinationals. This may have important political implications both for India's relationships with other developing countries as well as for itself. Plausibly, if present trends continue, Indian multinationals might outgrow their links with the Indian state capitalist base. As with multinationals elsewhere, this may result in situations in which the overseas companies act without reference or regard to their principal interests in India; if this happens they will arrive at the stage of true multinationals, disregarding sovereign state boundaries. The activities of Indian transnationals are less important thus far, as they have confined themselves to contract activity overseas. The only political impact of this is in the field of generalized pay-offs prevalent in winning international contracts.

Raw Materials

In the classic theory of imperialism the need to secure industrial raw materials is regarded as a primary motive for expansion. Raw materials exploitation is one of the key areas which invites foreign investment and this often results in charges of imperialist exploitation [33b]. India, a large mineral and commodity exporter, seeks investments abroad aimed at securing strategic raw materials and commodities for itself. Despite growing domestic production India is 60% dependent on oil imports, and each year must import large quantities of edible oils to make up for deficient domestic production. All, or most of the following minerals, some of which are crucial to defence and development [K12] have to be imported: antimony (Bolivia, USA, Australia); arsenic (China); some types of cadmium, molybdenite, nickel (USSR, Canada, Finland, Morocco, Indonesia); phosphates[23] (Nauru, Morocco, Algeria, USSR, USA, Tunisia, Chile); tin (Malaysia, Thailand, Indonesia, Bolivia); vanadium (USA, Finland). India also imports smaller amounts of sulphur, zinc, borax, fluorspar, and tungsten [D1]. Thus, obviously, Indian capital must seek supplies of raw materials [V2a: 138]. There is an accumulating body of evidence to show that the Indian state and industry have sought long term supplies of raw materials overseas through investment but with only a modicum of success. These ventures came to fruition in only a few cases, but where they have, as with tiny Nauru, or Iran, they have made only a slight difference to India's long term need for phosphates and oil.

In 1970, the Indian Minister of Foreign Trade declared that India needed raw materials on a long term basis from the then ECAFE region. In 1971, India signed an agreement with Peru specifically designed to obtain strategic 'non-ferrous' minerals. A 1974 article defended Indian arms sales on the grounds that they would help gain long term supplies from 'countries who have valuable raw materials for India.' In 1965, India expressed interest in investing in lead and zinc mines in East Africa; in 1970, Ethiopia offered a potash mining concession to India, and another African country offered a gypsum deposit. In the same year India was prospecting for coal in Nigeria, and information on mining concessions in Indonesia were conveyed to potential Indian investors. In the 1970s India was prospecting for minerals in Upper Volta and Zaire, exploring investments for mining graphite in Sri Lanka, planning to mine phosphates in Egypt, exploring mineral prospects in Tanzania, leasing a coking coal concession from Australia and concluding a similar mineral supply agreement with Indonesia.[24]

In the oil and petroleum field, India was extremely energetic in the 1960s in its search for supplies, but this resulted only in the conclusion of numerous unremunerative agreements with developing countries. In 1965 the Oil and Natural Gas Commission (ONGC) (India's seventh largest company, with assets of Rs.2,920 million in 1971) along with Italian and Dutch oil companies entered into a 25 year contractual venture with the National Iranian Oil Corporation; this secured for India 17% of all oil found in an offshore oilfield in the Persian Gulf. Problems arose when it was found that the crude was too heavy to be refined in India, and only several years later was India able to convert its Madras refinery to handle it. This early effort to secure oil supplies was seen as insufficient by the Petroleum Minister in 1971 and ONGC redoubled its efforts; it undertook drilling in Tonga, and was offered a concession in Somalia. In 1972, in order to obtain supplies of Bangladesh's natural gas, India offered to build a pipeline between the two countries. In the 1970s India prospected for oil in Egypt and Iraq, and entered into an arrangement with Libya for a 15% share in exploiting an oilfield in 1975. Oil exploration teams were also sent to Syria, Oman and South Yemen. None of these activities bore fruit.

A successful Indian Joint Venture in natural gas in Tanzania began in 1975. By 1977 the Songo-Songo gas field had been brought onstream by India. In the same year India had to abandon its Iraqi oil venture along with the potentiality of 15–30% of the total find. Added to India's general need for oil, another justification for overseas prospecting was that its underutilized skills in oil technology could be usefully employed in the Arab world; finds in India have been very low when set against the capital expenditure in exploration. However, for whatever reason India's overseas oil ventures have been unsuccessful.

Another type of Indian foreign investment was to secure raw materials needed for its basic economy and consumption. Since the mid-1960s the Indian government has put forward various plans for investments in such developing countries as Nigeria, Burma and Egypt, which would have buyback facilities. Proposals of this kind have been made in the fields of phosphates, cement and ammonia, whereby India would set up a local processing industry and thus obtain vital commodities in short supply in India.

Investment designed to maintain an existing monopoly position in the supply of certain commodities to the world market by investing in plantations overseas and co-opting foreign cultivation, which is having an effect on India's domestic production has been another venture. For example, a venture for a 50,000 acre cashew-nut plantation in Tanzania planned in 1978 which could be replicated for tea plantations in Kenya. India is seriously short of edible oil, and several Indian companies have monopolized its import − the second highest in the late 1970s. Several companies, and others with overseas–Indian connections, have invested in palm-oil plantations and industries in Malaysia and Indonesia in an attempt to retain the Indian domestic market, while maintaining high prices, (at least 10 companies were concerned in 1980) despite the fact that oil-palms could be grown on a commercial basis in parts of India.

Several Indian investments have been tied to setting up industries attached to supplies of raw materials. For example the huge Birla paper mill in Kenya, with its 30,000 acres of pine and cypress; and the earlier example of the Birla paper project in Sabah, which is tied to 450,000 acres of timber land; also the abortive sugar project which was to develop large scale plantations. In Uganda, the sugar project India planned in 1964 (government and business) had 25,000 acres of sugar estates attached. These examples demonstrate how, in a modest way, India has entered the agrobusiness foreign investment field to secure raw materials and commodities for its domestic and foreign industries. This, coupled with securing supplies of strategic minerals, clearly places Indian investment in a position where it could be open to the charge of second-tier imperialism.

Joint Ventures in Services

Not all Indian Joint Ventures are in the field of industrial production or directly related to it, but also include shipping and transport, trading, consultancy companies, restaurants and hotels.

In 1978, only one shipping Joint Venture (between India and Iran) was in operation, but a number of others were planned or had been abandoned. As part of India's commitment to UNCTAD's policy of promoting more direct shipping links between developing countries and breaking the monopoly control of a few countries, India established the Shipping Corporation of India (SCI), and encouraged the formation of joint shipping lines with other developing states. In 1964 India attempted to promote a Joint Indo-African shipping line.[25] Only in the 1970s did such collaboration plans begin to bear fruit. In 1974 SCI and Iran set up a 49/51% Joint Venture company, the Irano-Hind shipping line, with a sizable number of vessels. In 1977, SCI was planning another joint shipping line with Tanzania, designed to ship cattle to the Gulf. Shipping Joint Ventures in the Indian private sector were also planned with Nigeria and Singapore. As India attempts to wrest greater control over the quantity of cargo carried on its own vessels, it has sought advantages by entering into joint shipping ventures with those other developing countries with which its trade also increases; particularly where India has been unable to obtain unilateral control over this trade, but might succeed through multilateral efforts.

In road transport, two Indian trucking firms were planning in the 1970s to set up Joint Ventures in Kuwait and the UAE. This type of venture would have placed Indian companies in a position where a share of the internal trade of other countries might have been gained.

Trading Joint Ventures are a recent Indian investment activity. In 1975, the State Trading Corporation (STC) opened a company in Hongkong with a 50% share[26] and planned to open similar companies in Jeddah, Baghdad and Tehran. In the private sector, Tatas have invested in trading venture companies in Oman, Australia and Zambia, and by 1979 there were other Indian trading venture companies operating in Saudi Arabia, UAE, Singapore and Malaysia. In this way the Indian partners have sought to increase their participation in world trade by operating simultaneously from several bases. Trading too, has been a traditional activity among overseas-Indians who often have several overseas offices.

Consultancy company joint equity investments are an extension of India's growing consultancy contract activity in other developing countries. A few such companies have invested abroad in order to localize their offices and qualify as 'local' companies when making local bids; for this reason such companies have been set up in Saudi Arabia and Kenya.

Restaurant Joint Venture investments are a minor activity associated with overseas-Indians, and mostly confined to the industrialized world. Indian investment in hotels is, however, becoming an increasingly prominent activity in developing countries. In some cases this includes control of local real estate,[27] and some Indian companies are now taking an important part in tourism in Sri Lanka, Mauritius, Tanzania, Nepal, the Gulf and the Seychelles. In the USA, overseas-Indians have acquired a large portion of the motel business (20,000 units).[28] Indian Joint Ventures in banking and insurance are discussed in Chapter 8.

Clearly, Indian Joint Ventures with equity participation are increasingly found abroad in a wide variety of fields, reflecting the diversification and growing capabilities of the Indian state capitalist economy. As such they are a prime indicator of the nature of India's political economy and its growing relationships with other developing countries.

Contractual Ventures

Contractual ventures, or project contracts, in other developing countries are related to Joint Venture investments. They represent less an example of export of capital and more an indication of India's level of development and its progressive involvement in the industrialization of other developing countries. The growth of Indian 'turn-key' projects and consultancy contracts accelerated in the 1970s. By 1978 Indian industry as a whole had contracts worth $16,000 million in other developing countries − a figure regarded as inflated by some.

In some respects Indian contracts in other developing countries are associated with India's continued economic survival in its present form. Both to utilize idle industrial capacity and to earn foreign exchange with which to pay ever rising oil import bills, as well as to provide foreign exchange for consumption purposes, India has entered into contract activity. These ventures also illustrate some of the priorities for Indian industry and its state capitalist system.

Much of India's overseas contract activity is in the construction industry, i.e. building hospitals, housing, airports, roads, schools, factories and furnishing technical services (doctors, teachers and technicians) to oil-rich developing countries. The majority of people in India lack these facilities or services, but the government's and business rationale is that contracts earn foreign exchange and help overall domestic development. Yet, aside from paying oil import bills, money earned in this manner has been almost entirely spent on conspicuous consumption and defence.

The business pattern adopted by Indian companies in their contract activity has a history within India as well. The building of turn-key projects and consultancy capability are closely interlinked, and this has been reflected in Indian activity overseas [R16]. The Indian domestic experience in which Western turn-key projects were active in the 1950s and 1960s came under severe criticism by the Indian government and parliament by 1970 [F4: 318]. It was argued that turn-keys did not train, or utilize the existing skills of Indians; they were seen as an undesirable way to acquire an industrial base, because they required massive import of expensive capital goods without building the infrastructure and surrounding support base. Yet it is this very same turn-key business form which Indian industry has embraced in its own activity abroad. In the 1970s hundreds of contracts had been signed and in only a few was any provision made to train local nationals.

Turn-Key Contracts

Indian industry has built up an industrial base which has enabled at least 43 Indian companies to build large projects, mostly in the civil construction field but increasingly in more sophisticated fields. At least half of these companies are large scale units in the public sector, and active in over 30 countries, primarily oil-rich states such as Libya, Iraq, Saudi Arabia, Kuwait, Oman and the UAE. Success was so great in this field that in 1979 India was ahead of South Korea as the second largest Asian exporter (after Japan) to the Middle East.

The Indian public sector's predominance in large turn-key project contracts is a striking illustration of the Indian state capitalist system, in this case its state owned sector, seeking outlets abroad. Utilizing the superiority of its technical expertize and its cheap labour, Indian industry has sought to extract maximum benefits from capital-rich oil states that lack indigenous skills. Indian companies are fast learning to ingratiate themselves through massive pay-offs to the governments of the Gulf countries. In public sector companies, large sums have been allocated under disguised headings. Political involvement in other countries through contract activities has become prominent as some heads of public sector companies with large Gulf contracts have in the past channelled money from Arab rulers to Indian politicians, in an exercise of mutual purchase of interests. Such has been the level of Indian turn-key activity that, in the late 1970s, Western firms became worried about Indian competition, particularly where Indian concerns no longer acted as sub-contractors under a Western or Japanese prime bidder, but as prime contractors.

It is important to determine the extent to which India has acted autonomously as a major contractor or to which it has been a sub-contractor complementing the activities of larger industrialized capitalist countries from the West. The precise number of Indian sub-contracts is unknown but, particularly in labour intensive projects in Gulf countries, numerous. This sub-contract role is particularly prominent in cases where India supplies cheap labour to projects undertaken by Western and Japanese firms. Nevertheless, India increasingly takes on full contracts itself. In this way, first as a sub-contractor and then gradually as a full contractor, India may be starting to act autonomously, broadly a part of international capitalism but at the same time also manifesting itself as a full competitor in the field of international capitalism.

Another indication of India's growing capability in this field is the consortia of Indian firms engaging in turn-key contracts. In Tanzania a consortium of eight textile machinery manufacturers successfully bid for a turn-key project.[29] In 1976 a consortium of three other textile companies was set up in order to bid for contracts abroad. In 1977, nine Indian public and private sector engineering companies set up a consortium to undertake projects in Saudi Arabia. Indian firms have adopted the consortium approach, due to a growing realization that by pooling their efforts they can obtain the full benefits of independent contracting. Their ability to act independently is also one reason why huge public sector units have predominated in contract activity with companies such as RITES, WAPCO and IRC, specifically set up to bid for overseas contracts.

Some of these public sector companies are so large that they might be characterized as Indian based transnationals. Bharat Heavy Electricals (BHEL) which, in the 1970s was very prominent in turn-key contract activity, in 1971 was the tenth largest company in India with assets of Rs.2,330 million. Ironically, in the late 1970s India suffered from a severe power shortage with frequent breakdowns of equipment, much of which was manufactured by BHEL.[30]

As already noted, such companies as Indian Oil, and the Steel Authority of India are huge by international standards. This has fuelled the argument that the size and scale of these public sector companies is driving them abroad as opportunities for domestic expansion are restricted. More remarkably, according to some observers, these same companies may be at the forefront of Indian companies linking up with Western multinationals.[31] It may be premature to characterize such companies as transnationals but the distinction between these predominantly public sector and vast private sector firms is that the former do not encompass multiple companies.

Policy
In contrast to joint equity ventures, contracts are regarded by the Indian government as exports, and as such do not merit very close supervision, which may be one reason why Indian contract activity has grown so spectacularly. Neither the Economic Division of the External Affairs Ministry nor the Indian Investment Centre know much about Indian turn-key and consultancy contracts. In 1976 a projects cell was established in the Ministry of Commerce as a supervisory body, but actual approval of contracts rests with the Industrial Development Bank of India in Bombay and a working group within it, composed of bankers from the Reserve Bank of India, the State Bank and the IDBI. Thus, along with its own credit and loan activities, IDBI is intimately involved in fostering India's growing economic ties with other developing countries, acting autonomously from the central government's economic ministries in New Delhi. In addition IDBI involvement enters in its deferred payments schemes offered to Indian contractors on the following terms: 5% advance, 5% against shipping documents, 90% in 16 successive instalments at 8.25%.[32]

The Federation of Indian Export Organizations is also involved in Indian contract activity. Because contracts are regarded purely as exports, the FIEO, an apex body set up by the Government of India and having as its members export houses, chambers of commerce, commodity organizations, state trade development bodies etc., is intimately involved in encouraging contracts as an export promotion measure. FIEO acts as a promotion body, by directing contractors to bureaucratic incentive schemes and sources of finance, in an effort to build up India's non-traditional exports.[33]

Their definition of turn-key contracts as exports permits several bureaucratic relief measures. For example, the Export Credit and Guarantee Corporation of India announced in 1975 that it would issue risk insurance to all turn-key contracts, not only to those in the public sector as it had done thus far. The ECGC provides risk cover against loss of goods and services, and guarantees to banks, to enable exporters to obtain finance. Six types of schemes are extended by ECGC: 1) Packing credits; 2) Post shipment export credits; 3) Export finance; 4) Export production finance; 5) Export performance; 6) Transfer guarantees. In this way losses of up to 75% of Indian turn-key contracts are covered, and 90% of banks bonds issued by banks for bids against letters of credit can also be covered under the schemes.

Consultancy Contracts
Concurrently with turn-key contract activity has been the rise in consultancy contracting. Indian companies have engaged in two types of consultancy contracts: 1) managerial contracts, in architecture, industrial enterprises, hotels, auditing and managerial consulting. This is primarily connected with service industries and so far is a minor activity, though with some implications for India's relationships with developing countries in that,

for set contract periods, it vests managerial control over foreign enterprises with Indians, and it is thus reasonable to suppose that Indian industry could benefit from orders generated by these managerial contracts.

2) a more important activity is connected with the engineering industry and more closely linked to Indian finance capital. At least 49 Indian companies in the private and public sector have engaged in this type of contract venture in over 40 countries. Indian skills, like its industrial capacity, have in recent years suffered from severe under-utilization. Whether such skills can be gainfully employed abroad or whether this would fuel a net drain of them from India remains to be seen.

Industrial consultancy concerns a set of methods and organizational structures which can help technical knowledge and be converted into the construction of specific engineering projects [R16: 39]. Consultancy is a prime indicator of the level of development of industrialization in a given economy, and indicate a capital and skills intensive industrial base. When such skills are available this leads to consultants setting up independent consultancy companies in order to control the planning and execution of industries, irrespective of capital ownership and, in this manner, 'virtually substitute themselves for the owner during the important planning and design stages of industrialization' [R16: 39]. In other words they can determine the future of industrial development, just as Soviet blueprints helped China to shape its post-revolutionary development. This has important long term implications for India and its industries. If Indian consultancy firms are present at the planning stage, the industrial future of several Third World countries can be tied to India — for orders of equipment, reorders, turn-key contracts and ultimately joint-equity participations. Because consultancy contracts are often tied to subsequent turn-key project contracts, these firms can fix the prices of Indian equipment and services. In this way India, still short of capital, can compensate by materially influencing the industries in developing countries through its skills base. This can sometimes be counter productive for the recipient country where no provision exists for training its nationals, or where a diversification of sources of technology is hindered by the hiring of a particular consultancy company from a particular country.

The Indian government has long been aware of the necessity to build a domestic base of engineering consultancy companies and to utilize Indian know-how to boost exports to other developing countries. In 1955 an engineering consultancy company was established with Indian government help, and in 1966 the Planning Commission formed a committee (headed by Shri Thacker) to formulate a consultancy service policy. This committee issued a report which recommended that consultancy companies should be encouraged, so that they could project an image of an industrial India and promote exports, and urged that India open consultancy company offices abroad (as the Japanese had done) to bid for local contracts. In 1969, a symposium on consultancy services was held in New Delhi, and in the following year the government began to adopt a deliberate policy to encourage consultancy contracts. The Commerce Ministry commissioned a study on the business potential for Indian consultancies in the Gulf, funding for which was from US PL-480 funds. The government also held seminars and sent missions abroad to encourage consultancies. In 1970, one such delegation proposed Indian consultancy contracts in South-east Asia in return for raw materials. In the same year the government instructed the Export Credit and Guarantee Corporation to issue 90% risk cover to all consultancy contracts, and cover to Indian banks issuing advances to foreign banks on behalf of Indian consultancy bids. In 1971, the government aided the Indian Institute of Foreign Trade to set up a consultancy service centre, and in 1974 the Ministry of Commerce established a market development fund to aid consultancy contracts, by aiding market studies (60% of costs), opening offices abroad (25% of costs) and helping with publicity (50% of costs).

The Indian Investment Centre was entrusted by the government with the task of publicizing India's industrial skills abroad. As part of this exercise the government tried, with some success, to gain recognition by international development agencies of India as a potential source of consultancy skills; in 1978 India's status was recognized by IBRD, ADB, UNDP, ESCAP, IDBI, ECLA and UNIDO. Utilizing its consultancy skills through these agencies, India hoped to gain procurements for its industries and to utilize its idle skills.

By the late 1970s Indian consultancy contracts, though increasing, were not fully mature. According to some participants Indian consultancy companies began to move into high technology and sophisticated market fields only gradually. As in turn-key contracts, increasingly fewer Indian consultancy contracts are subordinate to Western firms, or merely sub-contracts.[34] The weakness of Indian consultancy companies remains in the realm of finance. India cannot offer long term credits and most Japanese and Western banks will not back Indian consultancy contracts, preferring their own national companies. Usually Indian consultancy companies do not train local nationals; this would put them out of business and the companies concerned prefer to maintain their skills superiority. Only the public sector National Industrial Development Corporation has made efforts to develop local consultancy organizations in Tanzania and Iran. At the same time, consultancy companies face a dilemma whereby India's skills base far out-strips its own productive capacity, which leads to situations where Indian companies place their orders with Western and Japanese companies, rather than with the less developed Indian engineering industry. The integration of Indian consultancy contracts with general Indian industry is thus still incomplete and the capacity of Indian state finance capital to sustain consultancy ventures was still limited in the late 1970s. To remedy this, the National Association of Consulting Engineers was formed in 1976, comprising consultancy firms both in public and private sectors, to lobby and act as a reference point for government and business, for consultancy contract activity abroad.

The examples of several huge public sector firms indicate how the priorities of the Indian state capitalist system show themselves. The National

Industrial Development Corporation was founded by the government to foster India's industrial development. By 1970, however, it had come under attack in parliament as having degenerated into a body dealing only in foreign contracts. It was exonerated in 1972 when the government stated that consultancy contracts boosted India's overall development. Just as in turn-key contracts, the big public sector companies, formed ostensibly to aid India's own domestic development, have instead fostered the development of oil-rich states. In such places, where there is much Indian contract activity, these companies can gain cash profits for the class that controls them and further prevent the development of Indian state capitalism beyond a certain stage. They can also divert attention from the fact that they have failed to build a self-sustaining Indian economy. By earning huge sums through contracts, domestic industrial stagnation can be ignored and a degree of domestic unrest diverted by the earnings which accrue to a small part of population participating as labour in contract activity. As Indian state capital's industrial base has reached the saturation point domestically, it goes abroad to build the houses, raise the factories, provide running water, which the privileged classes ruling India already have, and experience no need or desire to supply to the rest of the peoples of India. Indian firms go abroad according to their own capital imperatives and the capital earned is only utilized or reinvested to benefit the classes controlling them. This is why $16,000 million earned has had little appreciable effect on India's own development in the late 1970s.

The prospect is that this aspect of India's relationship with other develop-ing countries will continue to grow, but only according to the dictates of international economic and capital trends. This may see a reduction of Indian contracts in the Gulf and more such contracts in other areas of the capital-rich developing world where rapid industrial development is sought.

Notes

1. Interview, National Research Development Corporation, New Delhi, 22 February 1980.
2. Interview, NRDC, *Far Eastern Economic Review*, 12 January 1979.
3. There are several examples of the bureaucratically well-connected science educated mandarins, who have monopolized what they grandly call Indian 'science policy'.
4. In Mauritius, only the most modern West German salt plant was desired, despite the fact it was three times the cost of a similar plant from India.
5. *Government of India: Report of the Department of Atomic Energy*, 1959–60.
6. *BBC Summary of World Broadcasts*, FE/W512/A/14 21/3/1969, J1, Vol. 1, Appendix A, p. 176–9. Talks between Bangladesh and India began in March 1972, *Annual Report, Department of Atomic Energy*, 1972–73.

7. *Department of Atomic Energy, Annual Report,* 1970–71.
8. This was an attempt by Libya to gain a nuclear capability from India. There are reports that similar attempts with China were made in 1971. Libya subsequently collaborated with Pakistan for the production of a nuclear device. In September 1979 Libya cut off further oil supplies to India because of her unwillingness to supply further nuclear know-how. *Asian Wall Street Journal,* 26 September 1979.
9. *Foreign Affairs Record,* Vol. 24, No. 4, April 1978. Vietnam sought Indian help to revive the American built reactor at Dalat in southern Vietnam.
10. *RBI, Report on Currency and Finance,* 1973–74; B21; S27.
11. Interviews, Financial Consultants, Bombay, 7, 8 April 1980. Most of such investments are in the conventional form of stocks, bonds and securities on international financial markets. Overnight lending of spare capital was a popular method of utilizing such funds in early 1980.
12. From 1970 India did not classify travel by Indians to Mauritius, Sri Lanka and Nepal as foreign travel, thus there was no restriction on the outflow of funds. *Indian Economic Diary,* 9–15 July 1970. In 1978 Indians travelling to Mauritius and Seychelles came under a RBI 'Mauritius Travel Scheme' which allowed all Indians to visit without currency restrictions on alternate years.
13. Takeovers by Western multinationals may increase as it is realized that using Indian companies may be a way to alleviating political risks. In future this would bring Indian Joint Ventures more clearly into the agent role which Indian capital has not yet reached.
14. Interview, Economic Division, Ministry of Finance, New Delhi, 17 January 1980.
15. This statement was directly contradicted by those Indian government officials supervising Joint Ventures in the Ministry of Commerce in 1980. After approval is given, the only jurisdiction the Indian government observes is a RBI requirement that every company file an annual statement. This leads to many abuses which, while known, are officially 'undetected'. The balance sheets do tell a story however; many report losses year after year.
16. Most of investments in developed countries, except those in service industries, have failed.
17. In 1980, the Ministry of Commerce reported that much of the balance was filed under a catch-all term, as still being in a process of implementation (81 in 1980); most of these were subsequently abandoned. In Malaysia a 34% failure rate was reported. *Business India,* 8–21 December 1980.
18. Interview, Reserve Bank of India, Bombay, 7 April 1980.
19. IIFT *Report on Joint Ventures,* New Delhi, 1977.
20. Letter to the author from Mysore Government Soap factory, 26 December 1978; *Eastern Economist,* 14 May 1971 reports an investment of only Rs.150,000.
21. Through their foreign investments, the Birlas and several other Indian companies have sought to reproduce their monopoly position in other developing countries. Beside the Malaysian cases an even earlier example was the Indian sugar project planned in Uganda in 1964. Had it

materialized it would have given Indian business a monopoly over sugar production, refining and marketing throughout East Africa. Similarly, the Birla paper mill project in Kenya has given it a sizable share of the East African market. *Foreign Affairs Record*, Vol. 9, No. 9, September 1964; *Indo-African Trade Journal*, Vol. 1, No. 1, July 1965; *Eastern Economist*, 30 January 1970.

22. [H8] ; *Business India*, 20 August–2 September 1979; *Frontier*, 19 April 1980.
23. Phosphates are fertilizer components and thus an important input for capitalist farmers, the kulaks. This is one way the Indian state helps an important component of its domestic ruling classes.
24. Interview, Economic Division, Ministry of Commerce, New Delhi, 16 January 1980. *Commerce*, 22 February 1975; *Indian Economic Diary*, 28 May–3 June 1973; *BBC Summary of World Broadcasts*, FE/W870/A/22, 24 March 1976. The quality of India's own abundant coal is not always high enough for use in steel making.
25. *Indian Economic Diary*, 29 January–4 February 1977. China also has a joint shipping line venture with Tanzania.
26. *Indian Economic Diary*, 3–9 September 1975. By 1980 this venture was said to have collapsed.
27. An Indian company invested in a real estate development company in the USA in April 1980.
28. This by manipulation of US government loans given to prospective motel owners.
29. Letter to the author from the Textile Machinery Manufacturers Association, 27 December 1979.
30. For this reason, in early 1980, scandals involving BHEL pay-offs abroad began to emerge in India.
31. The author is indebted to A.K. Bagchi for this insight.
32. Letter to the author, from Textile Machinery Manufacturing Association, 27 December 1979.
33. Interview, Federation of Indian Export Organizations, New Delhi, 11 February 1980.
34. Interview, National Association of Consulting Engineers, New Delhi, 24 January 1980. This should not be exaggerated into a conception of a fully mature Indian industry. For example the sourcing of equipment used in such ventures.

6. Banking and Insurance

The importance of banking and, by extension, finance capital to any analysis of imperialism requires little elaboration. The two forms are, however, quite distinct and the importance of banking capital alone must not be exaggerated. Finance capital is examined here due to the stress placed upon it by analysts of imperialism ever since Lenin identified it as one of the key elements and motive forces of imperialism. For Lenin, imperialism was the articulation of the concentration of capital, the result of the merger of bank capital with industrial capital which, in turn, resulted in a new stage, the age of finance capital. Springing from this, Lenin believed, was export of this capital and the formation of world combines leading to territorial world division, i.e. imperialism [R20; N1].

It is, therefore, important to examine finance and bank capital and their expansion abroad, to determine how they apply to India since 1947. The degree of transformation that has taken place within Indian banking institutions, from strictly commercial activities to the beginning of industrial financing inside as well as outside India, is of particular importance. The expansion of Indian banks overseas and their role in the export, not just of banking but Indian finance capital, are directly related to this.[1] In order to determine if the description of India as a proto- and second-tier imperialist power is justified according to Leninist criteria, the nature of Indian banking operations, and their expansion overseas must be examined.

Capital Institutions

The formation of finance capital institutions in India has been one of the explicit designs of the Indian state which established a number of institutions in the public sector devoted to the financing of industry in India, that potentially could be invested in other countries [S30]. The first of these was the Industrial Finance Corporation (IFC) set up in 1948 to give credit to industry. The IFC works with the IBRD and raises some of its capital abroad.[2] The National Industrial Development Corporation (NIDC) was formed in 1954 but by the 1960s it had degenerated into a consultancy organization. The Industrial Credit and Investment Corporation of India (ICICI) was formed in

1955 as an associate of the World Bank specifically to aid private industry. It has provided loans as well as equity capital for industry in India and has never been answerable to the Indian parliament. The Industrial Development Bank of India (IDBI) was set up in 1964 as the apex development bank in India. Beginning as a subsidiary of the Reserve Bank of India it later separated and, as we have seen (Chapter 4) has been involved in extending rupee credits to other developing countries for the purchase of Indian goods. Its activities in the industrial finance field in India overlap with the NIDC and IFC. Yet another financial institution, the Industrial Reconstruction Corporation of India (IRCI) was formed in 1971, particularly to revitalize sick or stagnating industries, and those subject to closure. Another source of finance capital is the Unit Trust of India (TI) which, in 1964, began as a scheme for raising capital from small deposits as well as from subscriptions of the RBI, State Bank of India, and the Life Insurance Corporation. In addition, Indian finance capital is derived from 18 nationalized banks (which together mobilize 90% of the banking capital), the Life Insurance Corporation, General Insurance Corporation and the central bank itself, the Reserve Bank of India (see Chapter 5). So far, except in the limited cases of the IDBI and LIC, none of these capital institutions have invested in industries abroad, although Indian financial institutions have invested in foreign government securities and shares. As we have noted, however, Indian banking and finance capital is intimately involved in providing finance and risk cover to Indian Joint Venture investments and contracts abroad, and in this way is becoming involved in the industrial development of several Third World countries.

History

Banking in India has existed for at least three millennia. Traditional bankers were able to give bills of credit (hundis) which, depending on political circumstances were negotiable far beyond India. Many traditional Indian bankers were similar to traditional moneylending bankers of China and Arabia. Here, we are concerned with the rise of modern banking on the industrial capitalist model, which grew up alongside but did not completely supplant traditional banking. It is important to bear in mind that between traditional bankers and the 'modern' Indian banking system there are strong links which continue to this day, particularly in the domestic context.[3]

Modern banking in India began with the rise of the big European Agency houses in Bombay, Madras and Calcutta during the late 18th and early 19th centuries [M37]. To service these houses, colonial branches of European exchange banks were opened, concerning themselves with the commercial activities of Europeans [A12], financing the export of native commodities and the import of European goods. The management and finance of India's foreign trade was thus monopolized by European exchange banks even beyond independence in 1947. The first Joint Stock banks in India appeared after 1813 and were entirely in the hands of Europeans, but most of these early banks collapsed during a financial crisis of 1829-33 [P2]. In 1860 a British colonial act facilitating the formation of Joint Stock companies with limited liability was initiated. By 1870 there were already two Indian managed Joint Stock banks in operation [M37], of which the oldest was the Allahabad Bank set up in 1865, but this fell under foreign domination after 1922. By 1900 there were nine Indian Joint Stock banks, only the Allahabad and the Punjab National Bank, which was set up in 1895, survive today. For a long time, then, Indian native capital was involved in the formation of a modern banking sector in India, and these banks were not always the adjuncts of European capital.

A second type of modern banking emerged in the colonial period: the Presidency banks established by the British to facilitate payment of government salaries and administration expenses. Until 1862, these banks were under direct government control, but less stringently after then, and in 1921 the government Presidency banks (Bombay, Bengal and Madras) were amalgamated to form the Imperial Bank of India, a partially government-owned central bank engaged in normal commercial banking. This was considerably more extensive in assets and branches than the smaller Indian Joint Stock banks, and was the equal of the big European exchange banks.

Parallelling the development of a modern Indian industrial bourgeoisie, Indian capitalists, quite early on, saw the advantages of entering the joint stock and industrial banking fields. The early history of modern Indian banking was bedevilled with failures, collapses and wryly amusing frauds, but enough succeeded to lay the foundations for subsequent developments in Indian banking. Some indigenous bankers were also successful in making the transition and, as we will see, the small 'non-scheduled'[4] banks which they set up expanded overseas very rapidly, thriving in a colonial environment conducive to trade and the movement of merchant-moneylending capital.

The strongest impetus to Indian banking came as a result of the nationalist Swadashi movement after the partitioning of Bengal in 1905. In 1906, the Bank of India and the Canara Bank began to operate. In 1907, the Indian Bank was formed, with a strong element of Nattukottai Chettiar control. Under the Maharaja's patronage, the Bank of Baroda was set up in 1909, followed, in 1911, by the Central Bank and the Bank of Behar, and in 1912 the Maharaja of Mysore set up his own bank. A feature of this early period was that several fraudulent Indian banks, notably the 'Pioneer Bank' and the 'Kathiawar and Ahmedabad Corporation' bank, opened, or claimed to have opened, offices abroad. Indeed, this latter bank has the distinction of having had the earliest branch of a modern Indian bank abroad on record, in Nairobi in 1910-13 [M37: 296]. In 1921, the Bank of India opened a branch at Mombasa, but due to fraud and mismanagement it closed in 1923 [M37: 296].

In 1917 the first Indian industrial bank was opened, when the Tatas set up the Tata Industrial Bank which, for the most part, confined itself to financing Tata enterprises. Because its industrial financing was small and seemed to be at the expense of its other commercial activities, this bank was merged with the Central Bank of India in 1923. Just prior to its amalgamation, the Tata Industrial Bank had invested in a London based bank, the British-Italian Corporation. There were other Indian industrial banks in this early period, but of the eight in 1923 only four survived in 1939, and these were very small and localized banks.

During the late teens and in the 1920s few new Indian banks were formed, the Union Bank of India was established in 1919 and the Bank of Chettinad in 1929, this, by 1947 had at least 40 offices in Madras, Burma and Ceylon.[5] In 1938 the Dana Bank was formed and during the 1930s several Indian banks opened branches in Ceylon; the Bank of Chettinad and the Indian Bank in 1932, the City Bank in 1934, the Calicut Bank in 1936, the Travancore National and Quilon Bank in 1936, the Oriental Bank in 1937 and the Nadar Bank in 1937. Most of these branches collapsed and only the Indian Bank survived in Ceylon after independence [W5: 42]. At this time several Indian banks opened branches in Burma: the Mahalaxmi Bank, Kerala Provincial Bank, Krishnaiyer and Sons, Bank of Asia (1939) and Calcutta Commercial Bank. The Central Bank of India also maintained a branch and throughout the 1930s increasingly participated in financing Indo-Burma trade, bypassing British banks.[6]

In the 1940s the United Commercial Bank was set up by the Birlas in 1943 and the Bharat Bank by the Dalmias.

The Imperial Bank

After its formation in 1921 the Imperial Bank of India was permitted to open a branch in London, but its activities were restricted to acting as a custodian of the Secretary of State for India's cash balances. Although envisaged as potentially a central government bank in 1921, a 1924 government committee recommended that a separate central bank be set up, a proposal acted upon in 1934 when the Reserve Bank of India was formed. As part of this Bill, from 1935 the Imperial Bank was allowed to engage in normal banking in London and to open branches in Burma (six branches and one sub-office) and in Ceylon (one branch inherited from the Madras Presidency Bank, dating from 1864). After independence, the Reserve Bank (in 1946) and the Imperial Bank (in 1955) were nationalized [M32]. In 1949 the government was given full jurisdiction over the entire banking system in India.

By 1930 there was already a high degree of concentration in Indian banking, and by 1938 the Bank of India, Central Bank of India, Allahabad Bank, Punjab National Bank and the Bank of Baroda were referred to as the big five. Despite this, Indian banks for the most part remained outside the exchange business which continued to be the preserve of European exchange banks. Bills of exchange and financing foreign trade were weak points in Indian banking. Prior to independence, with the exception of Burma, Indian banks rarely financed trade. Rather, Indian banks opened branches abroad to service the needs of overseas–Indian populations, for remittance business and credits, as well as to extend the network of Indian merchant capital (traders–

moneylenders), notably in Burma, Malaya and Ceylon. Thus the Chettiars, acting through the modern banks they controlled, set up offices in Singapore and Malaya. In 1946 there were 628 scheduled, and 183 non-scheduled bank offices outside the Indian union (excluding Pakistan).[7] Whether the precipitate drop in the number of Indian bank branches overseas was a reflection of partition or of the decline of merchant capital links such as those forged by the Chettiars and other merchant groups during the colonial period is not clear. Certainly the sharp drop in non-scheduled banks operating offices outside India may have been a reflection of the latter, and an overlap may also have occurred with merchant moneylender-controlled scheduled banks, such as the Indian Overseas Bank.

In the late 1940s, as Indian industrialists increased their trade with the West, British companies' hold over such trade began to be eroded, and several Indian banks opened branches in London to participate in the exchange business.

The Context of Indian Banking Abroad

To return to the point raised at the outset: the necessity of defining the role that traditional Indian merchant bankers played in Indian bank expansion abroad, and their gradual demise, transition or replacement into what is today 'modern' Indian banking abroad. A static view of these merchant bankers, as well as Indian banks themselves, is untenable in that both these groups and institutions have been in a constant state of change and adaptation according to the exigencies of a wider global capitalist economic system.

Maxime Rodinson [R19:6-8] defined modern capitalism, in contrast to the capitalistic features found in pre-existing systems, as determined by the mode of production. Capitalism exists where there is an enterprise that pays wages to free workers in an industry which sells its production. By this definition capitalism is not synonymous with commerce, as obviously mercantile capitalism pre-dates modern industrial capitalism. Other forms of pre-capitalist production (possibly with capitalistic features) led to the formation of capital, whether merchants or usurers and sometimes formed a type of merchant's 'finance' capital. Modern capitalism, for Rodinson, differs by virtue of its organization of labour, and the fact that as a mode of production it can operate only in a surrounding capitalist sector which is already extensive on a world scale. Examining money capital prior to the advent of modern industrial capitalism, Rodinson saw it as being tied to landed property, land credit and lending, rather than as accumulation for purely monetary uses, i.e. finance capital. Capital was lent or utilized for non-monetary uses, i.e. consumption moneylending and land accumulation. A distinction is thus drawn between economies that possessed capitalistic features, that is, commercial mercantile capitalism, and those with modern industrial capitalism features. Rodinson, however, fails to stress the overlap which occurs between these two pure models, the constant process of change and transition from the previous or traditional mode of production to modern industrial capitalism and eventual finance capitalism. The relevance of this to any examination of Indian banking abroad is that such banking occurs against this background of transition, in which Indian banks reflect the level of domestic state capitalist development and transition within India as well as its external ties.

Indigenous banking in India has adapted itself according to political and economic conditions as capitalist development has taken place in India. For example, up to the mid-19th Century many indigenous bankers were engaged in internal money changing, a function largely eliminated after the British introduced a standardized currency. Discussing the links between indigenous and modern banking in India is complicated by problems of definition. Some [P2: Ch.2] have preferred to differentiate between moneylending and indigenous banking, the latter financing trade, the former consumption. Such a distinction is artificial, as, in practice, a great deal of overlap occurs. Indigenous bankers not only supplement (or parallel) the modern banking sector but some have successfully transformed themselves into modern bankers.

Nattukottai Chettiars: Sub-Imperialists?

While the role of overseas–Indians will be examined, as an element influencing India's economic and political relations with developing countries, in the next chapter, it is relevant here to examine one particular group who, when the British Empire was at its apogee, were able to build a network of banking, moneylending and trade activities unparalleled by the subsequent development of Indian banking overseas since 1947. Is it not possible that the Nattukottai Chettiars played a sub-imperialist role in pre-1945 Burma, Ceylon, Malaya, Thailand, Indonesia, Indo-China and Mauritius, which set the stage for the post-independence economic relations between India and some of these countries? This kind of question suggests that many features to be seen in India's post-independence thrust abroad in the developing countries have their roots in the pre-independence period. The formation of a rupee ambit, credit links, and contemporary foreign investments in industry were foreshadowed by the activities of groups such as the Nattukottai Chettiars in the late 19th and early 20th Centuries.

The Nattukottai Chettiar's home is in Chettinad in India's present day Tamil Nadu state [W5]. They are an ancient indigenous banking community; found in Ceylon in the pre-European period they started to gain prominence only after the advent of Europeans in Asia. By the 19th Century they were playing an important part in meeting local credit requirements in Ceylon and, after the British conquest, in Burma. Describing themselves always as bankers, the Nattukottai-Chettiars none the less engaged in trade, pawnbroking, and above all moneylending, primarily to agriculture. They thrived in the imperial climate and by the late 19th Century sustained the role – until 1945 – of compradore intermediaries, the middlemen supplying the credit needs of the local populations in Ceylon, Burma and Malaya; the credit for these activities was obtained from the British merchant banks. Because British banks were unwilling to enter local capital markets directly, the Nattukottai Chettiars monopolized this function. Their financial network linked India and South-east Asia; they acted as moneychangers, earning sterling, converting it to rupees and remitting large amounts of finance thus acquired back to India. Land foreclosures in Ceylon and Burma gained vast tracts of agricultural land for them. In Burma's case, by 1930 the Nattu-kottai Chettiars controlled 6% of the total occupied land [C10] and 25% by 1937, or 1/3 of the total land in Burma that had been under rice culti-vation in 1936 [A11]. As usurers the Nattukottai Chettiars were unparal-leled, the control they acquired cannot so far be compared with contem-porary Indian economic involvement and control in developing countries. The social costs of their activities was offset by their effect on the economic development of Burma, Ceylon and Malaya, where rice, tea and rubber production increased extensively as a result of the credit they provided.

The Nattukottai Chettiars well illustrate the features that Rodinson calls capitalistic, merchant usury capital going abroad to earn profits but putting their capital accumulation into land and trade rather than industry. It must be remembered that these activities were an integral part of the world capitalist economy, because in their middleman role the Chettiars channelled credit and production back and forth between the European and local sectors of the colonial economy. While losing this role in the post-independence period, the Nattukottai Chettiars and Indian banking abroad in general successfully made a transition. Whereas earlier, both were concerned merely with trade (the former with usury too), today they are more and more concerned with investing in industries, often in countries such as Malaysia, which were their former area of activity. They have increasingly taken on the features of 'modern capitalists', if as adjuncts to international capital, then as middle level agents who, on occasion, can act autonomously in their own interests.

Motives
With the nationalization of the Reserve Bank of India in 1946 and the form-ation of the Indian Banks Association in the same year, Indian banking reached a watershed. The basic motivation (earning profits and servicing overseas-Indians) for Indian banks to open branches abroad did not change dramatically after independence, but there was a gradual accretion of new motives affecting Indian banks' roles abroad. Banks have followed the expansion of India's trade and business abroad and become involved in international trade and money markets. The aim of providing retail banking and services to overseas-Indians, such as remittance facilities, deposit accounts, credits and so on, has remained from pre-independence. After independence participation in the import-export trade between India and the country of the branch locations was added. These two factors were the major influences in determining the business potential and expansion of

Indian banks going abroad up to 1970. Due to the overseas-Indian factor, the RBI correctly states that Indian banks abroad differ from large multinational banks in that they can rely on a captive form of business abroad.[8]

Policy

Until the 1970s little distinction existed in government policy between banks in the domestic sphere and the same banks establishment of branches abroad. In so far as there was a policy it was one of encouragement with a view to participation in the foreign exchange business — a field in which some banks entered in the 1960s. [P2]. According to a Central Committee Report of 1969, several difficulties were encountered by Indian banks venturing abroad. 1) They lacked the capital and resources to do it efficiently. 2) Most branches operating abroad do so at a loss. 3) They lacked trained staff and were subject to hostility from indigenous populations [P2: 312-13]. By the late 1970s, many of these difficulties, though not eliminated were considerably reduced.

Few private banks maintained overseas branches after 14 of them were nationalized in 1969, and following further nationalization, in 1980, no private bank maintained branches abroad. To study the effects of nationalization on foreign banking operations the Reserve Bank set up a Committee which recommended the amalgamation of all Indian banks with branches abroad into a single, overseas bank. This recommendation, however, was not accepted.

In the wake of nationalization, Indian business observers both at home and abroad urged that the establishment of Indian bank branches abroad should become a priority. There was an increasing awareness that Indian banks could effectively mobilize foreign exchange resources from overseas-Indian sources; and this was spectacularly borne out after the 1976 policy liberalizations, with a dramatic rise in the inflow of remittances.

The real impetus for Indian banking abroad occurred after 1973, with the Reserve Bank of India's policy decision not only to be more liberal in granting permission to those banks wanting to open branches abroad but also to promote such activity.[9] As a result, local banking operations in such places as Hongkong, Singapore and Bangkok flourished and Indian banks started financing some local businessmen, Third World trade and general finance. The government also began to promote the idea of a regional emphasis in targets for new branches, particularly in South-east Asia and the Middle East.

Performance and Profitability

Although the performance and profitability of Indian banks abroad has gradually improved, nevertheless in the late 1970s, due to inefficient methods and a lack of initiative, they still lagged behind their foreign competitors.

In 1966 the total deposits of Indian bank branches overseas was

Rs.15.70 million; in 1968 total credits were Rs.10.33 million. Between 1966 and 1968, the growth rate for Indian banks abroad compared to the overall bank growth in the countries of operation was:

Country with Branches	Deposits	Bank Credit
UK	− 3.7	+ 1.7
Japan	+ 19.2	− 2.2
Sri Lanka	− 16.4	+ 17.8
Kenya	+ 15.4	− 8.4
Malaysia	+ 3.7	+ 5.0

Thus, in Sri Lanka and the UK, growth in deposits was lower than the general rate of growth of other banks in these countries, while in Japan, Kenya and Malaysia, Indian banks recorded higher than average rates of growth. By 1973, Indian banks' total deposits abroad were Rs.26.10 million (Rs.27.248), with the level of advances at Rs.21.90 million. In 1975, this increased to Rs.68.00 (60.87) million in deposits and Rs.61.20 million in advances; total business generated by Indian banks abroad in the same year was Rs.80.718 million. The operating expenses in 1975 were 18.8% of the total costs of Indian banks abroad and the Reserve Bank was urging increased mechanization to improve profitability. This aspect has been a persistent problem.

Remittances to India from overseas-Indians form a large part of Indian bank operations abroad, as they do for Bangladeshi and Pakistani banks abroad. Remittances comprised Rs.30.96 million in 1973, rising to Rs.105.15 million in 1976 and continuing to rise in 1979. In the 1950s and 1960s low profitability was a severe problem. The net profit rate in 1967 was 8.8% rising to 11.9% in 1968 for a total of Rs.16 million in profits for that year. By the late 1970s, as some banks participated in currency markets and others became involved in the movement of capital from one market to another, profits continued to increase. Indian banks with foreign offices registered higher overall profit rates, with the percentage of earnings of foreign branches to total earnings of domestic banks rising from 4.5% in 1970 to 6.2% in 1975. The percentage of gross to total profits of all overseas branches was 5.68% in 1970 and 10.6% in 1975. Earnings of Indian banks abroad from interest, discounting, dividend commission and exchange were, according to the Reserve Bank report, slightly below the same banks in India in 1970 and 1975, but earnings from other sources (letters of credit, bills for collection, etc.), slightly higher compared to these activities in domestic banks, probably because, although higher rates of interest, commission and brokerage are paid by Indian banks abroad, working expenses are low.

Individual banks' branches abroad tend to be more profitable in the developed than in the developing world, and branches in developing countries sometimes take years to achieve profits; perhaps this indicates that Indian banks opening branches abroad are motivated less by the prospect of quick profits than of long-term benefits and possible gains in developing countries.

Indian banks operate in many developing countries whose laws require them to invest in local assets, and have necessarily opened local investment portfolios. Thus, Indian banks own shares of foreign government securities and company stocks in addition to their usual investment portfolios in India. Foreign investments demonstrate the growing involvement of Indian banks in the local financial structures of developing countries and, by extension, India's stake in the stability of many foreign governments. In Nigeria, for example, where RBI restrictions on the outflow of additional Indian capital pre-1975 threatened to impede Indian banking operations, the banks turned to local capital sources to raise funds from overseas-Indians.

The improved performance of Indian banks abroad was, in part, due to increased diversification of activities and expansion of their local base business. In the late 1970s, Indian banks began raising foreign currency loans for Indian shipping and airlines on currency markets; and began taking Euro-dollar deposits and generally enhancing their liquidity. New techniques were also introduced to mobilize the deposits of rural overseas-Indian populations. Mobile Indian bank branches in Fiji, Mauritius and Kenya deepened the Indian foothold in the local economies of these countries. In areas such as Malaysia and Indonesia where Indian banks previously had limited scope for expansion, financing industrial projects, particularly Joint Ventures [C11], led to increased Indian participation in local money markets. By 1969, in Singapore, Indian banks were lending to other clientele, besides overseas-Indians, to set up local industries, and 25% of their paid-up capital was contributed to the Singapore Government's Economic Development Board.

Indian Banks and Joint Ventures

In the mid-1960s, when Indian Joint Venture investments were having difficulties finding finance in situations where local banks demanded 200% security, it was suggested that Indian banks should assist more vigorously in financing these ventures. It was felt that Indian banks had a 'responsibility' to help, a view which overlooked their own shortfall in capital. For this, among other reasons (lack of experience, delays in approvals), until the mid-1970s many Indian companies preferred to raise their loan capital from foreign sources and banks, as well as lending institutions.[10] Indian Joint Venture investment activity and Indian banking abroad are related in that, for example, in Indian contract activity, the approval committee in Bombay always refers the applicant to the capabilities of Indian banks.

By the late 1970s, there was generally a greater awareness of the value of involving Indian banks more fully in investment servicing. The RBI stated that in 'promotion of Joint Ventures, Indian banks play a prominent role; by extending credit, providing information, arranging participation, and servicing capital movements'. The location of Indian bank branches abroad became of value to Indian capital seeking to invest abroad. In the late 1970s, Indian banks also began to play a promotional role for Indian investments. Representative offices, such as that of the Bank of India in Djakarta, provided information for prospective investment in Indonesia, and the same bank's Singapore branch claimed to be instrumental in setting up five Joint Ventures in Indonesia. Other promotional services increasingly provided by Indian banks abroad were rendered to Indian turn-key and consultancy contracts by issuing bid bonds, performance guarantees and credits; and in Seoul, efforts to promote mutual trade and investment, as well as Third World ventures with South Korea.

Nationalizations

Between 1969 and 1980 nearly all, and since 1980, all Indian banks operating abroad have been public sector institutions. Thus, Indian banking expansion has been, not an expression of private monopoly capitalism, but rather bureaucratic state capitalism.[11]

Indian banks overseas, as we have noted, often face the possibility of nationalization. Domestically, India seeks to restrict foreign banks' activities and, since 1979, besides those based in the developed world, only Bangladesh among developing countries maintains a branch in India. In 1977 there were 12 foreign banks in India, augmented in 1980 by a number of Arab banks. In responding to foreign nationalizations of Indian banks, the Indian government has adopted a moderate stand, to avoid accusations of hypocrisy. Generally, particularly since the late 1960s, when facing nationalizations in developing countries, India has adopted a sophisticated approach by devising compromises in the form of joint banking ventures.

In February 1963, the Government of Burma nationalized the branches of the State Bank of India, Punjab National Bank, Central Bank, United Commercial Bank and the Indian Overseas Bank with a total of seven offices. Total deposits held in Burma at the time was Rs.100 million or 10% of total bank deposits then held. The Indian government claimed that the amount of capital repatriated to India from Burma up to that time had been minimal, and that India wanted a fair and reasonable valuation for compensation.

In September 1965, Pakistan seized Indian bank branches operating there, along with other Indian assets, these were entrusted to a custodian of enemy property. Thirteen Indian banks were involved with at least 39 branches in East and West Pakistan. After 1971 branches in Bangladesh were not restored to India, although the State Bank reopened there.[12]

In February 1967 Tanzania nationalized the four branches of Indian banks operating there; in 1969 the South Yemeni government nationalized the Bank of India branch in Aden. In both cases a small compensation was paid.

Banking Joint Ventures

The domestic nationalization of 14 banks in India in 1969 was a politically motivated move which disregarded its effects on the operations of Indian banks overseas. In Thailand, where the operations of state owned banks was banned, this led to the setting up of the Bharat Overseas Bank. Formed in 1973 as a joint sector bank to continue Indian banking presence in Thailand, it was composed of seven Indian banks; the Indian Overseas Bank holding a 30% share, and a 70% share held by six other banks, which then remained in the private sector.

In Nigeria, the Bank of India was converted into a subsidiary company in 1969, and in 1976, the Nigerian government acquired a 60% equity share, converting it into a joint banking venture. Indian banks in Uganda converted into locally incorporated banks in 1969, and later into a single subsidiary of the Bank of Baroda, with the Ugandan government participating in an equity share of 51%. The Ugandan government later seized the whole operation; until this point Indian partners maintained control through management — as they did in Nigeria.

After bank nationalization in India in 1969, Malaysia was asked by the Indian government for time to consider the future of the three Indian banks which between them then had 11 branches in Malaysia. The problem was similar to that in Thailand and Nigeria: the Malaysian government prohibited the operation of any foreign government-owned bank due to fears of subversion — notably from the Bank of China. The value of assets of Indian banks in Malaysia at that time was Rs.220 million. No solution was found until 1973 with the formation of the United Asian Bank, made up of the three nationalized banks that had previously operated in Malaysia. Declared (inaccurately) at that time to be India's first Joint Venture in banking, it had directors from Malaysia's three ethnic communities. Its initial capital was Rs.70 million, 33 1/3% of the issued capital taken up by the Indian government, and 66 2/3% by Malaysians. Three of the ten directors were to be chosen by India. An attempt by India to solve the problem by involving the overseas-Indian community was resisted by the Malaysian government in that they insisted on a degree of Bumiputra participation in any agreement. By 1974, the United Asian Bank showed a good performance in profits and rate of expansion; the growth in deposits was 39% against a Malaysian average of 32%. One third of the advances extended by the Bank went to Bumiputras.

In November 1975, Sri Lanka began moves towards nationalization of foreign banks' operations; those concerned were British, Indian and Pakistani. In July 1976, Sri Lanka's Foreign Minister warned that unless these banks brought in foreign capital and expertize they would be shut down. In November 1976, British banks' operations in Sri Lanka were nationalized, but Indian and Pakistani banks were exempted because they were already nationalized at home and, in the words of the then Prime Minister, 'these banks will have an important role in expanding trading and bilateral relations between Sri Lanka and her immediate neighbours'.

In the face of these threats to the operations of its banks, the Indian government has demonstrated increasing ability to respond flexibly by entering into banking Joint Ventures, in order to avoid losing its economic presence gained through banking activities in developing countries. A response in contrast to the damaging nationalizations of the 1960s, when India's economic presence by way of banking was lost in many developing countries.

In the colonial era, Indian banking played an integral and sub-imperialist role for a wider colonial capitalist economy. After independence this role was supplemented by the imperatives of the Indian state capitalist system itself seeking external outlets for its goods, services and capital, and wishing to mobilize the capital resources of overseas-Indian populations. From the evidence presented thus far it should be clear that the traditional role of Indian banks abroad as a service centre for overseas-Indians is being supplemented by a new role which channels the Indian economy into overseas investments and capital flows. This is transforming Indian banks into capital investment institutions and conduits for funds raised on international capital markets. In this way Indian banks are part of the more generalized and deepening involvement of India in the economic, financial, and ultimately, the political structures of other developing countries. However, it must not be overlooked that Indian banks abroad have still not transcended their status as a conduit of Indian banking capital abroad, and are only just beginning to channel Indian finance capital overseas.

Indian General and Life Insurance

Related to the expansion of Indian banking abroad is Indian General and Life Insurance and its foreign business and investments. Parallelling the increasing involvement of Indian banking in the local economies of other developing countries, Indian insurance, particularly life insurance, has played an important role in the financial structures of some developing countries far longer. Instead of increasing over the years the Life Insurance Corporation of India's involvements overseas have, however, decreased and continued to do so up to 1980.

The role of insurance in the banking and financial structures of developing economies is a little explored field. Especially in those developing countries where local financial institutions are weak or non-existent, insurance companies can mobilize large quantities of local capital. Most insurance, particularly general insurance, remains under the control of developed countries which, through insurance-reinsurance networks, are enabled to maintain their dominance in the developing countries concerned. General insurance import and export trade is still primarily in the hands of European and American based companies. Reinsurance (i.e. spreading risks among many companies) is one of the primary institutions for world-wide interlinking of capital [V2b]. Developing countries are very weak in this field, and thus are dependent on countries with larger capital resources prepared to back bigger risks [U1e].

General insurance undertakes all risks, such as fire, marine, flood etc., usually renewable annually on a short term basis, with generally lower profits than life insurance which mobilizes capital by selling premiums that mature at death or a fixed time. Life insurance can mobilize enormous savings capital and, by careful examination of death rate patterns and good management, its assets generally exceed its liabilities and it is thus a potentially rich source of investment capital and profit.

Indian General Insurance Abroad

India is internationally involved in general insurance, with the import trade reserved for Indian companies [U1d]. Until recently, however, these companies remained closely tied to the industrialized world's insurance companies. Unlike Indian life insurance, which was nationalized after 1965, general insurance was nationalized only in 1972, when the General Insurance Corporation of India began business as a holding company for four subsidiaries which contained and amalgamated all the private general insurance companies (foreign and Indian) which had previously undertaken business in India.[13] In 1958, there were 184 insurance companies (91 Indian, 93 foreign) and in 1972, 107 (64 Indian, 43 foreign); a multiplicity that led to extreme weakness and an absence of outstanding performance both domestically and externally. This weakness was largely due to dependence on the West for reinsurance and to foreign companies operating in India (mainly from the UK). In the 1950s, the annual drain through reinsurance was calculated at Rs.10–15 million [G9; Gov.12, 1956]. To alleviate this problem a Reinsurance Corporation of India was formed in 1956, with a capital of Rs.100 million, but in 1960 the reinsurance capital drain abroad had grown to Rs.81 million, and in 1972 to Rs.132 million [Gov.12c, 1969; 1972]. Remarkably, in spite of being closely tied to the developed world, Indian general insurance began looking abroad for business — following trade and, more importantly, overseas-Indian links, even before 1945.

In 1954, Indian insurers wrote a gross direct premium abroad of Rs.50 million [G9] and between 1951 and 1957 the net premium income recorded by the Indian general insurance business abroad rose from Rs.9 million to Rs.26 million (from 23% to 33%) of their total business [Gov.12c, 1958]. In 1969, income from foreign business had grown to Rs.300.5 million of a total income of Rs.918 million, but this was balanced by an outgo of Rs.833 million, of which Rs.81 million was reinsurance payments. In 1972, foreign income was Rs.412.4 million of a total income of Rs.1,521 million, but the outgo was Rs.1,025 million. In the same year the only profits Indian general insurance made abroad was in fire cover [Gov.12c, 1972]. Thus, up to 1972, general insurance profits abroad were not very high, and premium rates charged by Indian companies were sometimes higher than their foriegn competitors.

An interesting aspect of Indian general insurance is its investment of foreign assets to partially meet its foreign liabilities as well as provide a capital base. This field can potentially involve India in the financial structures of developing countries. These foreign assets in the form of British, foreign and colonial government securities have, however, comprised a minimal part of the investment portfolios of Indian general insurance companies as is shown by the following:

Year	Amount (Rs. million)	% of total assets
1955	24.5	6%
1957	20.5	4.2%
1960	17.6	3.1%
1969	22.4	1.4%

While, by 1972, investments held by foreign general insurance conpanies in India totalled Rs.34,424,000 [Gov.12c, 1973]. By 1978 the total investment portfolio of Indian general insurance, the bulk of whose investments were in India, was Rs.7,070 million. The apex institution, the General Insurance Corporation of India, was the second largest non-banking financial institution in India and one of the five most important domestic investors. More importantly, following nationalization, from 1976 the Corporation began to issue reinsurance to foreign companies abroad, which may indicate that in future it will perhaps take a fresh look at foreign investments. Reflecting the general growth of the service sector of the Indian economy, with its long experience of conducting business abroad, Indian general insurance in the 1980s might become a major general insurance source in the developing world; one indication of this is that the Chinese were seeking Indian insurance expertize in 1981.

By extending abroad in the developing world, particularly in West and East Africa, and South-east Asia, Indian general insurance may become one more Indian economic institution which will become increasingly involved in local economies and capital markets in the Third World.

Life Insurance Corporation Abroad

Contrary to what might have been expected the Life Insurance Corporation of India's (LIC) foreign involvement does not lead to an exposition of India's growing economic involvements abroad. With the exception of Mauritius, LIC's operations overseas illustrate only a potential vis-à-vis the constricting reality of the absence of Indian involvement in other developing countries.

Indian life insurance's overseas operations began during the colonial period; as a locally based activity, life insurance in India paralleled that of banking. In the late 19th Century, Parsis in Bombay set up several companies, followed by Sindhis, Punjabis and, after the 1905 Swadeshi movement, Bengalis [R1]. Indian life insurance business from the time it first went abroad (probably following the First World War) was always closely tied to overseas-Indian populations. By the 1920s Indian based insurance companies were conducting business abroad and as they undertook to cover the liabilities of non-resident Indians, they necessarily had to increase their local investments [R11]. Before 1929, life insurance policies held by Indian companies abroad averaged Rs.2,848, Rs.1,000 higher than domestic policies. From 1929, amounts assured through foreign business by all Indian life insurance companies was Rs.8,979,000, and by 1935 Rs.12,409,000. The Indian life insurance company with the largest foreign business prior to the war was the Oriental, which had a large business in Burma. Most of foreign business of all Indian insurance companies was transacted in the then British colonies of East Africa and South-east Asia, a practice carried over into the post-independence period.

The nationalization of life insurance in India (in 1956) had immediate repercussions on Indian life insurance abroad. Previously 40 Indian companies were transacting life insurance outside India [Off.16a] with a total of 276,000 policies worth Rs.920 million [B3]. In 1957 this foreign business was consolidated and reduced in value to Rs.324.43 million as many policies were divested and transferred. For political reasons, LIC also curtailed foreign operations in a number of countries. Before 1956 these Indian life insurance companies were closely linked to big industrial houses and groups, such as Tatas, Singhanias, Birlas, Jalans, Goenkas, Chettiars and Dalmias.

Transfer to LIC entailed the integration of all these companies and their foreign offices. Because the LIC Act did not apply outside India, it was registered locally as a new company in: Kenya, Mauritius, Hongkong, Fiji, Aden (PDRY), Uganda, Malaysia, Singapore, UK, Pakistan, Burma and Ceylon (Sri Lanka). For the latter three this was for servicing existing accounts only and not for new business. A study [Off.16a] commissioned at the time decided that LIC would transact new business only in Kenya, Uganda, Tanzania, Mauritius, Aden, Malaysia, Singapore and Hongkong. It was also decided to open new business in the UK to mobilize the capital of overseas-Indians there.

In 1957, through LIC's foreign operations, India was poised to continue expanding its economic relationships with other developing countries by mobilizing foreign capital towards subsequent investment in foreign industrialization, as well as raise capital for India's own development and meet India's long term interests in economic and political fields. Yet this did not occur neither has it done so since. While inside India, LIC has become an enormous mobilizer of finance capital (Rs.12,600 million in 1970), investing in heavy industries, and a key support for government development strategies, outside there has been a curious apathy, as year by year LIC's foreign operations have dwindled.

As early as 1956 H.D. Malaviya [M4: 27-9] called LIC's inherited business abroad luxury and 'singularly unremunerative'. The expense ratio was higher abroad and he gave an example of one company whose asset deficiencies had to be augmented by a remittance of Rs.30.5 million from India. Malaviya complained that foreign business earned nothing for India but only drained it of capital without a return, a pattern which continues to this day.

LIC's areas of operations have contracted from the 12 countries in 1957 to three, plus two in 1980. In 1963 LIC had to close down its operations in

Burma due to the Ne Win coup and resulting nationalizations, but kept its investments. LIC's assets for the servicing of accounts in Pakistan were seized in 1965 and LIC lost everything. Business had to be terminated in Tanzania in 1967 due to nationalization, although 13 years later LIC was helping Tanzania to set up a state insurance company. In 1968 nationalization closed down LIC's operations in Aden (PDRY). Business was terminated in Uganda in 1970, and in Hongkong in 1971 [Off.16a]. In 1970 LIC launched new business in Nepal, run from their Muzaffarpur Divisional Office in Bihar, only to be directed by the Nepalese government, in 1979, to divest itself of the business. To conform with local legislation, LIC stopped new business in Kenya in the late 1970s, and transferred servicing of accounts to a new locally registered company: LIC-Kenya, a Joint Venture with the Kenyan government. In Malaysia too, a Joint Venture company, United Oriental, in which LIC has a share, has taken over LIC's business that was set up as a part of the Malaysian government's Bumiputra policy in 1977 [B3]. In the 1970s too, business was terminated in Singapore.

With this constant contraction, the growth rate of LIC's new policies abroad has obviously been low. The average annual increase of business in the 1960s was only Rs.20.3 million, but other figures show an average annual increase of Rs.100.66 million between 1962 and 1967 [Gov.1].

New policies issued each year between 1968 and 1979 averaged approximately 4,000, a very small number when compared to the tens of thousands of new policies within India. Annual sums assured for these new policies varied from year to year as the following shows:

	1968	1969	1970	1971	1972
Number of new policies:	4,663	4,203	4,661	3,945	3,809
Amount assured in Rs.millions:	90.07	87.00	102.8	80.50	150.92

Indian Life Insurance Corporation's Foreign Investments

The most interesting aspect of LIC's operations abroad are its foreign investments maintained to service their foreign policy holders (see Table 6.1). Most of these were inherited by LIC along with the operations of life insurance companies abroad. When comparing the distribution of LIC's total investments, the foreign component is the smallest even in comparison with certain regions of India. Between 1964 and 1969 foreign investment constituted only Rs.100,000 a year compared to Rs.600 million in new investments in West Bengal in the same period [Off.16b, 1969-75]. In 1956 the book value of foreign investments in government securities was Rs.113.6 million or 3.3% of LIC's total investments, and in foreign provincial securities (ex-colonies) Rs.7.3 million or 0.2% [Off.16a]. LIC's total assets

foreign investments between 1957 and 1968 were around 2% of total assets
and the percentage of foreign liabilities compared to total liabilities

Table 6.1
Life Insurance Corporation of India: Foreign Investments by Country
(Indicating rate of appreciation/depreciation of fixed investments:
1966–67 to 1970–71).

Country/Date	Type	Amount (Rs.)
Sri Lanka		
1966–7	Government loan	24,750
1967–8	Government loan	38,981
1968–9	Government loan	31,185
1969–70	—	—
1970–1	Government loan − 3%	31,185
Hongkong		
1966–7	UK Government securities	91,159
1967–8	UK Government securities	143,576
1968–9	UK Government securities	123,065
1969–70	—	—
1970–1	UK Government securities	131,010
Malaysia		
1966–7	Government securities	463,060
1967–8	Government securities	731,935
1968–9	Government securities	731,935
1969–70	—	—
1970–1	Government securities	731,935
Burma		
1966–7	Government securities	25,876,109
1967–8	Government securities	42,203,739
1968–9	Government securities	42,644,739
1969–70	—	—
1970–1	Government securities	63,520,227
	Municipal securities	540,000
	Bonds	37,075,815
Indonesia		
1966–7	Cash	67,114
1967–8	Cash	83,500
1968–9	Cash	83,500
1969–70	—	—
1970–1	Cash	83,500

(continued over)

Table 6.1 (continued)

Country/Date	Type	Amount (Rs.)
Singapore		
1966–7		–
1967–8	Government securities	918,750
1968–9	Government securities	918,750
1969–70	–	–
1970–1	Government securities	918,750
Pakistan		
up to 1965		15,056,300
South Africa		
1966–7	Government securities	3,086,298
	Municipal securities	351,517
	Bonds, shares, debentures	131,330
	Fixed deposits	2,803,050
	Cash	14,667
	Total	*7,571,197*

Total Foreign Investments	
up to 1956	*140.84 million*
up to 1966	*150.93 million*
1968	*44.50 million*
1971	*45.83 million* *

* Figures incomplete

Source: LIC Annual Reports

diminished from 7% in 1957 to 4.1% in 1968 [B3]. LIC usually follows a conservative foreign investment policy keeping money in government securities and making few new investments. While amounts in government securities are relatively small, they do have political implications such as the investments of Rs.7,571,197 in South Africa in 1966–7. LIC is probably unaware that it contributes to the continued stability of some governments by maintaining money in their securities; the Economic Division of the External Affairs Ministry were equally unaware of such investments in 1980. While LIC closed its operations in Sri Lanka, Burma and Hongkong for political reasons it still maintains investments in these countries. In Burma, in addition to funds in government and municipal securities, and bonds, LIC owns real estate in Rangoon. These investments have depreciated so much that encashing them is not worthwhile; LIC retains them hoping for a better day on which to sell LIC's foreign investments are handled by its general investment cell in Bombay, which is answerable to the insurance cell in the Finance Ministry. Foreign policy implications are not generally taken into account, particularly since in recent years new investments have been made only in the UK, Mauritius, and Fiji. Foreign investments are not very attractive to LIC; in 1968 returns from interest were only 4.62% compared to 5.22% on domestic investments.

The criticism of LIC's foreign operations made by Malaviya in 1956 remains valid in 1980, when they were still not self-sustaining and, therefore, contrary to expectation, no flowback of funds to India was earned through profits. In 1968 an official report [Gov.1] charged that Indian operations were subsidizing foreign operations by Rs.5 million a year. When the UK and Fiji operations were matching their local liabilities to assets, additional capital had to be sent from India in the mid-1970s.

The status of LIC's foreign operations are confined to three states, Fiji, Mauritius and the UK with two Joint Venture companies in Kenya and Malaysia, all of which employ LIC personnel sent from India. In the UK, LIC operations resemble those of a separate subsidiary company; following local laws and practices, setting its own rates and filing its own reports. Its business is confined to overseas-Indians only. In Fiji, LIC's operations are similar to the UK's with an important difference, the business is with local nationals of Indian descent. The profitability of Fiji offices is not high because of stiff competition from a single Australian company. Despite this, LIC in Fiji is an important part of the local economy, and in 1977 loaned the local government $250,000. Even in Kenya and Malaysia where LIC has converted its operations, the involvement of their staff is very great and Indian embassy officials frequently liaise with its local offices. This illustrates that in the eyes of embassy officials at least, LIC is an important local Indian institution.

The relative importance of LIC in India's growing economic involvements abroad is given credence by its presence in Mauritius where its operations are an extension of domestic business; rates are set at the same levels and, although the Mauritian government does not require LIC to maintain local investments, as a matter of policy it does maintain a 50/50 investment policy, matching local liabilities with local investments as much as possible. In Mauritius LIC is 'in a unique position in the economy and life of the country', and despite the fact it has eight competitors its operations have been successful. The Mauritian Prime Minister is a policy holder and LIC is an integral part of the local economy, being the second largest company in size and having assets which, they state, match those of the central bank in Mauritius. In the words of one Corporation official, 'LIC in Mauritius is stabilizing the local financial structure by helping to localize it'; this, of course, has political implications. LIC, and by extension India, is strengthening the hand of the Ramgoolam government and helping to mobilize the Indian descent population and its savings against the economic power vested in the Franco-Mauritians and the latter's links to Europe and South Africa. This involvement has gone unnoticed in India and abroad; it may foreshadow similar developments elsewhere involving LIC if a change in policy regarding its foreign operations ever occurred.

LIC's other operations abroad have suffered from total apathy and a policy of deliberate neglect on the part of the Indian government. Its potential to strengthen Indian economic relations in other developing countries has been disregarded. Inheriting such business LIC has been content to let it run down, helped by nationalizations which India was powerless to oppose. The alternative, of entering into insurance Joint Ventures, has been acted upon only recently and that as a reaction, not a result of planned policy. This lack of interest is doubtless due to LIC's involvement in domestic business, where it enjoys a monopoly. According to one official, the dynamic talent and skills of LIC are such that, if the signal were given, Rs.2,500 million in additional business could be generated abroad in five years. LIC thus illustrates both India's growing economic involvements in developing countries, and the lack of policy initiative in grasping the institution's potential at a time when Indian companies and banks are expanding their operations around the world.

Indian banking and insurance and their expansion abroad, as yet, clearly do not support the Leninist definition of imperialism. Curious anomalies and slow growing external banking ties have hindered the growth of what would be a full-blown Indian imperialism. There are, however, exceptions to this broad observation. In its relations to small neighbouring states, such as Bhutan, Nepal and Mauritius, nascent Indian finance capital, if sometimes in the form of banks or banking capital, is exercising itself in a domineering manner seeking to maintain or gain a hold over the economies of these small states. In their foreign operations therefore, Indian banks and insurance are just beginning to reach a scale in which charges of proto- and second-tier imperialism may become justified.

Notes

1. It is nevertheless true that this point needs elaboration, particularly as the amount of capital Indian banks import through remittances was, in 1980, still far greater than the amount they exported.
2. For some observers, along with ICICI, it constitutes an important direct link to Western capital.
3. Many have incorrectly denied this, but at the same time recognizing a limited relationship [M37: 126]. The link is strong in rural credit networks where modern banking has acted as an adjunct to traditional creditors rather than supplanting them. This has been particularly true since the extension of rural banking in the 1970s.
4. Banks with a capital base of Rs.0.5 million or less were non-associates of the Reserve Bank of India under its charter of 1935. Thus only with capital in excess of this could they be classified as scheduled.
5. Other reports have put the number of branches this bank had in Burma

alone, as over 45 [A11: 312].

6. [A11: 307]. According to the son of the manager of the Allahabad
   Bank in Rangoon in 1931 (Interview, Indian Institute of Foreign Trade,
   New Delhi, 5 February 1980), that branch's activities were confined to
   the refinancing of Chettiars who offered only chits against unseen rice
   in godowns as security. As Chettiars began to suffer losses in this form
   of speculation, the bank started losing heavily, and ultimately had to
   close down.

7. [P2]. These figures are unclear, elsewhere in the same book he states
   that between 1948 and 1953 the number of non-scheduled banks outside
   India fell from 4,674 to 3,943 and scheduled bank offices outside India
   from 272 to 106.

8. *RBI Bulletin*, March 1977. Captive business in the form of the State
   Trading Corporation accounts is also important to the State Bank's
   foreign operations. 35–40% of all Indian imports are with the STC and
   this in turn creates massive business for the State Bank. (Interview,
   IIFT, New Delhi, 5 February 1980).

9. *RBI Bulletin*, March 1977. Some bankers feel that instead of playing a
   constructive development role, the RBI through its attitudes has played
   the role of policeman towards Indian banks and hindered their
   operations abroad.

10. This merits closer study as it may jeopardize the view expressed in this
    work regarding the autonomy of Indian investment activity abroad.

11. The only private banks in the post-1971 period which remained under
    big private business control were the Hindustan Commercial Bank
    (J.K. Singhania), New Bank of India (Bangur), Oriental Bank of
    Commerce (Thapar) and the Bank of Madura (Thiagaraja). This position
    was further eroded in 1980 when some, such as the New Bank, were
    nationalized. None had branches or offices abroad.

12. *Commerce*, 8 February 1975. The SBI branch was allowed to operate
    only in Dacca and the agreement was on a reciprocal basis with a
    Bangladesh bank operating in Calcutta.

13. The four companies are: New India Assurance, National Insurance,
    United India Fire and General Insurance, Oriental Fire and General
    Insurance. *Indian Insurance Yearbook*, 1972; *Business India*, 23 July–
    5 August 1979.

7. The Overseas-Indian Populations

In the previous chapters we have seen how, as a reflection of its internal political economy, India today is forging economic relationships with developing countries based on aid, investment, contracts, banking and insurance.

One factor which impinges on all this and itself constitutes an important facet of India's relations with some developing countries, is the role of overseas-Indians. India's state capitalism has been inconsistent in its recognition of the potential represented by overseas-Indians in political and economic gains, whilst cautiously recognizing the liability they represent for India's relations with the Third World. On one hand, they are a pool of local contact men and women, ready at hand for India's economic and political activities, and a pool of capital in the form of remittances; on the other, they can jeopardize India's relations by their independent activities.

While the phenomenon of overseas-Indians resembles that of overseas-Chinese and their influence in China's foreign relations, it is the nature of the system in India and its relation to the world economy which help to determine the interrelationship between India and overseas-Indians. Overseas-Indians are seen as part of India's growing economic involvement in the Third World, and can themselves cast new light on hitherto obscure areas of India's foreign relations.

Overseas-Indians: Who Are They? How Many?

Confusion has existed between Indian nationals, those of Indian descent, those of South Asian descent (post-1947), those who are Indian government employees abroad and those who are first generation labour migrants. All these categories are included here under the general term, overseas-Indians, but, given the realities of post-1947 South Asia, some overseas-Indians are now overseas-Pakistanis and Bangladeshis; as such, they are largely excluded from discussion, even though they overlap in definition and play similar roles abroad, according to their place in the world economy. Some overseas-South Asians, by virtue of their differing political and emotional loyalties are, however, a minimal asset for Indian state capitalism abroad, and are sometimes its opponents.

A wide disparity exists in the assessments of how many overseas-Indians there are. According to one source [N4] in 1947 approximately 3.5 million were living in 51 countries. By the 1970s, their number and distribution had obviously changed, but, because of the confusing criteria adopted to define overseas-Indians the disparity continued. Tinker [T6] states that in 1970 there were not more than 5 million; another source [S22] produces figures totalling more than 21 million! Tinker's figures seem to be a gross under-estimate, considering that the combined figures for Malaysia, Nepal and UK alone totalled 4 million, and, as early as 1955 the number of overseas-Indians was assessed at 4 million.[1] Thus, it seems that the actual number is unknown, but employing the broad definition offered at the outset, higher figures offered from the mass of conflicting data are perhaps a more reliable approximation, as other evidence seems to bear out.

For example, in 1967 the total number of overseas-Indians was assessed at 7 million [N6]; in 1969, only 600,000 were said to be living abroad.[2] In 1970, it was declared that over one million were in Africa alone [G3a] although it is not clear how many subsequently emigrated to the industrialized world. The highest estimate of 10 million was offered by Vaid [V1] which, he maintained, meant 35–40 million when their families were included, but this is probably an over-estimate. In the late 1970s the rapid rise of overseas-Indians holding Indian passports probably augmented figures by around 2 million. In 1974, 300,000 Indian passports were issued, and 700,000 in 1976. In 1977, one million passports were issued, and 1.8 million in 1978. In addition, some Indians have gone to the Gulf without passports.[3] Thus, it may be safely assumed that by 1979, at least two million more overseas-Indians had joined those already established in communities overseas, so that, by the 1980s Vaid's figures seem less unreasonable.

Indian Government Policy

Indian government policy towards overseas-Indians is contradictory and, except in one respect, lacks coherence; more surprisingly, it reflects little concern[4] except for mobilizing remittances home. Before independence it was assumed that because of Indian nationalism greater concern would be evinced for overseas-Indians once independence had been achieved. Economic and judicial sanctions on behalf of any overseas-Indians who were ill-treated were advocated by some [B28]. In 1946, Nehru visited Malaya and declared that with independence all Indians overseas would become Indian nationals unless they decided otherwise [T6a: 291]. Despite this pre-independence concern, with the exception of early protests against South African treatment of its Indian population post-independence policy lapsed into total passivity [T6b; G3b]. A separate department concerned with the affairs of overseas-Indians was called for in 1950, such a department already existed in the Ministry of External Affairs, but was said no longer to exist in 1976, but in December 1977 it was revived and its work designated as classified (80% according to officials). Policy matters, not day-to-day dealings are the concern of this department which is deemed to be 'sensitive' because it works with non-Indian nationals. Up to 1979, it was not working as systematically as its equivalent in China.

In 1980, this department seemed to be restricted to dealing with established overseas-Indian populations in key countries such as the UK, though not at the level of top community leaders. Important to its work was monitoring overseas-Indian funds to the government. In 1979, still seeking a clear policy from the government it was only at the stage of compiling lists and gathering information.

The basis of India's overseas-Indian policy was that they should identify closely with the indigenous population among whom they lived. Krishna Menon, in 1950, stated that Indians abroad must give allegiance to the country where they lived. He stressed the affinities they had with the 'mother' country, but that this could not be a political tie. Even as India was publicly committed to supporting decolonization it was caught in a dilemma concerning overseas-Indians, who were urged to take out local passports, thus reducing India's responsibility; in the 1950s this led to a contradiction with India's stated decolonization policy.

For the most part the Indian government offers no protection to its nationals abroad, and whilst requesting them to identify with their country of residence has, on occasion, asked for their help [G14b].

The policy of urging overseas-Indians to identify with their country of residence fuelled opposition from right-wing groups in India, which in the past have urged the application of sanctions against government that 'squeeze' Indians. Nevertheless, Indira Gandhi expressed the government's view of the rising tide of nationalism in the Third World when, in 1967 she said of Uganda that 'freedom has its price and must be paid'.

In the early 1950s some overseas-Indians demanded to be allowed to participate in Indian elections and have their own representatives in government, as did the overseas-Chinese in their home government. This demand was refused; only Indian officials abroad have the right to vote. In 1978 overseas-Indians in the Gulf demanded representation in the Punjab and Kerala state assemblies, and representation in parliament for all overseas-Indians.

Indian policy in respect of overseas-Indians carrying foreign passports was stated to resemble that in operation between Europe and Europeans settled in the United States. But with the increase in emigrants in the 1970s, particularly to the Gulf, Indian government policy manifested greater concern, and plans to regulate emigration were discussed.

In Sri Lanka, with the growth in Tamil separatism in the early 1970s the Indian government declared that redress lay with the Sri Lankan government which it could only 'sound'. At the same time, however, the Indian High Commissioner in Canada investigated racial violence and expressed his concern. In 1975 those overseas-Indians holding Indian passports and earning over $12,000 a year were instructed by the government that unless they remitted 10% of their earnings annually to India they would not be permitted to renew their passports.

The advent of a Janata government in 1977 saw major changes in policy towards overseas-Indians. India's entry laws were amended to enable them to return to the 'motherland' — and this also applied to foreign nationals. The Indian Foreign Minister declared that India would neither disown or fail to appreciate the loyalty of overseas-Indians. A seminar was sponsored by the government and it was stated that the Indian Council for Cultural Relations would henceforth involve itself more fully with overseas-Indians. Indian diplomats in Sri Lanka were dispatched to camps to observe conditions under which Tamils were held preparatory to repatriation. The new policies seemed to be seeking a balance of India's own interests while simultaneously expressing legitimate concern for the conditions of its own nationals overseas. This line of policy will probably survive political changes in India because of the perceived utility of overseas-Indians to India's state capitalism and its need for finance and expertize, as well as in assisting its overseas investments.

Overseas-Indians and the World Economy

Particularly in the way they relate to the Indian state capitalist economy, the *raison d'etre* for the position of all South Asian migrants is economic. This has nothing to do with 'free choice', or the view of 'bettering oneself' that occurs in migration theory.[5] Unlike other migrants — i.e. mass migrations, 'national' migrations or political refugees and excluding inter-South Asian migration such as followed partition in 1947 — overseas-Indians have left India because of economic factors, in which 'free choice' does not play a major role.[6] The suggestion that emigration from South Asia is a result of demographic pressure and thus that the flow of Indian migrants overseas will continue is incorrect. Demographic factors play only a peripheral role in that India is a large country but with immense quantities of underutilized manpower as a result of uneven domestic development.[7] This labour force will go overseas for the role it can play there according to economic, not demographic needs. Beginning in the colonial period, overseas-Indians have performed a key intermediary function in world economy via their supply of skilled and unskilled labour acting on behalf of a world capitalist economic system. A function they continue to perform today. Although this has been modified or terminated in some places, due to political changes, new opportunities arise in others, which increasingly include acting as intermediary for Indian capital as it expands into developing countries.

From Colonial Traders to Modern Industrialists

The foundations of the contemporary role of overseas-Indians were laid in the colonial period. In South-east Asia, the Middle East and on the East

African coast, as merchants, priests and soldiers, for thousands of years
Indians played an economic, cultural and sometimes political role [T66].
Here, however, we are concerned with their role as intermediaries in the
world economy, which began with the establishment of a unified capitalist
economy after the advent of the European colonialist powers. India was the
centre of the British Empire, acting as a reservoir of manpower to serve the
aims of Empire elsewhere and further its economic and political interests
in Africa, Asia and the Caribbean. Some travelled abroad on their own initiative to exploit important niches created for them in the imperialist system,
acting as intermediary traders, agriculturalists or low-level administrators
opening up the hinterland for the penetration of imperial capital, or developing urban entrepot centres to facilitate the extraction of previously
untapped wealth for the metropolitan centre. After Africans, Indians were
numerically the largest colonial migrants to be taken abroad by a system
(indentured labour) akin to slavery.

Additionally, the colonial period also led some overseas-Indians to engage
in straight compradore activities. The activities of the Nattukottai Chettiars
in the economic field of pre-war South-east Asia have already been touched
upon.[8] Parsis — such as the Tatas — began quite early to act as intermediary
merchants of the British for Asian trade. Parsis firms owned ships that plied
between Calcutta and Canton, carrying opium and cotton[G11]; the British
East India Company was unwilling to be identified by the British parliament
as organizer of the opium trade. Resulting from these beginnings Parsi firms
had, by the late 19th Century, diversified their trading operations and
become transnationals with offices in Shanghai, Kobe, Osaka, London, Paris,
New York and Rangoon [V1]. Thus did Indian economic connections with
developing countries begin during the colonial period.

There were broadly two categories of Indian migrant in colonial times:
the indentured labourer and the petty-trader/moneylender or clerk. It was
those in the latter category who laid the foundations of India's contemporary
economic role in developing countries. Initially, the economic activities of
overseas-Indians — facilitated by small amounts of capital from India — was
based almost entirely on community ties. Later, however, some who were
involved in moneylending had massive capital to invest, so that by the end of
the colonial period, in most countries where they had a clear economic
presence, a popular belief grew among the indigenous peoples of all Indians
hoarding vast capital and of mythical India-based investment companies.
From petty trade and moneylending, a few Indian traders did acquire
economic power and in some places involved in commodity processing, e.g.
cotton-ginning in Uganda, flour and oil mills in Tanzania and Kenya [P6].
Generally, however, they remained at the level of retail and petty-traders.

An exception was Burma, where, by 1938 the Chettiars controlled 25%
of the land [V1] and a great deal of that country's trade was also in Indian
hands — Rs.350 million of a total of Rs.600 million in export trade. By 1940
the total Indian investment in Burma was put at Rs.1,889.9 million (in
1931 it was claimed to be only Rs.5,000 million). Indians owned 303

factories in Burma in 1939,[9] and even after independence, as Burmese nationalism compelled the Burmese government to initiate the liquidation of Indian interests, Rs.150 million worth of assets held by overseas-Indians was still in Burma in 1964.

In Malaya, overseas-Indian economic activities were more circumscribed due to the composition of the community (most were plantation workers) and the economic dominance of overseas-Chinese, but by 1950 they had laid the foundations for later, direct Indian investment by investing over £13 million themselves.

An important part of the overseas-Indian traders economic role has been their transition to 'modern' economic activities, though this has not occurred consistently.[10] The important shift of overseas-Indian activity has been away from trade and into local industries. Most such shifts received real impetus only after decolonization due to world economic and political changes brought by independence, forcing overseas-Indians increasingly to curtail their retail trading activities. Traders spoke of going into industry, but lacking capital, many were slow to implement their plans. In East Africa, in the 1950s, such industrialization as had occurred was the result of overseas-Indian activity [G3b]. In Sierra Leone Indian traders opened 10 small factories in the 1950s. In Nepal in the late 1950s Indians began several industries, particularly in textiles, and in countries where this transition had not begun in earnest such as Malaya, it was overseas-Indian community policy to try and encourage their move into industry.

This movement into industry by Indian traders tied in well with the promotion of India's own economic interests abroad. India explicitly stated that overseas-Indians going into industries can help India's own investment effort through mutual tie-ups. The government has seen, at least intermittently, the potential of overseas-Indians to build general export trade, and to this end has encouraged the establishment of overseas-Indian chambers of commerce, with which India has hoped to collaborate [V1]. This has been seen as part of a policy to build development in co-developing countries.

In some places the transition from trader to industrialist desired by Indian state capitalism has been slow, hindered by political fears, lack of opportunity and particularly a lack of capital. In societies with large working-class overseas-Indian populations, the economy is completely dominated by neo-colonial capital, the community lacks organization or the initial capital to become involved in industry. In Hongkong political fears deter overseas-Indians from going into industry [V1]. The basic insecurity and conservatism of Sindhi traders confines most of them to a petty-merchant money-lending role. There are exceptions, however, with one family's industries (Harilela) employing 40,000 workers and another Indian industrialist with factories worth $68 million.

Overseas-Indian Multinationals

An important aspect for contemporary overseas-Indian industrialists is the network of community and kin. Like the Chinese overseas, these links present built-in advantages for the multinationalization of some Indian business empires. Indeed, this development has already taken place with at least two or three overseas-Indian 'multinationals' emerging in the late 1970s. This development could assist India's own thrust abroad, with Indian based companies calling upon the expertize and collaboration of overseas-Indian multinationals.

These should not be seen as strictly extensions of India's contemporary capital thrust abroad, or as being tied in some way to the contract activities of India's own public sector companies like BHEL, EPIL or RITES. They are independent of India, having grown to a requisite capital scale and size (assets over £100 million) to qualify as multinationals, from their own bases in East Africa. Overseas-Indians like overseas-Chinese in this way have autonomously transformed their traditional compradore role to that of a new type of multinational company which acts in the interstices of international capitalism.

For these multinationals India is a target for investment like any other developing country, but with one vital difference: the desire to work more closely with the political structure in India in an effort to safeguard their investments on a long term basis; in their eyes, India is the final refuge if overseas-Indian multinationals are rejected or outlawed.

At least two family based companies may qualify for the title 'multi-national', both were originally based in East Africa [M38b]. By and large these companies have relied on family networks strengthened by marriage alliances to maintain their control as well as to guide the growth of the company. Where no immediate kin exist they rely on distant family or community ties to perform the same function.

Murray [M38b] has divided the growth of one overseas-Indian multi-national into three periods, with the final period leading to multinational-ization.[11] This final period was the real transition to manufacturing from trading by the Chandaria overseas-Indian conglomerate, a process which began in 1948–49 when it purchased a flour mill, and continued in 1952 when it expanded into metalware manufacturing. By 1978 this company had approximately 40 subsidiary companies and its assets were valued by family members at the somewhat inflated figure of £175 million. In 1980 its field of operations covered Tanzania, Kenya, Nigeria, Morocco, Ivory Coast, UK, Belgium, France, Italy, Canada, Australia, Papua New Guinea, Indonesia, Singapore, Philippines, India, New Zealand and Jordan. Products manufac-tured include, metalware, roofing materials, PVC products, paints, chemicals, matches, salt, palm oil, garments, textiles, electronics. Other investments include finance companies, mostly for in-house finance.

The rapid expansion of this particular overseas-Indian multinational has been very much predicated on its particular identity: security of investment and a safe haven for capital are of primary importance as well as the usual' economic forces impelling it to invest and seek profits. An examination of the pattern of investment reveals that the amount of risk capital is very small; most expansion has come from take-overs rather than fresh investments. In addition, most of the subsidiary companies in the group are managed by a separate service company to evade exchange controls which might otherwise prevent the repatriation of profits. This strategy is necessary because, as an overseas-Indian company, it has to overcome the dangers it faces from local nationalism and general hostility.

While Murray contends that it is inevitable that this overseas-Indian multinational's capital will continue to accumulate in metropolitan centres such as London, he recognizes that the newest field of expansion is Southeast Asia rather than the industrialized world. As an overseas-Indian company, it may in future take increasing amounts of capital to India rather than to metropolitan centres alone. The search for ultimate security may find this company increasingly buying into the political and economic structure in India. While overseas-Indian multinationals play a generalized supporting role to Western capitalism, explicit tie-ups with big Western firms are few. Local participation is usually with local partners, not multinationals and Indians overseas have yet to forge the strong links which increasingly tie some Chinese overseas companies to Japanese transnationals.

Economic Role of Overseas-Indians

Ultimately the economic role of many other Indians overseas will change according to the exigencies of a world economic system. What skews this simple picture of these roles is the superstructural elements of their presence in areas of the world where they are a minority or are faced with strong indigenous communities. In these settings, political and social factors cannot be ignored. Before returning to these aspects the role of Indian labour overseas and their remittances back to India must be considered.

The precursor to the modern movement of Indian labour overseas was the indentured labour system of the colonial period. The largest communities of overseas-Indians are in places such as Guyana, Trinidad, Mauritius, Fiji, Sri Lanka and Malaysia, where they are the descendants of indentured labourers. In countries such as Sri Lanka and Guyana acute racial tensions have resulted.

In the 1950s, with memories of the indentured labour system still fresh, India banned the export of labour. But labour movement to the oil-rich Gulf States began in the 1960s, when ambitious development plans there led to an insatiable appetite for labour.[12] Western Europe too, whose economy is built on cheap *gastarbeiter* labour, welcomed Indians to perform the dirty jobs that most Europeans refused to do.

While the Indian, Bangladeshi, Pakistani, Egyptian and Turkish governments welcome the export of their labour as a means of providing foreign exchange through remittances, the negative effects have been little studied; remittances fuel domestic inflation but do not compensate for the loss of skills [C16].

The idea that labour export somehow contributes to the development of the exporting as well as the importing country is specious, particularly when the use to which remittances are put are examined. It is also argued that it is a means to reduce unemployment in the Third World [B24]. According to the *Indian News* (a government publication) of 13 July 1978 'It is in the Arab world . . . that the Janata Party is likely to fulfil its election pledge to eradicate unemployment in India.' Some Indian opinion has taken an opposite view, being aware that the export of labour could become a modern indentured labour system.

The economic imperatives of the supply of Indian labour, overflow into other unsavoury sub-fields. One is the 'wife' or *burkah* trade from India to the Gulf, a form of semi-legal human traffic, which, since at least 1962 operates on a wide scale, with Indian and Pakistani girls being procured directly from poor parents for a payment of Rs.2,000.[13]

By 1977, Indian labour in the Gulf was big business, with a proliferation of recruitment agencies, over 500 recognized by the government and hundreds of illegal ones; attempts to regularize this activity were dismissed by the Indian Supreme Court. Over 80% of the total applications for Indian passports were for people destined for the Gulf. All professions, nursemaids, miners, watchmen, carpenters, masons, washermen etc. were involved, and in 1977 the government became concerned about their lack of protection. In October of that year the Kerala state government set up a state corporation (The Overseas Development and Employment Consultants Ltd) to regulate recruitment and earn revenue for sending labour overseas; the Maharashtra government set up a similar body later. The rapid rate of recruitment resulted in the depletion of vast areas of the Indian domestic economy as there was a massive migration of semi-skilled workers especially.[14]

The government was forced to respond to reports of ill-treatment; in February 1978 a team from the Labour Ministry was sent to investigate conditions in the Gulf. In Oman they found that Indians were living in slave-like conditions and, as a consequence, exports of Indian labour were temporarily banned. Because of recruitment malpractices the government proposed to set up a public corporation to look after Indian workers abroad.[15] Finally, in July 1978, Indian workers in Kuwait rioted over conditions and lack of unions. This strike was brutally put down by the Kuwaiti police and the 'ringleaders' sent back to India (*Hindu*, July/August 1978). A similar strike was said to have occurred earlier in Iran.

There is then, a basic continuity from the export of Indian labour under the colonial indentured labour system to the contemporary export of labour. Both served the desired function of expanding productive forces abroad, and both inherently had exploitative features based on the non-indigenous status of the migrant, whose position was and is kept deliberately insecure.

Role of Remittances

Tapping of remittances began during the colonial period, and continues under India's state capitalism, resulting in considerable wealth. In 1936, 71,999 overseas-Indians remitted a total of Rs.2,610,616 from Malaya for an average individual remittance of Rs.36, and in 1937, Rs.60, making a total of Rs.6,624,718. In 1940, the total was Rs.7,600,740. According to one writer [N1] this money was soaked up like water in sand. Remittances from Burma averaged Rs.26 million a year in the pre-war period [C2]. Even in 1950 Rs.100,000 worth of Burmese currency notes were flowing to Calcutta every day for smuggling and black-market purposes. As a result, in 1960, when the Burmese government began to expel Indians it allowed only Rs.75 to be taken out by each repatriate.

Until the government liberalized its remittance facilities for overseas-Indians official figures increased very slowly, although large sums flowed into India each year undetected. With liberalization came a massive growth in remittances through legal channels, reaching $1,000 million by 1977. In the same year India had become the third largest labour exporter to the Gulf. The impact of this drain on India was enormous, a labour aristocracy was formed and discrepancies between classes, in wealth and between regions, have widened. Certain areas like Kerala, Punjab and Gujarat in India, or Sylhet in Bangladesh have felt the impact of its *nouveau riche* migrants who remit funds which are used for consumption purposes only. Like the Oporto region of Portugal this has only fuelled local social and economic tensions. The impact on the economy in general has been inflationary, despite the use of some remitted funds to purchase essential imports like oil.

Concomitant with this growth in remittances has been a rise in the awareness of the Indian government that the skills as well as money of overseas-Indians should be tapped. As early as 1950 special tax exemptions were offered to returning overseas-Indians who brought home profits accrued abroad. When overseas-Indians were expelled from various countries, the government liberalized facilities to encourage them to bring assets into India. In 1957 the Indian government collected information on overseas-Indians with a view to offering them jobs in India, but this activity fell into oblivion until 1970. Punjab was a region with one of the highest numbers of emigrants overseas, and an awareness of their potential utility grew, and in 1970 the Punjab Chief Minister declared that he wished to encourage Punjabis overseas to invest in their home state. In 1973 central government drew up a plan to encourage overseas-Indian investment in India.[16] In 1974 the government became concerned by press reports about India's 'brain drain'. Only 6,000 scientists were registered with the government as working abroad, but a 'National Register' of Indians abroad was drawn up which totalled 16,000, 40% of whom were scientists; a scheme was formulated to attract the scientists (only a fraction of the real total) back to India, by permitting them to keep their savings in foreign bank accounts for three years. As part of this plan a conference was held in Washington to liaise with Indian scientists abroad, and the post of scientific attaché was created for the embassy there. The Indian mission registered only 600 names of overseas-Indians by November 1974. It was reported in the press (*Hindu*, 21 November 1974) that these schemes attracted only 22 enquiries out of a possible pool of at least 18,639.

In 1975 yet another scheme was drawn up to tap overseas-Indian funds for investment in India. This plan led to the 'non-resident external accounts' policy which, by allowing freely transferable accounts in foreign exchange, led to the massive inflow of legal remittances to India.[17] External deposits in 1971 were valued at Rs.800 million; in 1980 at Rs.9,170 million. In April 1976 new incentives were announced for overseas-Indian investment in 19 Indian industries for up to 70–74% of the equity, and in other industries if 60–70% of the production were exported. In May 1976 a separate department in the Ministry of Industry was formed specifically to encourage overseas-Indian investment and the inflow of funds. A further expansion of this plan was announced in September 1976 under which India would utilize the skills and technological know-how of overseas-Indians. Indian embassies were instructed to screen and select individuals, this process being limited to those 'retaining links to India'.

Awareness of the potential of overseas-Indian resources and skills increased, but implementation lagged, and where there has been success, as in increased remittances, little thought has been given on how to use these funds. Ultimately the role which overseas-Indians play in relation to India is double edged. They are an asset in so far as their skills, resources and local entrée are concerned and at the same time a liability in so far as they antagonize local populations and provoke suspicions of India's policy towards those countries where large numbers of overseas-Indians live.

Impact of Overseas-Indians on Indigenous Communities

This has been complex, influencing cultural and social as well as political and economic spheres, thus complicating India's relations with some countries in the developing world.

A characteristic of overseas-Indian populations which affects their continued economic role, and more distantly their relation to India, is their sense of identity, or its absence. Almost everywhere overseas-Indians have settled they have segregated themselves from the indigenous population. This characteristic is intimately tied to their economic role, as well as springing from social culture in India itself, where compartmentalization along caste, community and religious lines is the norm, and each community holds aloof from others, particularly when it comes to marriage (endogamous). Overseas-Indians not only remain aloof from indigenous populations, but form separate, exclusive groups within their own broad community. In East Africa one has the spectacle of a multitude of caste clubs, such as the Patel Club, a situation repeated wherever Gujaratis, Tamils and Bengalis, who seem particularly susceptible to this form of identification, are to be found. This exclusiveness serves the function of self-preservation, seeking to maintain the group's identity in face of a hostile environment. This group identity is important to the economic function of the community, particularly to the wider application of exclusiveness as it applies to the overseas-Indian community as a whole. Like that of their kin in India this attitude is consistent with pre-capitalist modes of behaviour and is increasingly incompatible with modern 'rationalized' capitalism and social behaviour. In the pre-independence period overseas-Indians' exclusiveness was a matter of pride to Indian nationalists [14b] and, on India's independence, invoked an even stronger sense of national consciousness among overseas-Indians [T6a].

In the colonial era overseas-Indians tended to identify with the white, European colonial power and not with India or the local population, a form of identification, particularly in the political field, that persists up to the present day. The overseas-Indian has a ghetto mentality, particularly as, except in Mauritius, Fiji and Guyana, his position is everywhere that of a minority. Remaining separated perpetuates the overseas-Indian's sense of defensiveness and vulnerability; this has led to repeated calls for their expulsion as rising local nationalisms conflict with what are perceived as egocentric aloofness. Thus, economic exploitation alone has not fuelled local resentment and racial tension, but also the behaviour pattern of overseas-Indians, rooted as it is in their basic insecurity of identity. India is a dreamland, a mythology of idealized culture; sentimental ties are highly important to the individual and this, as will be shown, has directly affected economic behaviour. Maintaining ties with India is a form of insurance, most overseas-Indians feel that if 'things go wrong' they can return to India.

A facet of overseas-Indian behaviour, rooted in their sense of identity, is the problem of racism, which has wider implications for India's relationships with co-developing countries, particularly in Africa. As an ideology, racism, nurtured by European colonialism is a disregarded and taboo subject [T6c]. In the past this problem has been particularly acute in Africa where overseas-Indians have played the 'brown man' intermediary role [N2] and have perceived themselves as superior to Africans, and yet, like other colonized people, inferior to Europeans. Colour consciousness, or more accurately caste consciousness − viewing other human beings as less than human − is rooted in South Asian culture and a vast literature exists concerning it. Its history concerns us here only in so far as this internal group differentiation affects political and economic behaviour abroad.

Marriage, being primarily endogamous, has its effects on overseas-Indian economic behaviour where certain language groups such as Punjabis, Gujaratis, Tamils and Sindhis predominate. Each of these, and caste and religious groups within them, also keep aloof and, through community ties fostered by family and marriage, constitute strong interlinked economic groupings uniquely suited to trading behaviour. This may be why some traders maintain a certain business ethic in which all outsiders are 'ignorant Africans'. The degree of localization that cuts them off from India, and the lack of full acceptance in their foreign surroundings, leaves them in limbo. This lies at the heart of their relation to India, and of India's relations with developing countries with an overseas-Indian population. It is a situation of constant ambiguity, a mutual opportunity and liability for both sides.

At times overseas-Indians have been seen as the vanguard of Indian expansion and imperialism. Idi Amin declared that Indians were the 'worst imperialists'; the French in Madagascar in 1960 in an effort to maintain their influence there propagated the potentiality of Indian expansion. In 1955 India's representative there was charged with undermining French rule by inculcating Merina intellectuals with romantic ideas of past links with India, and purportedly utilized the 15,000 overseas-Indians to support Malagasy nationalism [N4; A4: 276]. The pro-South African Creole press in Mauritius also accused India of using overseas-Indians to advance its imperialist interests. A similar charge has been made from time to time in Nepal, Sri Lanka and Pakistan.

In Fiji and Guyana the effect of overseas-Indians' presence has been more superficial; India opened Indian cultural centres in both. In 1971 Fiji's Prime Minister stated that a channel of communication could be established between India and Fiji through the local people and Indian traders; thus making a Fijian role mandatory. In Guyana, Indians were prevented from acquiring political power and, in an effort to assuage them, the Guyanan government built up ties with India, asking for aid and for an Indian cultural centre in 1971; India was charged with having so much to gain there that it favoured Cheddi Jagan against Burnham [I1].

In Malaysia in 1950, the local Indian government representative (John Thivy, later posted to Mauritius and Madagascar) was quite influential in guiding the Malaysian Indian community. Through him, Indian traders came together to form an association of chambers of commerce, and the Malaysian Indian Congress agreed to co-operate with the then colonial government to fight Communists. Such official Indian guidance in overseas-Indian affairs lapsed as Malaysia neared independence. A Malaysian government minister publicly warned overseas-Indians not to take their complaints to the Indian government.

As India has moved abroad in its investments, Malaysia has become a prime target. Overseas-Indians had high hopes that they might be linked with this activity and thus enhance their own economic position, but this has occurred only to a minor extent. Indian investments have found a good business climate in Malaysia, but this was not due to the presence of overseas-Indians alone.

In states where the overseas-Indian population is minimal their impact is variable. In the Maldives, where India was seeking base facilities in 1978, a Hindi speaking Shi'ah minority remains separate from the Maldivian Sunni majority population, and this may influence India's links with the Maldives.

Indian nationals sent abroad by the government on short contracts direct from India – technicians, advisers and teachers – are prominent in some African, and the Himalayan, states. Bringing a qualitatively different presence from that of resident overseas-Indians, they are usually welcome as their role is to assist development. As aid personnel they are probably the most effective of all Indian expatriate groups in extending India's interests. This is particularly true of such military personnel as pilots and advisers.

Overseas-Indians inevitably project negative or positive images of India which can affect the economic and political fields. Indian traders and officials can present a picture of a venal and grasping country in a state of abject poverty. Banda of Malawi's anti-Indian feelings based on his own experience, can influence Malawi's relations with India [D20].

Perhaps the most important instrument for projecting India's image amongst the masses in many developing countries is the Bombay film. Its link to overseas-Indians' presence becomes weaker as many audiences in the Third World find the semi-Westernized dreamland India appealing in its own right. Nevertheless, there is resentment in some Third World countries – e.g. Nigeria – where the ready availability of Indian films is seen as a form of cultural imperialism.[18]

In several Third World countries the colonially established presence of overseas-Indians became unwelcome with independence. With the strong emphasis on 'indigenization' there were calls to expel foreigners, many of whom were Indians.

Their first response to this mounting post-colonial hostility was an attempt to form community-wide organizations to lobby for overseas-Indian rights.[19] While most expulsions and repatriations of overseas-Indians have been due to rising nationalism, some have been the direct result of a break-down in political-diplomatic relations. This feature illustrates the Indian government's dilemma. While trying to disassociate itself from those overseas-Indians who hold foreign passports, expulsions have presented humanitarian problems that it would have preferred to avoid;[20] similarly in the case of stateless overseas-Indians. Politically motivated expulsions and migrations back to India have taken place; for example, in 1963 many Indians chose to leave China when India expelled its Chinese populations; in 1961, 2,000 Indians were expelled from Portuguese territories after the take-over of Goa; and in 1964, following the Zanzibari revolution, those overseas-Indians who could, fled, to avoid massacre.

Sri Lanka, Burma and Uganda present some of the most notable examples of anti-Indian sentiments leading to expulsion and repatriation. Expulsions from Burma and Sri Lanka began on a large scale after India's defeat by China in 1962. The Indian government maintained almost total silence, quietly acceding to the decision on expulsions taken by the Burmese and Sri Lankan governments.

The presence in Sri Lanka of numerous Tamil labourers and civil servants had, since the 1950s, been the basis for Sinhala political mobilization that led to communal violence in the 1970s. In 1960, it was urged that the problem be quickly settled to obviate future difficulties between Sri Lanka and India. With the advent of Mrs Bandaranaike's first government the problem became acute, culminating in the 'Sirimavo-Shastri' pact of 1964, in which India agreed to take back half a million stateless Tamils in exchange for the Sri Lankan government extending citizenship to 300,000. By 1972 only 79,025 Tamils had been repatriated to India under the agreement, and

the 'Tamil problem' was even further from a solution; armed Tamil
secessionists began to be active in the same year. The economic importance
of Indians in Sri Lanka may be illustrated by the fact that with the continued
expulsions the production of tea has been disrupted; and in 1972 the Sri
Lankan government wanted to *import* 2,000 toddy tappers from Kerala due
to labour shortages caused by the expulsions! To the Sinhala, India's
proximity and history suggests that the Tamils in Sri Lanka are precursors
of Indian colonization.

In Burma, after 1947, of the 40,000 Indians who applied only 10,000
were granted citizenship, and in 1964, the Ne Win government took
unilateral action against overseas-Indians by nationalizing all retail and
wholesale trade. In the rapid exit of Indians that followed, the Indian
embassy acted as a repository for overseas-Indian assets — until the Burmese
government protested. Despite this, India reaffirmed its friendly relations
with the Burmese government, thus distinguishing people-to-people from
country-to-country relations. Six flights daily, as well as ships had been sent
to repatriate Indians in 1964 and up to 1970 Indian ships were sent to
Burma three times a year, but in 1971 overseas-Indians stormed their
embassy protesting at the slow rate of repatriation. By 1972, over 1,960,518
had been repatriated from Burma, joined by 2,300 from Mozambique and
3,000 from Nepal.

The expulsions of overseas-Indians from East Africa began in the 1970s.
Because many of them held British passports and elected to go to the UK and
Canada they did not represent such an acute problem for India. The
expulsion of all overseas-Indians from Uganda is well known; the revolution
in Ethiopia in 1976 displaced others, and in Kenya and Tanzania legislative
measures made the situation difficult; in Malawi, after issuing sanctions
against 'Asians' in 1970, all were expelled in 1978.

Other countries have acted similarly to a lesser degree. In 1967 Singapore
dismissed all Indian dockworkers and offered free passage to India to all
those who relinquished Singaporean citizenship and those who were stateless. In 1969, as race riots began in Malaysia so did an exodus to India. In
1970, Ghana's select expulsion of corrupt Indian and Lebanese businessmen
led to fears of wider expulsions.

The Indian government reaction to all this has been subdued, because
expulsions of overseas-Indians can be a liability to Indian state capitalism
abroad. Nothing is to be gained for India by taking a hard line, and the
feeling has been that once tempers cool and the presence of overseas-Indians
rationalized, they can resume their role as a great resource for India.

Socio-Cultural Organizations

While, after 1957, the Indian government largely disregarded overseas-Indians
and their potentialities, private organizations since then have sought to
promote Indian and overseas-Indian interests.

In 1945 the Indian National Overseas Congress was founded to discuss problems of overseas-Indians, and organized a convention in 1950. In 1951, the Malaysian Indian Congress called a conference of all overseas-Indians in South-east Asia; and in 1953 a two day conference was held in London by the Council for Indians Abroad.

In 1955, a tour of East Africa by S.K. Patil, the Congress Party leader, was sponsored by the Brihad Bharatiya Samaj, an organization committed to linking-up all overseas-Indians, and funded by Gujarati businessmen. An overseas-Indian centre in Bombay was built by this organization.

Other organizations have been set up with the aim of providing a link between overseas-Indians and India, such as the 'Jambo' club of Bombay; and in 1969 one writer urged the establishment of an institute for the study of overseas-Indians [N3]. In 1977, the Janata government helped sponsor a meeting of the Friends of India Society International that demanded a separate government department of overseas-Indian affairs. The Indian government has unofficially sponsored the founding of organizations and newspapers from time to time in certain places among overseas-Indian communities to build up a network of support and informal liaison. In Hongkong the Indian Chamber of Commerce was formed in 1950 at the behest of Joginder Singh, the Indian Trade Commissioner, and the India Association is recognized as the apex organization by the Indian High Commission, a pattern repeated in many countries [V1]. In the US in the early 1970s the Indian embassy was creating overseas-Indian organizations and newspapers for the same purposes.

Thus as Indian state capitalism expands its relations with developing countries, overseas-Indian populations will increasingly be drawn into the process, for the most part as an added asset. The position of these populations, determined by economic factors, will increasingly be linked with the economic imperatives of an Indian economy extending itself abroad in the fields of investment, aid, banking, contracts, technology transfer and insurance.

Notes

1. *Times*, 10 April 1955. This figure was repeated in 1967 in the *Hindu*, 4 September 1967.
2. *Indian and Foreign Review*, 15 September 1972.
3. *Hindu*, 1 September 1977 reported that 3,000 persons were issued with passports in the UAE to protect stateless Indians.
4. In 1979 a plan for an Overseas Indian Centre in New Delhi was being implemented.
5. These theories are highly Eurocentric and deal for the most part with transatlantic migration excluding the movement of slave labour.
6. It is a position they share with the more recent labour migrants in Europe (*gastarbeiter*), Latins in North America or Arabs to the Gulf.

Froebel, Heinrichs, and Kreye, 'The New International Division of Labour', *Social Science Information,* Vol. 11, No. 1, 1978; and Mervi Gustafsson, 'Migrant Workers of the Arab World', *Current Research on Peace and Violence*, Vol. 11, No. 1, 1979.

7. As long as the productive forces within India are not providing employment equitably to its labour or even of utilizing it, some will seek to go abroad. It is this, a question of unequal internal development in India and not population surplus which is at the heart of South Asian emigration.

8. Today many Indian based Chettiar companies are involved in industrial Joint Ventures in Malaysia.

9. Indian companies in Burma were: a Birla starch factory, Adamji Haji Dawood (later an important Pakistani industrial family) owned match factory, the Nath Singh Oil company, and the Jewanlal aluminium metalware factory [C2].

10. In Hongkong most Sindhi firms are not interested in moving away from trade and money-lending [V1].

11. Murray incorrectly classifies the Chandarias as a Kenyan multinational overlooking the primary importance of its overseas-Indian personality in which expansion abroad is predicated upon fear and a wish for quick profits outside Kenya. This then is opposed to the view that supposes that there would have been no difference in their expansion had they been Kenyan African.

12. In Bahrain, Indians and Pakistanis are the largest group. In Oman Indians are 50%, Pakistanis 36.6% of the total expatriate community. In Kuwait in 1965 there were 11,699 Indians or 4.7% of total foreigners. In 1970 17,336 or 4.4%; in 1975 32,105 or 6.1%. By that date in Kuwait Indians were fifth after Lebanese, Jordanians, Egyptians and Palestinians. The breakdown was 1.0% professionals, 9.0% technicians, 21.6% clerks, 12.9% semi-skilled, and 51.8% unskilled labour.

13. *Hindu*, 27 April 1976.

14. *Guardian*, 3 January 1978. Despite efforts at regulating the recruitment business, profits were so high and the resulting pay-offs to politicians so ubiquitous that several businessmen continued to make fabulous fortunes in 1980. In one agency (Interview, Bombay, 7 April 1980) the whole system of recruitment was formalized. Labourers were chosen like the slaves of old, having their hands placed in a vice to watch their endurance of pain and prospective candidates deliberately kept in the hot sun all day to test their stamina. Bricklayers are asked to identify different types of cement and engineers are given tests. The most preferred South Asian workers are said to be Sri Lankans, the most docile and the second lowest paid after Bangladeshis. These last are not liked so much by Gulf employers because of their penchant for organizing into groups and unions. Indian and Pakistani labour, while more highly paid, is easier to control and remains competitive because it is still cheaper than other Asian labour.

15. Reminiscent of the colonial commissioners for indentured labourers. *Hindu*, 1 March, 31 March 1978. In 1979 the cell in the Labour Ministry responsible for worker welfare abroad was dismantled. Interview, Ministry of Commerce, New Delhi, 21 January 1980.

16. *Indian Economic Diary*, 8–14 October 1973. This investment was to be up to Rs.500,000 in cash, Rs.100,000 in machinery to be channelled through the Indian Investment Centre.
17. *Hindu*, 12 June, 24 August 1975. External Deposit schemes in Indian banks abroad differ from straight remittances: the former has an investment potential, in India or abroad, the latter is utilized for consumption spending by relatives.
18. Indian films have an audience in Greece, West Africa, South-east Asia, East and West Africa, West Asia and the USSR. In 1965 the Indian film industry was producing films in Swahili. *Indo-African Trade Journal*, September 1965.
19. In Sierra Leone the Indian Mercantile Association was founded in 1966 to deal with African hostility. It instituted public relations programmes such as giving scholarships to Africans and engaging in civic improvements [M27].
20. This is particularly true of East African Asians holding British passports. In the early 1950s an Indian diplomat (Apa Pant) told them to take British passports. In the early 1960s they were urged by India to take local passports. The Indian government position has been that since most overseas-Indians took British passports it is a British problem.

8. Conclusion

Like many other ex-colonial countries India has sought to develop its own productive forces. This in turn has gradually led to India's increasing involvement in the economies, societies and politics of other developing countries. The ties developed with these countries are based on the internal structure of the Indian state, that is, its particular political economy. These overseas ties have been manifested through Indian aid programmes, contracts, Joint Venture investments, loans, grants, technology transfers, banking, insurance and the sale of military equipment. Studies of India's foreign relations, and by extension its foreign policy, have hitherto given insufficient recognition to these tangible forces and resulting ties.

The nature of the Indian system is important to an understanding of its relations abroad and the possible emergence of India as a proto-second-tier imperialist power. The development of Indian state capitalism is now stimulating it to look abroad for markets and resources, added to which, the ruling classes in India already share an ideology that sees India as a potentially great power. This combination of structure and perception has led India to build missile systems, computers, nuclear technology and a blue-water navy. The origin and nurturing of these perceptions can be traced both to the colonial period when India had already begun to act as a sub-imperial agent for Britain, and to the structure of the contemporary Indian state.

From the material presented in previous chapters, it is evident that any examination of Indian proto-second-tier imperialism, must be hedged with qualifications, one of which is geographical. Indian power has, as yet, been unable clearly to establish itself beyond South Asia, or in many cases even beyond its own borders within South Asia. While the structural ingredients for its expansion abroad exist, this thrust is not yet fully developed. In other words, India's second-tier imperialism is only at the 'proto' stage, that is, in a process of formation.

A crucial area in which this study remains incomplete is in balancing the analysis with the large body of published material which clearly shows India's continuing and overwhelming dependence on the industrialized world for finance, expertize and ultimately political support. How far India has transcended its links of dependence to the superpowers through its own state capitalist development is still a moot point. This is particularly important if we are to translate a political economic analysis of the Indian state to the study of India's foreign relations. India is unmistakeably prone to super-power pressures in determining its foreign policies and relations, yet at the same time, the autonomy it has exhibited in this field has been based on the degree of autonomous industrial development that it has achieved, not on its dependence.

Indian state capitalist development and relations abroad also help to illustrate the degree to which Indian overseas activity is related to domestic mass poverty. A major criticism of the present study may be that, while illustrating the panoply of Indian state and economic power overseas, it ignores the fact that India remains a poor country with many oppressed people. In answer to this, it is maintained here that the structures of power that the Indian state has built have actually been predicated upon growing numbers of impoverished people. In other words, as the Indian state has developed and a small class of people have gained benefits, this development has been at the expense of the majority of people in India. The fact that India contains numerous poor and oppressed people as well as pre-capitalist social formations is, however, an important constraint on its foreign relations and economic thrust abroad. Because the majority of the population continues to exist at below subsistence level, the Indian state can only mobilize its potential productive capacity up to a certain point. This is a fatal weakness for Indian state capitalist development and its outward expansion, as well as the ultimate future of its domestic development strategy. Nevertheless, this domestic mass poverty can, up to a point, act as an impetus for India's outward economic expansion. Mass poverty effectively creates a small domestic market which necessitates India's industries turning abroad. Many impoverished people in India are unable to gainfully use their labour, except in a marginal subsistence fashion due to archaic political, social and, in many rural areas, economic structures. Further, they act as an encumbrance on existing resources, which are reserved for the rich, and necessitate continued import of aid from the superpowers, thus keeping India in a dependent position. As long as India's ruling classes are unwilling to make such domestic, political and economic changes as would spell their own doom, this situation will continue. This continuing dependence imposes constraints on the Indian state, of which the most important is India's massive foreign debt. The constant threat of mass internal unrest which could abort India's new overseas ambitions is also a result of this continuing mass poverty and internal social oppression.

Nevertheless, through a unique combination of features — of size, scale, history and international position — and as a consequence of its industrial development thus far, the Indian state has emerged as a rising second-tier power, and perhaps in the future as a 'proto' imperialist.

State Capitalism: a Force for a Change

Much literature has emerged dedicated to the hypothesis that developing countries remain subordinate to the industrialized world through a myriad economic and political ties which keep them in a state of continual dependence. Just as this view has spawned a whole host of studies, in more recent years a second literature has emerged dedicated to refuting or at least drastically modifying, this view. This study could be characterized as a part of the latter school.

In the Third World today a number of states are graduating to a new stage of development. This has been sometimes grandly characterized as 'rising middle powers'. Without subscribing to this last hyperbole, there is nevertheless an undeniable change in the position of a number of Third World states. How did this come about?

If as dependency theorists propound, Third World states have remained bound in a subordinate fashion to the industrialized world, and without discarding completely many of the insights which dependency theory offers, how has it been possible for these states to change their position? The answer lies in the nature of their development and, in particular, the role which the state plays in each.

As we have seen in the Indian case it is the role of the state in its capitalist development, as a planner, owner and supporter, which lies at the heart of the process.

India ia not, as some have posited, either a pure bourgeois capitalist country nor a semi-feudal dependency of international monopoly capital. India is composed of a coalition of ruling classes, of big business, traders, money-lenders, landlords, kulaks, army and bureaucracy. This ruling class, utilizing the apparatus of the state, has built a type of capitalism which has brought them increased power and a degree of autonomy on the world stage.

Indian state capitalist development has gradually begun to expand abroad as it faces continual domestic stagnation and crisis; this has affected the entire gamut of India's relationships with the outside world. It is posited here that if the present system within India persists, then the present outward expansion will also persist, barring major international obstacles. This will be due not to any sinister plan, but more to the imperatives behind all capitalist expansion. Nor is India alone in this, other Third World states with large developing industrial economies, such as Brazil and South Korea, are also expanding abroad into the Third World, and also in the future might be characterized as proto-second-tier imperialist powers. State capitalism today is a fundamental force for change in contemporary international relations, particularly in the Third World.

Until recently the relations between the states of the developing world have been little explored. Because of the priority given throughout the developing world to the major international economic and political inequalities between the industrialized and the less-developed countries, assumptions of an undifferentiated Third World have often been made [R21].

In the West, in contrast, increasing emphasis is being placed on the growing differences among the developing countries, particularly the oil-rich and the non-oil producing states, in an effort to counter the organized presence of the 'Group of 77' on international economic issues. No doubt Western writers, and even more Western statesmen, have their own motives in highlighting these differences. None the less, it cannot be denied that a growing number of developing states are forming structural ties in their relations with one another which establish differences of interest and reward that may in the future become more significant than the problems they also share. For this reason the example of India has some relevance to an examination of an emerging pattern of intra-developing state, or 'South-South' relations.

In the past India has been seen by some observers as a test case of the development process itself. Similarly it may be worth considering the Indian experience as a model of the kind of relations with other Third World countries which are likely to develop at a particular historical stage. At the same time, India is unique in some respects, and in others can be compared only with China amongst the developing countries. The type of relations India is forging with developing countries may, however, give some indication of an emerging trend within the developing world. If, as is argued here, India is illustrative of such a trend, her experience may provide insights into the future pattern of relations which, particularly economically medium-sized states, may take vis-à-vis both the industrialized and the less developed world.

In every post-colonial state a certain set of productive forces was inherited at the time of independence. How these forces have been unleashed or developed (or constrained) since 1945 lies at the heart of these states' policies and relations with the outside world. In other words, the level and type of post-colonial development largely determines the role such states play in international affairs.

It is also true that the type of development is determined, to a large degree, by the external forces issuing from the industrialized world. Yet, for the larger post-colonial states that are 'newly-industrialized', their survival and future direction is no longer solely tied to the industrialized world, but are also increasingly linked to other developing countries. These 'newly-industrializing' states may develop such new ties to secure strategic raw materials to feed new industries, or basic commodities such as foodstuffs. Other developing countries may also serve as markets for the expanding manufactures of the newly industrializing states' own nascent industries, or as manufacturing sub-contract outposts due to even lower labour costs and access to Third World markets. This pattern, then, will not differ radically from that developed under traditional imperialism via the fully industrialized world.

In this manner, India's economic as well as political fortunes are increasingly tied to, and supplementing its links of dependency to the West and the USSR, a world that the government likes to characterize as 'co-developing'. India will in future seek to draw some of its sustenance from the developing countries as well as to sell many of its new goods and services there. Thus, the imperatives of India's own domestic political economy may translate themselves into the external political field with long term implications for all India's foreign relations. Rhetorical postures in international forums bear little resemblance to objective realities, which increasingly show India's changed position in international relations. Given new external interests, India is likely to share developed world positions on a number of issues in international affairs,[1] particularly in the economic field. Like them, and for similar political and economic reasons, India needs a Third World constituency, a group of states over which it can exercise a degree of influence; a need that will continue and become increasingly apparent as long as the Indian state continues to follow its current path of development.

The near universal goal of nurturing development in the Third World in the post-1945 period, particularly regarding industrialization, has had profound effects on international relations which are only beginning to be discerned. The urgency given by many governments to the professed goal of ameliorating poverty on a domestic and international scale is increasingly widespread. Paradoxically, as development continues, it has increased poverty levels as, simultaneously, certain sectors in individual national economies have prospered; development in fact exacerbates contradictions, both within the domestic and international spheres. This has its application to the study of international relations, where the 'dynamic' aspect, the observable facts of change, are brought about by these forces, thus refuting most international relations studies which adopt a static view of events.

Indian state capitalist development is dependent on the mobilization and continuous supply of resources. Wherever this process continues it needs to be fuelled by some other sector of a society/national economy on a domestic or international scale.

As long as equitable development does not occur in the domestic sphere unequal development will be extrapolated into situations where one state confronts another less developed than itself. The potential political gains of the relatively more, over the relatively less, developed state will manifest themselves through economic forces.

The transference of these realities of economic development to international relations has been little understood and as yet incompletely analyzed. Past and familiar assumptions in the study of international relations have prevented most writers from detecting the new changes constantly modifying the set patterns from which many assumptions are derived. This may seem an obvious tautology but one which has been often ignored. These new patterns must result in a reassessment of the image as well as the actual analysis of medium-sized states like India. This is not to suggest that the exercise pander to the Indian ruling classes' self image of a successful India. In any such reassessment the fact that India is continually beset by overwhelming mass poverty cannot be ignored, it is the very basis of its new, enhanced position.

Extent and Nature of Indian Influence

What we are searching for, therefore, is a political interpretation, using the concepts of Indian state capitalism and proto-second-tier imperialism to highlight India's ties with the developing world.

Bearing in mind that the essence of imperialism is control over another state or society, can we state that Indian proto-second-tier imperialism controls any other place beyond its own confines? Or can we state that as a concept proto-second-tier imperialism helps to explain the conduct of the Indian state in international relations? These questions can only be partially answered as the process on which they are based is as yet incomplete.

While preserving their primacy, notions of control that might apply to Indian proto-imperialism must encompass not just political and economic control, i.e. through the vehicle of capital export or political-military interference, but also through the far more subtle forms of technological and social control. Thus, through technological superiority, and at times by means of overseas-Indians, the Indian state can exercise some degree of influence in several developing countries, though this would not be immediately apparent if these relations were examined in light of classic Leninist definition of imperialism. Whether these cases actually constitute imperialistic control is another question.

In looking for places where India can be said to control the economic and political life we shall look in vain beyond Bhutan and Nepal, and even in these there are important qualifications. India's weaknesses are as important as its strengths in any examination like that presented here.

The clearest manifestations of Indian power, its shortcomings and strengths based on its internal development can be seen within South Asia. It is from neighbouring South Asian states that charges of Indian imperialism have most often been made in the past 35 years. Adhering to our analysis of the economic forces actuating the recent outward thrust of Indian state capitalism it becomes apparent that, where Indian influence has been exercised, it has been for a longer period than its recent state capitalist development, nor has India always sought immediate economic gains from some of these neighbours. Indian influence in small South Asian states is based more on colonial inheritance than on new economic dynamism; India's own economic infrastructure has only recently caught up with its older political-strategic influence in these states.

In the Himalayan states Indian influence can be seen most clearly. Arguably, by virtue of the Indian rupee ambit and control over most of their foreign trade, Nepal and Bhutan are already almost totally integrated into the Indian domestic economy, despite their efforts to diversify their trade.[2] Influenced by the legacy of the colonial period, India has followed a neo-colonial strategy of maintaining influence in its own sphere in these two states for perceived defence reasons. As the economies of Bhutan and Nepal develop, partly through Indian aid efforts (which bring advantages for the

Indian economy) they will be subjected to increasingly sophisticated forces of the Indian political and economic systems. Meantime, they are clearly part of the Indian economic, but not always political, orbit. Nepal represents India's fourth most important export market and a large proportion of Nepal's trade (80%) is solely with India which finds a widening trade gap each year. Bhutan does not enjoy even a modicum of autonomy in its national economy, being fully integrated into the Indian economy. This picture must be qualified, however, by the fact that both Nepal and Bhutan have, with some success, sought to diversify their dependence by seeking aid and ties with other countries in the international community, with a result that, with increasing success, both have asserted a separate political identity for themselves.

In Bangladesh, where charges against Indian control were most often made in the period immediately following secession from Pakistan, these could be partly supported by examining the record of loans and credits India gave Bangladesh in the period 1972–75. At the same time it is important to remember that Bangladesh, then as now was receiving much greater aid from international organizations and other fully industrialized countries. Following Mujib's assassination, as Bangladesh successfully switched to total dependence on the West, the Gulf states and to China, India's real ability to control events there was seen to be very small.

Sri Lanka and Pakistan have always entertained doubts about India's intentions in South Asia, focussing on what they see as its big power pretensions. What these fears may have overlooked is that if India exercises itself abroad in the future, it will do so because of the nature of its own development and economic power, and not solely from political aspirations.

Pakistan well illustrates how India's weaknesses militate against achievement of predominant power even within South Asia [B14]. Indian capital cannot hope to match the role of patron that some other Third World states, such as Saudi Arabia, now play in Pakistan. Additionally, Pakistan itself now plays an important second-tier role through the supply of its labour, technicians and military personnel, in several parts of the Arab world.

If Indian proto-second-tier imperialism has never fully emerged in South Asia this is because of its own continuing dependence and weaknesses, resulting in the repeated intercession of outside powers who can prevent the Indian state from exercising its full influence in the South Asian region. Whether this factor will continue to act as a brake in the future remains to be seen. Further complicating factors may be that external interests in South Asia may be perpetuated by new oil-rich Third World proxies.

India's growing naval presence in the Indian Ocean can be related to its growing defence industries, as well as to a desire that her future position might enable her to enter the markets of states bordering the Indian Ocean basin. As was seen earlier, Indian insurance mobilizes local capital equal to that of the central bank in Mauritius. Overseas-Indians there, as in other Indian ocean islands, afford India an ideal entry into these micro-states' political economies. This has already mildly manifested itself in Mauritius, the Maldives and Seychelles. Tanzania and India were performing joint security duties in the Seychelles in late 1980. Whether this becomes a type of proto-second-tier imperialism in the Indian Ocean remains to be seen. Two examples will suffice to show that any such characterization is premature. Firstly, Indian ability to project itself in the region can hardly match that of the superpowers with their steady build-ups of bases and naval forces in the area. Secondly, as the case of the Maldives shows, India often cannot match the superior financial power of other Third World patrons, in this case that of Libya, with whom it vies for influence in the island nation.

India's relations with the oil-rich states of the Middle East are more complex than those with other developing countries, as they illustrate potentially mutual interests as well as growing differentiations. On the one hand, through its superior skills, technological base and labour, India has some advantages over these states. On the other, the oil-rich states have superior capital, as well as oil resources, both of which India needs. Superficially then, there is here the complementarity of interest which UNCTAD co-operative rhetoric proclaims. Indeed, the quality of relations Indian state capitalism maintains with the oil-rich states is different from that with other developing countries; these are a source of cash remittances, an outlet for a small proportion of under-utilized Indian labour, and a field of business activity for India's under-utilized industries. However, if the nature of these states' national development is compared to India's, the long term advantages may lie with India rather than with the Middle East, despite their short-term advantages of oil and finance. A state must not only possess capital and resources (or access to them) but have the ability to reproduce this capital and, more importantly, the skills base and labour force upon which to utilize them effectively. How the oil-rich states meet this challenge in the future will have a bearing on their relationship with Indian state capitalism and its economic imperatives.

Indian state capitalism has, on occasion, sought to build relations of dependence with weak, developing economies of several African states. As markets for its goods, investment fields, banking expansion areas, or, as in Nigeria, capital rich states for massive contracts, India has been aware of the potential for its political and economic interests in Africa since the 1960s. Arguably arms sales or investment in South Africa or the presence of large numbers of overseas-Indians will jeopardize Indian efforts to gain influence in Africa, but in the long term this is debatable. India has also aided Southern African liberation movements, a policy that will achieve some political and economic advantages in the future. Through its aid activities (notably military) India has gained a measure of influence in several African states, such as Ghana, Nigeria, Ethiopia, Somalia, Zambia and Tanzania. Whether these will be translated into other, more concrete gains for the Indian system in the future remains to be seen. One factor will continue to inhibit Indian influence in Africa however, and this is competition both from the fully-industrialized world with its superior finance and technology, and the rivalry of newly-industrializing states such as South Korea and Brazil.

Because of its perceived historic ties South-east Asia has always been a special target for Indian political and economic interest. Add its overseas-Indian populations with their connections to India, and it can be seen as a natural area for Indian investment and economic expansion. In 1969, the Singapore Prime Minister openly expressed the desire for India to shoulder responsibilities in the region to offset possible threats from China. South-east Asia is also an obvious natural market and source of raw materials for India. As was seen in a previous chapter, in a minor way Indian companies are already involved in the political process in Malaysia, and Indian banks are investing in the political and economic stability of a number of governments in the region. While in the short term the Indian presence rests more lightly than that of the Japanese, Americans, Australians or overseas-Chinese, in future India may become increasingly involved in the region and exercise a degree of influence based on a tangible presence. The competition to be faced from Japanese, South Korean and, within the region, Singaporean economic and then political influence, might effectively keep India in fourth or fifth place for a long time to come.

Elsewhere in the developing world India, through its economic imperatives, will also attempt to build relations that formally are co-operative, but are at times unequal. Latin America presents an ideal field for Indian state capitalist activities with the resources, markets and investment opportunities that are found there. There are problems for India however, in the form of regionally based Third World rivals, namely, Brazil, Argentina, Mexico and Venezuela, who are also expanding in other countries of the region, as well as the economic and political activities of industrialized countries. It is, therefore, in the Caribbean and Central American states, with their smaller economies and in some cases overseas-Indians, which perhaps in the future will find themselves playing host to a growing Indian economic presence, and perhaps political interest. In Oceania India faces a similar situation with a basic foothold in the region through overseas-Indians in Fiji. Already in Tonga and Nauru, India has experimented with new forms of economic relations, but these are only in their beginning.

India's Third World Rivals

As already noted a key point to emerge in the analysis is the role that India's Third World rivals will play in the future. Such countries as Brazil, South Korea, Taiwan and Singapore have expanded their investment, aid and banking activities in many places in the Third World even more dramatically than has India. If, in accordance with sub-imperialist theory, we view these states as agents of an increasingly differentiated Western capitalism the question arises: Is the Indian case in any way different?

The answer suggested by the present study is tentative: India may be marginally different. The evidence for this, as many observers have noted, is that India has retained an autonomy in international relations despite its overall dependence; at the same time it is not clear just how secure this autonomy is. Possibly, for example, it may be forfeited in the future if Indian state capital integrates itself even more closely with Western capitalism or, alternatively, joins the Soviet bloc. Moreover, even if this does not occur, India will continue to be overshadowed by 'fast-developing' economies such as South Korea, Singapore and some of the oil-rich Arab states, all of which are currently investing in the Third World. In this case, only India's relative autonomy from the West will commend Indian aid and investment to Third World countries, and offset a competitive disadvantage it may have with other 'proto' imperialist states. At present these are only hypotheses, but it is clear that the concepts of sub-imperialism and proto-second-tier imperialism have not yet been fully tested. Only similar studies to this, conducted for countries such as South Korea, Argentina, Singapore, Brazil, Venezuela, Pakistan, Saudi Arabia, Libya, Algeria and Iraq will enable us to clearly establish whether the phenomenon of proto-imperialism exists in the Third World.

In the meantime, two questions arise in any comparison of the economic performance in Third World markets of the 'fast developing' countries and the more sluggish performance of India. First we must identify areas for comparison. In this study, for reasons set out earlier, it has been assumed that trade flows, viewed in isolation, provide an insufficient basis for understanding political economy [C7a]. Goods offered for export have to be manufactured, it is therefore the productive capacity of the national economy that we must analyse.

Second, how are we to establish the causes behind contemporary Third World expansion? A prime motive in all industrial expansion, private or state, is clearly to ensure the profitability and, therefore, the continued viability of an enterprise. In the face of an internal crisis threatening the long term viability of Indian industry Indian state capitalism has gone abroad in search of new markets, investments and profits. The nature of this crisis was stagnation of India's domestic market and thereby its industries [J6]. It might be argued that other state capitalist countries have expanded abroad without the impetus of similar stagnation at home, but this does not undermine the argument. What matters for comparative purposes is the size of the domestic market, this is determined not by population alone (India after all has a huge population) but by per capita income, and the nature and scope of the modern economy, as well as domestic political structures. In India an adequate potential market for its industries has not been mobilized, but remains stagnant for reasons outlined earlier. In other state capitalist countries the limitation of the domestic market may have other causes, but the resultant outward expansion is the same.

Real poverty in India, in which wide areas of the economy have not been fully integrated into the modern industrial sector, has no parallels in scale in either South Korea or Argentina, and can be found only on a much lesser scale in Brazil and Mexico. What we must consider in comparing the Indian experience with that of other developing countries is the nature of

India's economic development when compared to others and the basis and historical development of these economic systems. A brief examination of similar Third World states to India reveals unexpectedly strong resemblances. Except for Hongkong, the economic history of all the newly-industrializing countries of the Third World is characterized by substantial state intervention and ownership, particularly in the initial foundation period of their industrializations. This is contrary to the view that only a few Third World countries, such as Tanzania or Iraq, can be characterized as state capitalist. Yet using the definition that state capitalism means not simply intervention, but ownership of industrial enterprises, the definition can still be sustained in the cases of Brazil and South Korea, for example. The point of departure may occur where the rate of state divestment of these enterprises eventually outstrips its development of new enterprises, obscuring its earlier predominant role.

Before examining the similarities between the newly-industrializing states of the Third World it is important to note an important difference between India and the 'success stories' of South Korea, Taiwan and Singapore. In his wide-ranging comparative study Chenery found that the early stage of industrialization was invariably one of state capital investment, and in several cases, of substantial foreign private investment too. In his view the input of foreign capital eased domestic consumption demands at a time when the expansion of the industrial base was putting pressure on domestic savings.[3] The Indian case is different. It is well established that due to mass poverty in India, the propensity to save is much lower than in South Korea, and the tendency to consume is very high, thus putting a great strain on existing resources. In addition, while India has lagged far behind the other 'newly industrializing' economies in attracting foreign capital for industry, this has actually been an indication of India's different position in international relations, that is, its autonomy and lower level of integration with international capital and the Western system generally. In so far as it has relied on foreign capital, India's industrial base has certainly gained from Western technology imported under technical agreements, but the development of most of its public sector industries (and of its heavy industry) it has relied on Soviet, not Western aid. Thus, a difference between India and some other comparable countries lies in their differing political positions. Much initial foreign capital input in Brazil and South Korea was available in the form of cheap Western loans. By contrast, India's dependence on foreign aid, which it received from both camps, was diversified and not always targetted towards industrialization. Much of the Western aid given to India has been for subsistence needs, food etc. Because South Korea and Brazil were more completely integrated into the Western alliance system they had the support of Western donors and were guaranteed a continuous flow of new investment capital for industry.

In other respects, India fits a general pattern in Third World industrialization. As in India, the recent growth of South Korean industry that is now beginning to extend itself abroad, had its roots in a much earlier period.

Despite the destruction occasioned by war, and the suffering imposed on the Korean people by the Japanese during their colonial occupation, Japan built an impressive infrastructure, an industrial base to suit their own imperial needs. Between 1933–39 there was an 80% growth in industry in Korea, mostly in mining (one-third of all industries), textiles, fertilizers, machine tools, ceramics and chemicals. The rail and port systems were the second most extensive in Asia.[4] After the Korean war southern industry survived the bifurcation of the country and the loss of the concentrated industrial belt in the north. Under the American occupation Japanese industrial assets were vested in public corporations and, during the administration of Syngman Rhee which followed, respectable growth levels began to be reached as the state took upon itself the role of building up industry and, to some degree, encouraging import substitution. Land reforms and mass education were also a feature of the 1950s. By the advent of the Park Government in 1962, the basic features of Korean development were already well established. At that stage they did not include sizable manufactured exports as a development 'strategy'. Indeed, the Park Government increased rather than decreased state intervention and ownership in the economy; it was only after the Second Plan was launched in 1966 that import substitution gave way to a deliberate policy to expand manufactured exports. And only after 1966 too, did the South Korean government begin to divest itself of industries which it had built and owned, for example; Inchon Heavy Industry, Dai Han Iron Mining, Han Kuk Mining, Korea Airlines, Korea Express etc., only to turn to building new even more strategic industries in the ship-building, petro-chemical and defence sectors. The Government also actively encouraged the formation of huge Japanese-style industrial and trading corporations to help extend the Korean economic presence abroad. As in the Indian case, some authorities have also argued that defence industries and spending have helped to stimulate growth in the Korean economy again, often irrespective of general welfare considerations.

It would appear on the basis of preliminary investigations, the South Korean case is not so radically different from India. The South Korean government has continuously intervened to foster growth, and market forces have often played a relatively minor role. A deliberate policy decision was taken for South Korea to expand its exports, but this in itself was not the foundation for its growth. Korea is a highly planned economy, with a hierarchy of formalized structures beginning with the Economic Ministers Conference, the Economic Science Council, the Office of Planning and Co-ordination and finally the Economic Planning Board itself. When allowance is made, as it must, for political differences, global position and history, the Korean analogy offers many useful insights to the understanding of India's own state capitalist development.

Brazil, which is the subject of a growing volume of literature, presents even more striking parallels with India. In some ways the success of Brazil over the last few years in thrusting itself overseas has been a measure of its more advanced vertical integration into the international capitalist system. As in India, Brazil was originally integrated horizontally, i.e. as a recipient market for manufactures and a source of raw materials for the industrialized world. The pace of its movement away from this horizontal role to become the supplier of intermediate manufactures, has taken place much more rapidly than has India's. As in South Korea, the period of fast growth, 'export led' in Brazil was preceded by a period of heavy state intervention to build an industrial base, starting in the 1930s under President Vargas. Of this first period of industrialization, Faucher[5] states that growth was slowed by the limits set by the nature of the domestic economy which state capitalism could only partially remedy. Between 1956–61 the development of state capitalism was continued in Brazil by the Kubitschek Government when planned targets were drawn up for the establishment of heavy industries. Even after the military regime installed itself in 1964 the state maintained a strong guiding hand in the economy, and indeed tightened this hold after 1965. In 1974, of 5,113 of the most important companies, 37% were state owned, 15% belonged to multinational corporations, and 48% were in the private sector. State investment also exceeded private sector investment during this entire period (mid-1960s to mid-1970s). Some examples of government industrial ownership are found in the fields of steel, oil and electricity as well as the development bank (BNDE). Thus, although the Brazilian state has been more dynamic than the Indian state with regard to both the import and export of capital, the basis of its economic development and foreign expansion have been quite similar. Namely, state capitalism, finding itself in conditions of restricted domestic demand, therefore goes abroad. Brazil's domestic economy is too small to sustain by itself the massive industrial base which the state has sponsored, nor will this feature change as long as Brazil takes no steps to change, for example, the conditions of its impoverished north-east. Like India then, the defining factor in Brazil's present expansion abroad has been the nature of its development.

It seems clear, therefore, even on the basis of a cursory investigation that there are distinct and shared elements among all those 'newly industrializing' Third World countries that are currently expanding into other Third World markets. This in turn is a part of a growing pattern of 'South-South' relations, the political effects of which have not yet been properly studied. India is not the only country whose particular economic development experience has ultimately led in its own small way to wider repercussions on the whole range of international relations. Many other Third World states, based on their own development, are also beginning to forge unequal relations with their lesser developed brethren.

Perhaps one of the most important impacts which India's growing relations with developing countries may have, is the challenge they may present to India's existing relationships to the industrialized world.

If through its own development, the Indian system continues to autonomously seek outlets abroad for its economic institutions, it will inevitably draw itself into conflict with established economic power centres in the developed world. In the short term, this will lead to a degree of autonomy, but in the longer term perhaps to attempts by the industrialized world to co-opt or rein-in the Indian state in order to make India once more a subservient agent, lest it upset present international patterns of relations. India's manpower, army, industries, expertize, even to some extent its capital, could then be used to play a direct supporting role to a superpower which sub-imperialist theory suggests; so far this has not occurred. Perhaps because the superpowers are in contention, allowing India a place for manoeuvre, as well as the non-recognition with which Indian capabilities have been received. Undeniably, the Indian state does enjoy some autonomy on the world stage. In recent years more explicit backing of Indian ambitions has been given by the Soviet Union, and this may help India play a more active political and economic role. This will come about not solely through superpower sponsorship, but also based on the tangible political and economic weapons it has been able to develop. Only internal upheaval in India is likely to abort this process.

In conclusion, Indian proto-second-tier imperialism is only in process of formation. While India exercises forms of influence in a few states, this does not extend beyond the confines of South Asia where a colonial inheritance is at work. Nevertheless, India is increasingly involved in the local political and economic structures of a number of developing countries, not all of which are found within South Asia. This involvement may eventually lead it (in some cases unwittingly, as the business activities of Indian companies abroad show) to exercise mild forms of influence in other developing countries.

What this study has sought to demonstrate is that there are a wide variety of forces operating within the Indian state which give rise to a growing structure of power, based on economic structures that have been built through state capitalism. These structures, and the forces they give rise to, are important in assisting our understanding of India's foreign relations.

In this sense, India's development and its new economic relations with other developing countries, provide an insight into the way the growth of state capitalism in the Third World is changing the face of international relations.

Notes

1. 'Capital to Export', *Economic and Political Weekly*, 25 November 1978.
2. Caroe, Olaf. 'The Mongolian Fringe', minute, *India Office Records*, Political and Secrets Department, Collections 38/4, 44/5 L/P&S/12/ 4369. He wrote in 1946 that the Himalayan states should be irrevocably tied to India through economic means. Interestingly Indian political influence has sometimes lagged behind economic realities, perhaps due to its weaknesses. It must also be clearly stated that the more modern

aspects of India's current economic thrust abroad in the fields of Joint Ventures, banking, etc. have been severely lacking in these states.

3. Chenery, Hollis. *Patterns of Development: 1950–1970*, Washington, 1970 and *The Changing Composition of Developing Country Exports*, Washington, 1979.

4. Grajdanzev, Andrew J. *Modern Korea*, New York, 1944. George M. McCune and Arthur L. Grey, *Modern Korea*, Cambridge, 1950.

5. Faucher, P. 'Industrial Policy in a dependent state: The case of Brazil', *Latin American Perspectives*, Issue No. 24, Vol. 7, No. 1, Winter 1980.

Glossary of Abbreviations

ADB	Asian Development Bank
ASEAN	Association of Southeast Asian Nations
BHEL	Bharat Heavy Electricals Ltd.
CFTC	Commonwealth Fund for Technical Cooperation
DANJAK	Indian Roadbuilding Mission — Bhutan
ECAFE	Economic Council Asia and the Far East
ECDC	Economic Cooperation among Developing Countries
ECGC	Export Credit and Guarantee Corporation
ECLA	Economic Commission for Latin America
EPIL	Engineering Projects India Ltd.
ESCAP	Economic and Social Council for Asia and the Pacific
FICCI	Federation of Indian Chambers of Commerce and Industry
FIEO	Federation of Indian Export Organizations
HAL	Hindustan Aeronautics Ltd.
TAEA-TAP	International Atomic Energy Agency-Technical Assistance Programme
IBRD	International Bank for Reconstruction and Development
ICICI	Industrial Credit and Investment Corporation of India
IDBI	Industrial Development Bank of India
IFC	Industrial Finance Corporation
	International Finance Corporation (World Bank)
IIFT	Indian Institute of Foreign Trade
IMTRAT	Indian Military Training Team — Bhutan
IRC	Indian Road Construction Ltd.
IRCI	Industrial Reconstruction Corporation of India
ITEC	Indian Technical and Economic Cooperation
LIC	Life Insurance Corporation of India
MITI	Ministry of International Trade and Industry (Japan)
MIC	Malaysian Indian Congress
MRTP	Monopolies and Restrictive Trade Practices Act
NACE	National Association of Consulting Engineers
NEP	New Economic Policy (USSR-1920s, Malaysia-1970s)
NIDC	National Industrial Development Corporation
NRDC	National Research Development Corporation

OECD	Organization of Economic Cooperation and Development
ONGC	Oil and Natural Gas Commission
PDRY	Peoples Democratic Republic of Yemen (Aden)
PLO	Palestine Liberation Organization
RCD	Regional Cooperation for Development
RBI	Reserve Bank of India
RITES	Railways India Technical Economic Services
SBI	State Bank of India
SCI	Shipping Corporation of India
SCAP	Supreme Commander of the Allied Powers (Japan)
SCAAP	Special Commonwealth Africa Assistance Plan
SWAPO	South-West Africa Peoples Organization
TASF	Technical Assistance Special Plan (IBRD)
TCDC	Technology Cooperation among Developing Countries
UNCTAD	United Nations Conference for Trade and Development
UNDP	United Nations Development Programme
UNIDO	United Nations Industrial Development Organization
WAPCOS	Water and Power Development Consultancy Services Ltd.

Bibliography

A1   Abbott, George C., *International Indebtedness and The Developing Countries*. London, 1979.

A2   Acharya, Gopal, 'Export of Indian Capital: Real Import', *Marxist Review*, Vol. 10, No. 1, July 1976.

A3   Acheson, Dean, *Present at the Creation*. New York, 1972.

A4   Adloff, R. and V. Thompson, *The Malagasy Republic*. Stanford, 1965.

A5   Agarwal, Vinod, *Initiative, Enterprise and Economic Choices in India*. New Delhi, 1975.

A6   Agmon, Tamir and Charles Kindleburger (eds.), *Multinationals from Small Countries*. Cambridge, 1977.

A7   Aharoni, Yair, *Foreign Investment Decision Process*. Boston, 1966.

A8   Alagh, Yoginder K., 'Indian Industrialization: Fact and Fiction', *Economic and Political Weekly*, Special No., July 1971.

A9a   Alavi, Hamza, 'Indian Capitalism and Foreign Imperialism', *New Left Review*, No. 37, May–June 1966.

A9b   ——— 'The State in Post-Colonial Societies: Pakistan and Bangladesh', *New Left Review*, No. 74, July–August 1972.

A9c   —— 'India and the Colonial Mode of Production', *The Socialist Register*, 1975.

A10   Amin, Samir, *Accumulation on a World Scale*. New York, 1974.

A11   Andrus, J. Russel, *Burmese Economic Life*. London, 1948.

A12   Anstey, Vera, *The Economic Development of India*. London, 1936.

A13   Arasaratnam, Sinnapah, *Indians in Malaysia and Singapore*. London, 1970.

B1   Bagchi, A.K., 'Some International Foundations of Capitalist Growth and Underdevelopment', *Economic and Political Weekly*, Special No. Vol. 7, No. 31–32, 1972.

B2   Bagchi, S.K., 'Trade Development in South Asia', *Foreign Trade Review*, No. 5, Vol. 9, April–June 1975.

B3   Bajpai, O.P., *Life Insurance Finance in India*. Varanasi, 1975.

B4   Balakrishnan, K., 'Indian Joint Ventures Abroad: Geographic and Industry Patterns', *Economic and Political Weekly*, 9 May 1976.

B5   Balsekar, R.S., 'Roles of Indian Banks Abroad', *Commerce*, 1 March 1969.

B6   Banerjee, Datta, Dayal and Mathur (eds.), *Dynamics of Formulating Policy in Government of India Machinery for Policy Development*. New Delhi, 1974.

B7   Banerji, Ranadev, *Exports of Manufactures from India: An Appraisal of the Emerging Pattern*. Tubingen, 1975.

B8   Barman, Kiran, *India's Public Debt and Policy since Independence*. Allahabad, 1978.

B9a   Barrat-Brown, Michael, *Essays on Imperialism*. London, 1972.

B9b   —— *The Economics of Imperialism*. London, 1974.

B10   Basu, Saraj Kumar, *A Review of Current Banking Theory and Practice*. London, 1974.

B11   Bauer, P.T., *Indian Economic Policy and Development*. New York, 1961.

B12   Becker, James F., *Marxian Political Economy: An Outline*. London, 1977.

B13   Beguin, Jean-Pierre (ed.), *Joint International Business Ventures in Developing Countries*. New York, 1971.

B14   Benoit, Emile, *Defense and Economic Growth in Developing Countries*. Lexington, 1973.

B15   Bergman, Theodor, *Development Models of India, Soviet Union and China*. Amsterdam, 1978.

B16   Berman, R.S., 'Natural Resources: State ownership and control Based on Article 180 of the Revised Constitution', *Journal of Ethiopian Law*, 1966.

B17a   Bettelheim, Charles, *India Independent*. London, 1968.

B17b   —— *The Transition to Socialist Economy*. Hassocks, 1975.

B17c   —— *Economic Calculation and Forms of Property*. London, 1976.

B18a   Bharati, Aghenanda, 'Indians in East Africa: A Survey of Problems of Transition and Adaptation', *Sociologus*, 14, 1964.

        —— 'The Unwanted Elite of East Africa: An Indian Minority's Wealth and sense of superiority stir African Resentment in Kenya, Uganda, Tanzania', *TransAction*, July–August 1966.

B19   Bhatia, Prem, *Indian Ordeal in Africa*. Delhi, 1973.

B20   Bhatt, Trikamlal A., *A Biographical Sketch of Indians in Africa*. Nairobi, 197?.

B21   Bhatt, V.M., 'Indian Investment and Collaboration in Foreign Countries', *Industrial Development of India: Policy and Problems*, Editor, C.N. Vakil, New Delhi, 1973.

B21a   Bhattacharya, Debesh, 'A Critical Survey of Indian Planning and its Achievements', *Journal of Contemporary Asia*, Vol. 3, No. 2, 1973.

B21b   —— 'Development and Technology in the Third World', *Journal of Contemporary Asia*, Vol. 6, No. 3, 1976.

B22   Bhattacharya, Sauripada, *Pursuit of national interests through Neutralism: India's Foreign Policy in the Nehru Era*. Calcutta, 1978.

B23   Bhattasali, B.N., *Transfer of Technology Among the Developing Countries*. Tokyo, 1972.

B24   Birks, J.S. and C.A. Sinclair, 'The International Migration Project: An Enquiry Into the Middle East Labor Market', *International*

Migration Review, Vol. 13, Spring 1979.

B25   Blackburn, Robin (ed.), *Ideology in Social Science*. New York, 1972.

B26   Boulding, K. and T. Mukerjee, *Economic Imperialism*. Ann Arbor, 1972.

B27   Bounkina, M., 'Inter-imperialist contradictions at the present stage', *International Affairs*, No. 9, 1974.

B28   Bozeman, G.S., 'The Future of Indians Overseas', *Indian Institute of International Affairs*, Paper No. 9, New Delhi, 1943.

B29   Braun, Dieter, 'Changes in South Asian Intra-regional and external relationships', *The World Today*, October 1978.

B30   Braunmuhl, Claudia von, 'On the Analysis of the Bourgeois Nation State within the world market context. An Attempt to Develop a Methodological and Theoretical Approach', *State and Capital*, Editors, John Holloway and Sol Picciotto, London, 1978.

B31   Brecher, Michael, *Nehru: A Political Biography*. New York, 1966.

B32   Bowles, Chester, *Ambassadors Report*. New York, 1954.

B33   Brown, Richard, *The Theory of Unequal Exchange: The End of the Debate?*, ISS Occasional Papers No. 65, Hague, 1978.

B34   Buchanan, Daniel Houston, *The Development of Capitalistic Enterprise in India*. New York, 1934.

B35   Buick, A., 'The Myth of the Transitional Society', *Critique*, No. 5, 1975.

C1   Caldwell, Malcolm, *The Wealth of Some Nations*. London, 1978.

C2   Chakravarti, Nalini Kumar, *Indians in Burma*. London, 1971.

C3   Chandra, Bipin, 'The Indian Capitalist Class and Imperialism Before 1947', *Journal of Contemporary Asia*, Vol. 5, No. 3, 1975.

C4a   Chattopadhyay, Paresh, 'State Capitalism in India', *Monthly Review* March 1970.

C4b   —— 'On the Political Economy of the Transition Period', *Economic and Political Weekly*, Special No., July 1971.

C5a   Chattopadhyay, P., 'Joint Ventures Abroad: A Policy Needed', *Indo-African Trade Journal*, Vol. 7, No. 11–12, November–December 1971.

C5b   —— 'Scrutinising the Accounts of Joint Ventures Abroad', *Capital*, 9 September 1976.

C6   Chaudhuri, Asim, *Private Economic Power in India*. New Delhi, 1975.

C7a   Chaudhuri, Pramit, *Aspects of Indian Economic Development*. London, 1971.

C7b   —— 'A Note on the Irrelevance of Trade', *Economic and Political Weekly* Annual, 1976.

C8   Chawla, Sudershan, *The Foreign Relations of India*. Encino, 1976.

C9   Chelliah, R.J., 'Tax potential and Economic Growth . . . in the ECAFE Region', *Economic Bulletin for Asia and Far East*, Vol. 17, No. 2, September 1966.

C10   Cheng, Siok-hwa, *The Rice Industry of Burma: 1852–1940*. Singapore, 1968.

C11   Chettiar, R.N., 'Role of Indian Banks in Singapore', *Commerce*,

13 December 1969.

C12   Chhabra, H.S., 'India's Economic Co-operation with Developing Countries', *Indo-African Trade Journal*, Vol. 8, No. 11-12, November–December 1972.

C13   Childers, Erskine, 'Technical Co-operation Among Developing Countries: History and Prospects', *Journal of International Affairs*, Vol. 33, No. 1, Spring–Summer 1979.

C14a   Chishti, Sumitra, 'India's Economic Co-operation with Developing Countries', *Foreign Trade Review*, April–June 1973.

C14b   —— 'India's Foreign Economic Policy', *Indian Foreign Policy*, Editor, Bimal Prasad, New Delhi, 1979.

C15   Chopra, Maharaj K., 'India's Oil Strategy and its Consequences', *AussenPolitik*, 2nd Quarter, 1977.

C16   Choucri, Nazli, 'The New Migration in the Middle East: A Problem for whom?', *International Migration Review*, Vol. 11, No. 4, Winter 1977.

C17   Claessen, Henri J.M. and Peter Skalnik (eds.), *The Early State*. Hague, 1978.

C18   Clark, Eric, *Corps Diplomatique*. London, 1973.

C19   Clarke, Simon, 'Capital, Fractions of Capital and the State. A Neo-Marxist Analysis of the South African State', *Capital and Class*, No. 5, Summer 1978.

C20   Clarkson, Stephen, *The Soviet Theory of Development: India and the Third World in Marxist–Leninist Scholarship*. Toronto, 1978.

C21   Cliffe and Saul (eds.), *Socialism in Tanzania*. Dar es Salaam, 1973.

C22   Conant, Charles A., 'The Economic Basis of Imperialism', *North American Review*, September 1898.

C23   Connelly, P. and Robert Perlman, *Resource Conflicts in International Relations*. New York, 1975.

C24   Cornelius, W.A. and F.M. Trueblood, *Latin American Urban Research 5*. London, 1976.

C25   Crane, Robert (ed.), *Aspects of Political Mobilization in South Asia*. Syracuse, 1976.

D1   Dagli, Vadilal, *Natural Resources in the Indian Economy*. Bombay, 1971.

D2   Dalal, K.C., 'Indian Technical and Economic Co-operation', *Foreign Trade Review*, March–June 1975.

D3   Dalaya, Chandra, *The External Debt of the Government of India*. Bombay 1970.

D4   Dar, Usha and Pratap, K., *Investment Opportunities in ASEAN Countries*. New Delhi, 1979.

D5   Das Gupta, Jyotirindra, 'A Season of Caesars: Emergency regimes and development politics in Asia', *Asian Survey*, April 1978.

D6   Das, Nabagopal, *The Indian Economy under Planning*. Calcutta, 1972.

D7   Dasgupta, Diplab, *The Oil Industry in India*. London, 1971.

D8   Davey, Brian, *The Economic Development of India*. Nottingham, 1975.

D9   Dayal, Ishwar, *Dynamics of Formulating Policy in Government of India, Machinery for Political Development*. Delhi, 1976.

D10   Dedijer, Vladimir (ed.), *Spheres of Influence in the Third World*. Nottingham, 1973.

D11   Delf, George, *Asians in East Africa*. London, 1963.

D12   'Dependency in the Global System', issue of *International Organization*, Winter 1978.

D13   Desai, Meghnad, 'Vortex in India', *New Left Review*, No. 61, May–June 1970.

D14   Desai, V.R. Mutalik, *Banking Development in India*. Bombay, 1967.

D15   Deshmukh, C.D., *Economic Developments in India 1946-56*. Bombay, 1957.

D16   Deutscher, Isaac, 'Roots of Bureaucracy', *The Socialist Register*, 1969.

D17   Diaz-Alejandro, Carlos F., 'Foreign Direct Investment by Latin Americans', *Multinationals from Small Countries*, Editors, T. Agmon and C. Kindleberger, Cambridge, 1977.

D18   *Directory of Foreign Collaborations in India* (2 Vols.). New Delhi, 1974.

D19   Dore, Ronald, *Shinohata*. New York, 1978.

D20   Dotson, F. and Lillian O., *The Indian Minority of Zambia, Rhodesia and Malawi*. New Haven, 1968.

D21   Dubashi, J., *Perspectives for India's Trade with Developing Countries*. New Delhi, 1966.

D22   Dumont, Louis, *Homo Hierarchus*. London, 1970.

D23   Dutta, Amlan, *Perspectives of Economic Development*. London, 1973.

D24   Dutt, Rajani Palme, *India Today*. London, 1940.

E1   Elliot, Charles, *Patterns of Poverty in the Third World*. New York, 1975.

E2   Elliot, David, *Thailand: The Political Economy of Underdevelopment*. London, 1977.

E3a   Emmanuel, Arghiri, *Unequal Exchange*. London, 1972.

E3b   —— 'Myths of Development versus Myths of Underdevelopment', *New Left Review*, No. 85, May–June 1974.

F1   Fanon, Frantz, *The Wretched of the Earth*. London, 1967.

F2   Frank, Andre Gundar, *Capitalism and Underdevelopment in Latin America*, New York, 1967.

F3a   Frankel, Francine, *India's Green Revolution*, Princeton, 1972.

F3b   —— *India's Political Economy 1947-1977: The Gradual Revolution*, Princeton, 1978.

F4   Friedmann, W.C. (ed.), *Joint International Business Ventures in Developing Countries*, New York, 1971.

F5   Froebel, Heinrichs and Kraye, 'The New International Division of Labour', *Social Science Information*, Vol. 11, No. 1, 1978.

G1a   Galtung, Johann, 'A Structural Theory of Imperialism', *Journal of*

Peace Research, Vol. 13, No. 2, 1971.

G1b   Galtung, Johann, 'Social Imperialism and sub-imperialism', *World Development*, March 1976.

G2   Ganguli, B.N., *Integration of International Economic Relations*, New Delhi, 1968.

G3a   Ghai, Yash P. and Dharam P., *Portrait of a Minority: Asians in East Africa*, Nairobi, 1965.

G3b   —— *The Asian Minorities of East and Central Africa*, Minority Rights Group Report No. 4, London, 1971.

G4   Ghosh, Alak, *Indian Economy, Its Nature and Problems, A New Look at Indian Economics*, Calcutta, 1976.

G5   Gillion, K.L., 'The Sources of Indian Emigration to Fiji', *Population Studies* 10, 1956.

G6   Goldman, Marshal I., *Soviet Foreign Aid*, New York, 1967.

G7   Gopal, Madan, *India as a World Power*, Delhi, 1948.

G8   Gough, Kathleen, 'Imperialism in South Asia', *Monthly Review*, March 1972.

G9   Gregg, Davis M. and Dan M. McGill (eds.), *World Insurance Trends*, Philadelphia, 1959.

G10   Grow, Roy F., 'Soviet Economic Penetration of China, 1945–1960: Imperialism as a Level of Analysis Problem', *Testing Theories of Economic Imperialism*, Editors, S.J. Rosen and J.R. Kurth, Lexington, 1974.

G11   Guha, Amalendu, 'The Compradore Role of the Parsi Seths, 1750–1850', *Economic and Political Weekly*, 28 November 1970.

G12   Guha, Partha Subir, *Bibliography of publications from Economic Research Centres*, Calcutta, 1974.

G13   Gupta, Alka, *India and UN Peacekeeping Activities: A Case Study of Korea 1947-53*, New Delhi, 1977.

G14a   Gupta, Anirudha (ed.), *Indians Abroad: Asia and Africa. Report of International Seminar*, New Delhi, 1971.

G14b   —— 'India's Overseas Children', *Third World*, Vol. 1, No. 3, November 1972.

G15   Gupta, Shyam Ratna (ed.), *India: A Study in Futurism*. New Delhi, 1976.

G16   Gupta, Sisir, 'Foreign Policy for the Seventies', *India: A Study in Futurism*, Editor, S.R. Gupta, New Delhi, 1976.

G17   Gustafsson, Mervi, 'Migrant Workers of the Arab World', *Current Research on Peace and Violence*, Vol. 11, No. 1, 1979.

H1   Halliday, J., *Political History of Japanese Capitalism*, New York, 1977.

H2   Halliday, J. and G. McCormack, *Japanese Imperialism Today*, London, 1972.

H3   Handa, Rohit, *Policy for India's Defence*. New Delhi, 1976.

H4   Harris, F.R., *Jamsetji Nusserwanji Tata: A chronicle of His Life* (2nd Edition). Bombay, 1958.

H5   Hasan, Masood, *India's Trade Relations with Rupee Payment Countries*. Aligarh, 1972.

H6   Hayter, Teresa, *Aid as Imperialism*. London, 1972.

H7a   Hazareesingh, K., 'The Religion and Culture of Indian Immigrants in Mauritius and the Effect of Social Change', *Comparative Studies in Society and History* 8, 1966.

H7b   —— *History of Indians in Mauritius*. London, 1975.

H8   Heenan, D.A. and W.J. Keegan, 'The Rise of Third World Multi-nationals', *Harvard Business Review*, January–February 1979.

H9   Hobson, John A., *Imperialism: A Study*. (2nd Edition), London, 1968.

H10   Hollingsworth, L.W., *The Asians of East Africa*. London, 1960.

H11   Holloway, John and Sol Picciotto (eds.), *State and Capital*. London, 1978.

H12   Hymer, Stephen, 'The Multinational Corporation and the Law of Uneven Development', *International Firms and Modern Imperialism*, Editor, H. Radice, London, 1975.

I1   Ince, Basil A., 'Race and Ideology in the Foreign Relations of Independent Guyana', *East Indians in the Caribbean* Conference Proceedings, University of the West Indies, St. Augustine, 1975.

I2   'India in Africa', *New African*, October 1979.

I3   'Indian Capital Abroad', *Economic Weekly*, 31 October 1964.

I4   'India Re-emergent', *Banker*, January 1977.

I5   'India as a World Power', *Foreign Affairs*, Vol. 27, No. 4, July 1949.

I6   *India and the UN*, Indian Council of World Affairs (2nd Edition), Westport, 1974.

I7a   Institute of Asian Economic Affairs, *Intra-regional co-operation and Aid in Asian Countries*. Tokyo, 1968.

17b   —— *Asia's Economic Growth and Intra-regional Co-operation*. Tokyo, 1967.

I8   Irfan Habib, *The Agrarian System in Mughal India 1556–1767*. Aligarh, 1963.

I9   Ito, Shoji, 'On the basic nature of the investment company in India', *Developing Economies*, September 1978.

J1   Jain, J.P., *Nuclear India*. (2 vols.). New Delhi, 1974.

J2   Jaipaul, Rikhi, 'Indian Nuclear Explosion', *International Security* Spring 1977.

J3   Jalee, Pierre, *Pillage of the Third World*. New York, 1968.

J4   Jannuzi, F. Tomasson, *Agrarian Crisis in India: The Case of Bihar*. Austin, 1974.

J5   Jaura, Ramesh, 'The Malaysian Way', *Economic and Political Weekly*, 17 June 1978.

J6   Jha, Shiva Chandra, *Studies in the Development of Capitalism in India*. Calcutta, 1963.

J7   Jomo, K.S., 'Restructuring Society: The New Economic Policy Revisited', unpublished paper, Fakulti Ekonomican Pengurusan, University Kebangsaan, Malaysia.

K1a   Kalecki, Michael, *Selected Essays on the Economic Growth of the Socialist and the Mixed Economy*. London, 1972.

K1b   Kalecki, Michael, *The Last Phase in the Transformation of Capitalism*. London, 1972.

K2   Karkal, Gopal Linga, *Perspectives in Indian Banking*. Bombay, 1977.

K3   Kashkari, Chaman, *Energy Resources, Demand and Conservation*. New Delhi, 1975.

K4   Kaul, T.N., 'India's Economic Co-operation with Developing Countries', *Foreign Trade Review*, January–March 1973.

K5   Kay, G., *Development and Underdevelopment: A Marxist Analysis*. London, 1971.

K6a   Kidron, Michael, *Foreign Investment in India*. London, 1965.

K6b   —— *Capitalism and Theory*. London, 1974.

K7a   Kobayashi, Ushisaburo, *War and Armament Taxes of Japan*. New York, 1922.

K7b   —— *War and Armament Loans of Japan*. New York, 1922.

K8   Kochanek, Stanley, *Business and Politics in India*. Berkeley, 1974.

K9   Kodikara, S.V., *Indo-Ceylon Relations Since Independence*. Colombo, 1965.

K10   Kotwal, O.P., *Indian Economy in Soviet Perspective*. New Delhi, 1972.

K11   Krishnamurti, B.V., 'Power and Elite Planning', *Economic and Political Weekly*, 27 May 1967.

K12   Krishnaswamy, S., *India's Mineral Resources*. New Delhi, 1972.

K13   Kurth, J.R. and S.J. Rosen (eds.), *Testing Theories of Economic Imperialism*. Lexington, 1974.

L1   La Guerre, John, *Calcutta to Caroni: The East Indians in Trinidad*. London, 1974.

L2a   Lal, Dipak, *New Economic Policies for India*. London, 1973.

L2b   —— *Appraising Foreign Investment in Developing Countries*. London, 1975.

L3   Lall, Sanjaya, 'Developing Countries and the Emerging International Technological Order', *Journal of International Affairs*, Vol. 33, No. 1, Spring–Summer 1979.

L4a   Lamb, Helen B., 'Indian Business Communities and Evolution of an Industrialist Class', *Pacific Affairs*, Vol. 28, No. 2, June 1955.

L4b   —— 'The Indian Merchant', *Journal of American Folklore* 71, 1958.

L5   Langer, W.L., 'A Critique of Imperialism', *Foreign Affairs*, October 1935.

L6   LeCraw, D., 'Direct Investment by Firms from Less Developed Countries', *Oxford Economic Papers*, Vol. 29, No. 3, November 1977.

L7a   Lenin, V.I., *Imperialism: The Highest Stage of Capitalism*. New York, 1939.

L7b   —— *Selected Works* Vol. 2, Moscow, 1970.

L8   Levkovsky, A., 'The State Sector: Its Social content and Development', *Social Science* 5, 1974.

L9   Leys, Colin, *Underdevelopment in Kenya: The Political Economy of Neo-Colonialism 1964–1971*. London, 1975.

L10   'Libya's Dependence on Foreigners is Likely to increase', *Middle East Economic Digest*, 27 April 1979.

L11   Lichtheim, G., *Imperialism*. London, 1971.

L12   Lockwood, L., 'Israeli Subimperialism?', *Monthly Review*, January 1973.

L13a   Lokanathan, P.S., 'Economic Reconstruction of Asia and the Far East', *United Asia*, Vol. 1, 1948.

L13b   —— 'Regional Economic Co-operation in Asia', *India Quarterly*, Vol. 7, No. 1, 1951.

L14   London, Paul A., *Merchants as Promoters of Rural Development: An Indian Case Study*. New York, 1975.

L15   Luxemburg, Rosa, *Accumulation of Capital An Anti-Critique*. New York, 1972.

M1   Mack, A., 'Theories of Imperialism', *Journal of Conflict Resolution*, Vol. 18, No. 3, September 1974.

M2a   Mahajani, Usha, *The Role of Indian Minorities in Burma and Malaya*. Bombay, 1960.

M2b   —— 'India and the people of Indian Origin Abroad', *India's Foreign Relations During the Nehru Era*, Editor, M.S. Rajan, Delhi, 1976.

M3   Makhijani, Arjun, 'Structural Retrogression in the Indian Economy: A Comment', *Economic and Political Weekly*, 11 November 1978.

M4   Malaviya, H.D., *Insurance Business in India*, Indian National Congress, New Delhi, 1956.

M5   Malaysian Indian Congress, *The NEP and Malaysian Indians: MIC Blueprint*. Kuala Lumpur, 1974.

M6   'Maldives, Republic of the', *MF Survey*, 23 January 1978.

M7   Malenbaum, Wilfred, *Prospects for Indian Development*. London, 1962.

M8   Mamoria, C.B., *Organization and Financing of Industries in India*. Allahabad, 1960.

M9   Mandel, Ernest, *Late Capitalism*. London, 1974.

M10   Marini, R.M., 'Brazilian Sub-imperialism', *Monthly Review*, February 1972.

M11   Marwah, Onkar, 'India's Nuclear and Space Programme: Intent and Policy', *International Security*, Vol. 2, No. 2, Fall 1977.

M12a Marx, Karl, *Value, Price and Profit*. New York, 1935.

M12b —— *Wage Labour and Capital*. New York, 1969.

M12c —— *Capital*. Moscow, 1976.

M13   Mates, Leo and W. Friedmann (eds.), *Joint Business Ventures of Yugoslav Enterprises and Foreign Firms*. Belgrade, 1968.

M14   Mattick, P., *Marx and Keynes: The Limits of the Mixed Economy*. Boston, 1969.

M15a Mayer, Adrian C., *Indians in Fiji*. London, 1963.

M15b —— *Peasants in the Pacific*. London, 1961.

M16   McEachern, Doug, 'The Mode of Production in India', *Journal of Contemporary Asia*, Vol. 6, No. 4, 1976.

M17   McFarlane, Bruce, 'Imperialism in the 1980s', *Journal of Contemporary Asia*, Vol. 6, No. 4, 1976.

M18   McMichael, P., James Petras and Robert Rhodes, 'Imperialism and the Contradictions of Development', *New Left Review*, No. 85, May–June 1974.

M19   Mehta, Asoka, *India Today*. New Delhi, 1974.

M20   Mehta, Balraj, *India and the World Oil Crisis*. New Delhi, 1975.

M21   Mehta, G.L., 'As Others See us: An Indian View', *Foreign Affairs*, October 1958.

M22   Mehta, S.S., 'Possible Forms of Economic Co-operation in Asia', *Indian Trade Review*, Vol. 8, No. 4, January–March 1974.

M23   Mehta, Vinod, *Soviet Union and India's Industrial Development*. New Delhi, 1975.

M24   Meillassoux, Claude, 'A Class Analysis of the Bureaucratic Process in Mali', *Journal of Development Studies*, Vol. 6, No. 2, January 1970.

M25   Mellor, John W. (ed.), *India: A Rising Middle Power*. Boulder, 1979.

M26   Mende, Tibor, *From Aid to Recolonization*. London, 1975.

M27   Merani, M.V. and H.L. Vanderlaan, 'Indian Traders in Sierra Leone', *African Affairs*, Vol. 78, No. 311, April 1979.

M28   Miliband, Ralph, *The State in Capitalist Society*. London, 1969.

M29   Mishra, B.B., *Bureaucracy in India*. New Delhi, 1977.

M30a   Misra, K.P., *India's Policy of Recognition of States and Governments*. Bombay, 1966.

M30b   —— *Studies in Indian Foreign Policy*. New Delhi, 1969.

M30c   —— *Foreign Policy and its Planning*. Bombay, 1970.

M30d   —— *Foreign Policy of India: A Book of Readings*. New Delhi, 1977.

M31a   Mitra, Asok, *Economic Theory and Planning*. Oxford, 1979.

M31b   —— *Terms of Trade and Class Relations: An Essay in Political Economy*. London, 1977.

M32   Mittra, S., *Monetary Politics in India*. Bombay, 1972.

M33a   Moran, T.H., 'Foreign Expansion as an Institutional Necessity for US Corporate Capitalism: The Search for a Radical Mode', *World Politics*, April 1973.

M33b   —— 'The Theory of International Exploitation in Large Natural Resource Investments', *Testing Theories of Economic Imperialism*, Editors, Rosen and Kurth, Lexington, 1974.

M34   Morris, H.S., *The Indians in Uganda*. London, 1968.

M35   Mukerji, I.N., *Towards Economic Integration in Asia*. New Delhi, 1978.

M36   Muni, S.D., 'Major Developments in India's Foreign Policy and Relations', *International Studies*, Vol. 15, No. 3, July–September 1976.

M37   Muranjan, S.K., *Modern Banking in India*. Bombay, 1940.

M38a   Murray, Robin, 'The Internationalization of Capital and the Nation State', *New Left Review*, No. 67, May–June 1971.

M38b   —— 'The Chandarias: The Development of a Kenyan Multinational', *Readings on the Multinational Corporation in Kenya*, Editor Kaplinsky, Nairobi, 1978.

N1 Nabudere, Dan, *The Political Economy of Imperialism*. London, 1977.

N2 Naipaul, Shiva, *North by South*. London, 1979.

N3 Nair, Balakrishnan N., 'The Indian Presence in the Indian Ocean', *Journal of African and Asian Studies*, Vol. 3, No. 1, Autumn 1969.

N4 Namjoshi, M.V., *Monopolies in India, Proposals for a Mixed Economy*. Bombay, 1966.

N5 Nanjundan, S., *Indians in Malayan Economy*. Office of Economic Advisor, Government of India, New Delhi, 1950.

N6 Nanporia, N.J., 'The Overseas-Indians', 4 parts, *The Asia Magazine*, 19 November, 26 November, 3 December, 17 December 1967.

N7 Nath, Dwarka, *A History of Indians in Guyana*. London, 1970.

N8 Navaratnarajah, A.S., *Export Credit Financing and Export Credit Insurance and Guarantee Scheme in India*. UNESCO, Economic Commission for Africa, 1974.

N9 Nawab, A.W., *Political Administration of Indian Economy*. Delhi, 1974.

N10 Nayyar, Deepak, *India's Exports and Export Policies in the 1960s*. Cambridge, 1976.

N11 Nehru, Jawaharlal, *India's Foreign Policy: Speeches of Prime Minister Nehru 1946–1963*. New Delhi, 1964.

N12 Nkrumah, Kwame, *Neo-Colonialism, the Last Stage of Imperialism*. London, 1965.

N13 Norman, E.H., *Origins of the Modern Japanese State*. New York, 1975.

O1 Ono, Giichi, *War and Armament Expenditures of Japan*. New York, 1922.

O2 Ostheimer, John M., *The Politics of the Western Indian Ocean Islands*. New York, 1975.

O3 'Overseas-Indians, The', *Far Eastern Economic Review*, 23 November 1979.

O4 Owen, Bob and R. Sutcliffe (eds.), *Studies in the Theory of Imperialism*. London, 1972.

P1 Palmer, Norman D., *The Indian Political System*. London, 1961.

P2 Panandikar, S.G., *Banking in India*. Revised Edition, Bombay, 1975.

P3 Pandey, K.L., *Development of Banking in India Since 1949*. Calcutta, 1968.

P4 Pannikkar, K.M., *India and the Indian Ocean*. London, 1951.

P5 Park, Richard, *India: Emergent Power?* New York, 1978.

P6 Patel, Hasu H., *The Indians in Uganda and Rhodesia: Some Comparative Perspectives on a Minority in Africa*. Denver, 1973.

P7 Patel, S., 'Growth in Income and Investment in India and China 1952–1960', *Indian Economic Review*, February 1957.

P8 Patnaik, Prabhat, 'Imperialism and the Growth of Indian Capitalism', *Studies in the Theory of Imperialism*, Editors, Owen and Sutcliffe, London, 1972.

P9a Pavlov, V.I., *India: Economic Freedom Vs. Imperialism*. New

Delhi, 1963.

P9b   Pavlov, V.I.,and R. Ulyanovsky, *Asian Dilemma: A Soviet View and Myrdal's Concept.* Moscow, 1973.

P10   Payer, Cheryl, *The Debt Trap.* London, 1973.

P11a   Petras, James F., 'New Perspectives on Imperialism and Social Classes in the Periphery', *Journal of Contemporary Asia,* Vol. 5, No. 3, 1975.

P11b   —— 'State Capitalism and the Third World', *Journal of Contemporary Asia,* Vol. 6, No. 4, 1976.

P11c   —— *Critical Perspectives on Imperialism and Social Class in the Third World.* London, 1978.

P12   Pilling, G., 'Imperialism, Trade and "Unequal Exchange" the work of A. Emmanuel', *Economy and Society,* Vol. 2, 1973.

P13   Poulantzas, Nicos, *Classes in Contemporary Capitalism.* London, 1975.

P14   Pollack, J.D. and O. Marwah, *Military Power and Policy in Asian States: China, India, Japan.* Boulder, 1980.

R1   Radice, Hugo (ed.), *International Firms and Modern Imperialism.* London, 1975.

R2   Raghavan, N., *India and Malaya: A Study.* Bombay, 1954.

R3   Rajan, M.S. (ed.), *India's Foreign Relations During the Nehru Era.* Delhi, 1976.

R4a   Ram, Mangat, 'Regional Plan Harmonisation and Trade Co-operation in South Asia', *Foreign Trade Review,* July–September 1973.

R4b   —— 'The Theory of Customs Union as applied to South Asia', *Foreign Trade Review,* Vol 9, No. 4, January–March 1975.

R5   Rana, Swadesh, 'Brazil's Armament Industry', *Strategic Analysis,* Vol. 3, No. 8, November 1979.

R6   Rangnekar, D.R., *Poverty and Capital Development in India.* London, 1958.

R7   Rao, B.S., *Surveys of Indian Industries* (2 Vols.). Calcutta, 1958.

R8   Rau, B.R., *Present Day Banking in India.* Calcutta, 1938.

R9   Rau, Chalapathi, 'India: A Power in Foreign Affairs', *Indian and Foreign Review,* 1 March 1976.

R10   Rawat, P.C., *Indo-Nepal Economic Relations.* New Delhi, 1974.

R11   Ray, R.M., *Life Insurance in India.* Bombay, 1941.

R12   Reddaway, W.B., *The Development of the Indian Economy.* London, 1965.

R13   Reddy, Nagi, *India Mortgaged.* Anantapuram, 1978.

R14   Resnick, Stephen A., 'The Second Path to Capitalism: A model of International Development', *Journal of Contemporary Asia,* Vol. 3, No. 2, 1973.

R15   Roach, E. Hugh, 'The Transfer of Technology, the Need for Pragmatism', *Behind the Headlines,* Vol. 37, No. 5, 1979.

R16   Roberts, John, 'Engineering Consultancy, Industrialization and Development', *Journal of Development Studies,* Vol. 9, No. 1, December 1972.

R17   Robinson and Gallagher, *Africa and the Victorians: The Official*

Mind of Imperialism. London, 1961.

R18a   Robinson, Richard D., *International Business Policy*. New York, 1964.

R18b   —— *National Control of Foreign Business Entry*. New York, 1976.

R19   Rodinson, Maxime, *Islam and Capitalism*. London, 1974.

R20   Roy, Ajit, *Monopoly Capitalism in India*. Calcutta, 1976.

R21   Roxborough, Ian, *Theories of Underdevelopment*. London, 1979.

R22   Rungta, R.S., *The Rise of Business Corporations in India: 1851–1900*. Cambridge, 1970.

S1   Sandhu, K.S., *Indians in Malaya: Some Aspects of their Immigration and Settlement 1786-1957*. Cambridge, 1969.

S2   Sarker, Jayanti, 'India's Builders head Overseas', *Far Eastern Economic Review*, Vol. 93, No. 36, 3 September 1976.

S3a   Sau, Ranjit, 'Theory of Unequal Exchange, Trade and Imperialism', *Economic and Political Weekly*, 6 March 1976.

S3b   —— *Unequal Exchange, Imperialism and Underdevelopment*. Calcutta, 1978.

S4   Saul, John S., 'The State in Post-Colonial Societies: Tanzania', *The Socialist Register*, 1974.

S5   Sauldie, Madan, 'India and Africa: Bridging an Ocean', *Africa*, No. 74, October 1977.

S6   Schumpeter, J.A., *Imperialism: And Social Class*. New York, 1971.

S7   Schwarzenberger, G., 'An International Insurance Agency', *Yearbook of World Affairs*, 1969.

S8   Sen Gupta, Bhabani, 'The Emerging Concept of South Asia and the Soviet Union', *Asia Pacific Community*, Summer 1978 No. 1.

S9   Servan-Schreiber, Jaques, *The American Challenge*. London, 1969.

S10   Sethuraman, *Institutional Financing of Economic Development in India*. Delhi, 1970.

S11   Shaw, T.M., 'Kenya and South Africa, Sub-imperialist states', *Orbis*, Summer 1977.

S12   Shee, Poon-kim, *Roots of Sinophobia in the Asian Countries*. Singapore, 1977.

S13   Shelvankar, K.S., *The Problem of India*. London, 1940.

S14   Shenoy, B.R., *The Bombay Plan*. Bombay, 1945.

S15   Shetty, S.L., 'Structural Retrogression in the Indian Economy since the mid-Sixties', *Economic and Political Weekly* Annual No., February 1978.

S16   Shibuya, Yukio and Shoichi Yamashita, *Foreign Aid and Economic Growth of Developing Asian Countries*. Tokyo, 1968.

S17   Shivarama, Shivanna, *Foreign Ventures in India*. Uppsala, 1967.

S18   Shivji, Issa G., 'Tanzania: The Silent Class Struggle', *Socialism in Tanzania*, Editors, Cliffe and Saul, Dar es Salaam, 1973.

S19   'Shoshas', *Journal of World Trade Law*, May–June 1979.

S20   Singer, Milton, *Traditional India: Structure and Change*. Philadelphia, 1959.

S21   Singh, Charan, *India's Economic Policy*. New Delhi, 1978.

S22   Singh, I.J. Bahadur (ed.), *The Other India*. New Delhi, 1979.

S23   Singh, Jyoti Shanker, *A New International Economic Order, Toward*

A Fair Redistribution of the World's Resources. New York, 1977.

S24 Singh, Tarlok, *India's Development Experience.* Delhi, 1974.

S25 Singh, Uma Shanker, 'Burma's Economic Relations with India, 1948–67', *International Studies*, January–March 1978.

S26 Smythe, Hugh H., 'The Indian in Africa: A Problem for Sociological Research', *Sociology and Social Research 39*, 1954.

S27 Sodhia, K.C., 'Indian Investment Overseas', *Indian Journal of Public Administration*, Special No. 20(3), July–September 1974.

S28 Spulber, Nicholas, *The Economics of Communist Eastern Europe.* Cambridge, 1957.

S29 Srivastava, P., *Capital Funds in Underdeveloped Countries.* Allahabad, 1976.

S30 Srivastava, P.K., *Foreign Collaboration: its Significance in India's Industrial Progress.* Agra, 1975.

S31 Strange, Susan, 'International Economics and International Relations', *International Affairs*, April 1970, Vol. 46, No. 2.

S32 Subramanyam, K., 'Planning Defence Production', *Times of India*, 24 January 1980.

S33 Swainson, Nicola, *The Development of Corporate Capitalism in Kenya 1918–1947.* London, 1980.

S34 Szentes, Thomas, 'Status-Quo and Socialism', *Socialism in Tanzania*, Editors, Saul and Cliffe, Dar es Salaam, 1973.

T1 Tandon, Yash, 'Role of Transnational Corporation and Future Trends in Southern Africa', *Journal of International Relations Association*, Vol. 2, No. 1, June 1978.

T2 Taneja, S.K., *India and International Monetary Management.* New Delhi, 1976.

T3a Thomas, Raju, *The Defence of India.* New Delhi, 1978.

T4 Thomas, R.G.C., 'Politics of Indian Naval Rearmament', *Pacific Community*, Vol. 6, No. 3, April 1975.

T5 Timberg, Thomas A., *The Marwaris.* Delhi, 1978.

T6a Tinker, Hugh, *Separate and Unequal.* London, 1976.

T6b —— *The Banyan Tree: Overseas Emigrants from India, Pakistan and Bangladesh.* Oxford, 1977.

T6c —— *Race, Conflict and the International Order.* London, 1977.

T6d —— 'Mauritius: Cultural Marginalism and Political Control', *African Affairs*, Vol. 76, No. 304, July 1977.

T7 Tomlinson, J.W.C., *The Joint Venture Process in International Business.* Cambridge, 1970.

T8 Trimberger, E.K., *Revolution from Above: Military Bureaucrats and Development in Japan, Turkey, Egypt and Peru.* New Brunswick, 1978.

U1a United Nations, UNCTAD, *Trade Expansion and Economic Integration Among Developing Countries.* New York, 1967.

U1b —— Department of Economic and Social Affairs, *Foreign Investment in Developing Countries.* New York, 1968.

U1c —— UNCTAD, *Reinsurance Problems in Developing Countries.*

New York, 1973.

U1d   United Nations, UNCTAD, *Insurance Legislation and Supervision in Developing Countries*. New York, 1972.

U2   Uppal, J.S. (ed.), *India's Economic Problems*. New Delhi, 1975.

V1   Vaid, K.N., *The Overseas Indian Community in Hongkong*. University of Hongkong, Centre for Asian Studies, Monograph No. 7, 1972.

V2a   Vakil, C.N. (ed.), *Industrial Development of India: Policy and Problems*. New Delhi, 1973.

V2b   —— *Social and Economic Significance of Insurance in Modern Economic Life*. Bombay, 1970.

V3a   Vayrynen, R., 'Comments on Imperialism Research', *Instant Research on Peace and Violence*, Vol. 5, No. 3, 1975.

V3b   —— and L. Herrera, 'Sub-imperialism from Dependence to Subordination', *Instant Research on Peace and Violence*, Vol. 5, No. 3, 1975.

V4   Venkata-Subbayya, Hiranyappa, *Enterprise and Economic Change: 50 Years of FICCI*. New Delhi, 1977.

V5   Vohra, Dewan Chand, *India's Aid Diplomacy in the Third World 1947-1975*. PhD. Thesis, School of International Studies, Jawaharlal Nehru University, 1978. Published New Delhi, 1980.

W1   Wallerstein, Immanuel, 'Dependency in an interdependent world: The Limited Possibilities of Transformation within the Capitalist World Economy', *African Studies Review*, Vol. 17, No. 1, April 1974.

W2   Walton, J., 'Internal Colonialism: Problems of Definition and Measurement', *Latin American Urban Research* 5, Editors, Trueblood and Cornelius, London, 1976.

W3   Wariavwala, Bharat, 'Timid Search for Status', *Seminar*, December 1980.

W4   Warren, Bill, 'Imperialism and Capitalist Industrialization', *New Left Review*, No. 81, September–October 1973.

W5   Weerasooria, W.S., *The Nattukottai Chettiars Merchant Bankers of Ceylon*. Dehiwala, 1973.

W6   Weiskopf, Thomas E., 'Dependence and Imperialism in India', *The Review of Radical Political Economics*, Vol. 5, No. 1, Spring 1973.

W7   Winder, R.B., *Lebanese in West Africa*. Hague, 1962.

Official Documents and Annual Reports

Off. 1   Asian Development Bank

Off. 2   Bharat Overseas Bank

Off. 3   Botswana, Government Information Services: *President Khama in India 1976*.

Off. 4   Colombo Plan

Off.5   Economist Intelligence Unit: *Quarterly Economic Reviews . . . of (India etc.)*

Off.6   Engineering Export Promotion Council: *Seminar on Trade and Industrial Co-operation Between India and EEC Countries.* Report No. 77, New Delhi, 1979.

Off.7   Export Credit and Guarantee Corporation

Off.8   Federation of Indian Chambers of Commerce and Industry: *Workshop on Indian Joint Ventures and Project Exports Report.* New Delhi, 1979.

Off.9   Fiji, Government of: *Report on Small Industry: Opportunities and Policies in Fiji Islands.* ITEC Study, Suva, 1969.

Off.10   Indian Bank

Off.11a   Indian Institute of Foreign Trade: *India's Joint Ventures Abroad.* New Delhi, 1977.

Off.11b   Indian Institute of Foreign Trade: *Report on Indo-Ethiopian Trade Prospects.* New Delhi, 1973.

Off.11c   Indian Institute of Foreign Trade: *India's Trade and Economic Co-operation with Asia.* New Delhi, 1973.

Off.12   Indian Overseas Bank

Off.13   Industrial Development Bank of India

Off.14   International Finance Corporation Special Commonwealth Africa Assistance Programme State Bank of India

Off.15   International Institute of Strategic Studies (London): *Strategic Surveys.*

Off.16a   Life Insurance Corporation of India: *Interim Report on the Activities of the Corporation.* Bombay, 1957.

Off.16b   Life Insurance Corporation of India

Off.17a   National Council of Applied Economic Research: *India's Export Potential in Selected Countries.* New Delhi, 1970.

Off.17b   National Council of Applied Economic Research: *The Managing Agency System.* New Delhi, 1959.

Off.18   Nigeria, Ministry of Foreign Affairs: *Nigeria: Bulletin on Foreign Affairs*, 1972.

Off.19   Stockholm International Peace Research Institute: *Yearbooks.*

Off.20   *Thapars Industrial Directory*, 1974.

Off.21   *Times of India Directory*, 1978, 1979.

Off.22   United Nations Development Programme – The Administrator Reports

Off.23a   World Bank – International Bank for Reconstruction and Development

Off.23b   World Bank – World Development Report

Government of India: Annual Reports and Other Publications

Gov.1   Administrative Reforms Commission, 1968, *Report of Working Group on Life Insurance Administration*, 2 Vols.

Gov.2   Department of Atomic Energy (Annual Report)

Gov.3   Department of Company Affairs, *Company News and Notes*

Gov.4   Department of Industries, *Journal of Industry and Trade*

Gov.5   Directorate of Commercial Intelligence and Statistics, *Indian Trade Journal*

Gov.6   Directorate of Public Relations and Publications, *Handbook of Foreign Collaboration 1974*

Gov.7a   Economic Survey — (Ministry of Finance) (Annual Report)

Gov.7b   Economic Yearbook (Annual Report)

Gov.8   India High Commission, London, *India News*

Gov.9a   Ministry of Commerce (Annual Report)

Gov.9b   Ministry of Commerce, *Economic and Commercial News*

Gov.9c   Ministry of Commerce, *Monthly Statistics of Foreign Trade*

Gov.9d   Ministry of Commerce — 1977, *India's Trade Agreements as in force 1 May 1976*

Gov.10a   Ministry of External Affairs (Annual Report)

Gov.10b   Ministry of External Affairs, *Foreign Affairs Record*

Gov.10c   Ministry of External Affairs, *Indian and Foreign Review*

Gov.11   Ministry of Defence (Annual Report)

Gov.12a   Ministry of Finance (Annual Report)

Gov.12b   Ministry of Finance, *Pocket Book of Economic Statistics 1973*

Gov.12c   Ministry of Finance, Controller of Insurance, *Indian Insurance Yearbooks 1956–1973*

Gov.13   Ministry of Home Affairs (Annual Report)

Gov.14   Ministry of Information and Broadcasting, *India 1974 A Reference Annual*

Gov.15a   Planning Commission, *Yojana*

Gov.15b   Planning Commission, *Plan Documents 1st–6th Plan*

Gov.16a   Reserve Bank of India (Annual Report)

Gov.16b   Reserve Bank of India, Report on Currency and Finance (Annual Report)

Gov.16c   *Reserve Bank of India Bulletin*

Gov.16d   Reserve Bank of India, *Report on Banking and Currency*

Pamphlets

CFTC, Commonwealth Skills for Commonwealth Needs, Commonwealth Secretariat, London, n.d.

CFTC, Commonwealth Secretariat, London, June 1974.

Engineering Projects (India) Ltd., n.p., n.d.

Indian Joint-Ventures Abroad, Indian Investment Centre, n.p., n.d.

MECON, Metallurgical and Engineering Consultants (India) Ltd., Ranchi, n.d.

MECON in Nigeria, op. cit.

MECON a Moving Force, op. cit.

NIDC — Major Assignments, NIDC, New Delhi, n.d.

NIDC — Consultants and Engineers, New Delhi, n.d.

Syndicate Bank your bank in India, Manipal, 1979.

Periodicals and Newspapers

Asian Wall Street Journal — Hongkong

BBC Summary of World Broadcasts; Asia and the Far East — Reading

BBC Summary of World Broadcasts; Asia and the Far East, Weekly Economic Report — Reading

Business Week — New York

Business India — Bombay

Capital — Calcutta

Christian Science Monitor — Boston
Colombo Plan Newsletter — Colombo
Commerce — Bombay
Dawn — Karachi
Eastern Economist — New Delhi
Economic and Political Weekly — Bombay
Economic Weekly — Bombay
Far Eastern Economic Review — Hongkong
Financial Times — London
Frontier — Calcutta
Guardian — London
Hindu — Madras
Hsinhua — Beijing
Indian Economic Diary — New Delhi
Indian Investment Centre Bulletin — New Delhi
IMF Survey — Washington
Indo-African Trade Journal — New Delhi
Japan Times — Tokyo
Le Monde — Paris
Le Monde Diplomatique — Paris
MEED — London
Mideast Markets — London
NACE Bulletin — New Delhi (National Association of Consulting Engineers)
New African — London
New York Times — New York
Observer Foreign News Service — London
Statesman — Calcutta
The Straits Times — Singapore
Times — London
Times of India — Bombay
Yogakshema — LIC, Bombay